Praise for *The History of Havana*

"This is a very good book . . . a rich and readable social and cultural history, which incorporates popular culture—film and radio, dance music and popular religion—to weave a historical tapestry as beguiling as a Havana night."—*History Book Club*

"In fine prose, with academic rigor, clarity that shows respect for the reader, and a good dose of lyricism, the co-authors serve us up the trajectory of the Cuban capital."—*Diario Las Américas*

"What a wonderful read! Dick Cluster and Rafael Hernández' stories read like late night conversations on a dark, humid Havana terrace: marvelous, sly, and frequently incredible. And that's the real kick, because they're meticulously researched, and smoothly well-chosen and arranged. This is a history that feels more like literature: palpable, personal, full of secrets revealed and the occasional, and necessary, melancholia."—Achy Obejas, author of *Days of Awe*

"Serious and easily readable. *History of Havana* employs conventional documentary, written and visual sources, and a variety of testimonials from throughout the world to bring to life the complex portraits and challenges of contemporary Havana—a historical crossroad of the New World, a stage of scenic architecture, rhythmic sound-scapes, remarkable artistic genius, foreign invasions, struggles for personal and national freedom and independence—today a vibrant, complex, world-renowned city, in a new global moment, creating its future in the throes of the fall of the Soviet Union, the lure and hooks of tourism, natural disasters, and the challenges of Empire."—Harry Belafonte, singer, actor, UNICEF Goodwill Ambassador

"*History of Havana* by Rafael Hernández and Dick Cluster invites general readers to enter and experience modern-day Havana as the product of its past. They will find a city whose citizens developed and changed in moments of revelry and times of crisis, responding to local history and world history, and making history as well. This diverse population negotiated when possible, fought when required, and sought to imagine and sustain revolutionary visions and life-ways of new men and women."—Danny Glover, actor and activist

"This riveting and highly readable historical document is bittersweet. 'Bitter' in that throughout the history of Havana, weather, wars, and economic strangulation have forced this great city to periodically deteriorate. 'Sweet' in the seemingly infinite optimism and sense of humor of its citizens, and even sweeter because the city will rise again and reclaim its proper place amongst the great urban centers of the world."—James Stewart Polshek, architect of The Rose Center for Earth and Space at the American Museum of Natural History

"Gorgeous, feisty, savvy, cosmopolitan, sexy, defiant, and yes, at times decadent and decaying, yet always resilient and ribald, battered repeatedly but never beaten—the city of Havana, where everyone deserves to have been born, is the star of this loving, gritty history. The authors lead the reader from Columbus' stumbling into Cuba in his quest for the Orient in the fifteenth century to our own decade. They tell the story of Havana's people, their physical space, their welcoming and unwelcome encounters with foreigners, and their capacity for re-invention. It's a great read."—Jorge I. Domínguez, Clarence Dillon Professor of International Affairs, Harvard University

PALGRAVE ESSENTIAL HISTORIES

General editor: Jeremy Black

This series of compact, readable, and informative national histories is designed to appeal to anyone wishing to gain a broad understanding of a country's history.

Published

THE HISTORY OF HAVANA

by Dick Cluster
and
Rafael Hernández

palgrave
macmillan

THE HISTORY OF HAVANA

First published in 2006 by
PALGRAVE MACMILLAN™
175 Fifth Avenue, New York, N.Y. 10010 and
Houndmills, Basingstoke, Hampshire, England RG21 6XS
Companies and representatives throughout the world.

PALGRAVE MACMILLAN is the global academic imprint of the Palgrave Macmillan division of St. Martin's Press, LLC and of Palgrave Macmillan Ltd. Macmillan® is a registered trademark in the United States, United Kingdom and other countries. Palgrave is a registered trademark in the European Union and other countries.

ISBN-13: 978–0–230–60397–4 (paperback)
ISBN-10: 0–230–60397–1 (paperback)

Library of Congress Cataloging-in-Publication Data

Cluster, Dick, 1947–
     The history of Havana / by Dick Cluster and Rafael Hernández.
         p. cm.
     Includes bibliographical references and index.
     ISBN 1–4039–7107–2 (alk. Paper)
     ISBN 0–230–60397–1 pbk
         1. Havana (Cuba)—History. 2. Havana (Cuba)—Description and travel.
I. Hernández, Rafael. II. Title.

F1799.H357C58 2006
972.91′23—dc22   2006045750

First PALGRAVE MACMILLAN paperback edition: April 2008

10 9 8 7 6 5 4 3 2 1

Printed in the United States of America.

Contents

List of Illustrations

MAPS

PHOTOS

Acknowledgments

"What seemed like mystery," sang Jimmy Cliff on an island not far from Cuba, "were only untold history." Many people have initiated us into Havana's mysteries, far too many to thank them all individually here. Among those who contributed leads and sources that helped us shape this book in particular, we wish to acknowledge Antolín Bárcenas, Luisa Campuzano, Mario Coyula, Denia García Ronda, Antonio José Ponte, Reina María Rodríguez, Daniel Taboada, and those who generously agreed to be interviewed about their family histories: Raquel Cañizares, Carlos Larrinaga, Verónica Loynaz, Daniel Motola, Teresita Roca and Juan Valdés Paz. In the Office of the City Historian we received valuable contributions from Zenaida Iglesias and Yamira Rodríguez, researchers in the Dirección de Arquitectura Patrimonial, and from Magda Resyk, director of Habana Radio. Cuban historians Oscar Zanetti Lecuona, Gustavo Placer Cervera and Oscar Loyola read and commented on parts of the manuscript. In the José Martí National Library, Eliades Acosta and Teresita Morales aided our research, and staff members Olga Vega, Ana Gloria Valdés, and Martha Haya, as well as Marisel Caraballo, collaborated in our search for information and illustrations. We are also grateful for help from specialists at the archives of the Institute of History.

For encouragement and aid in the process of turning our interest in Havana into a book proposal and then a published book, we are indebted to our editor at Palgrave, Gabriella Pearce, as well as to Tom Hallock, Gayatri Patnaik, and Alex Smithline. Nancy Falk supported this goal throughout, contributed her own perspective on the city, consulted on many drafts and put up with the U.S. author's servitude to the project and all the obsessions that came with it. Daybel Pañellas lent her critical judgment and her support to the Cuban author's work.

Havana and surroundings, from a map illustrating the British siege of 1762, modified to show a portion of the new barrios and old towns incorporated over the next two centuries. The walled city of the 18th century is in the center, with street grid. The Royal Ditch can be seen bringing water from the Almendares or Chorrera River (at left separating the modern nieghborhoods of Miramar and El Vedado). Locations of Spanish fortresses built before and after the British invasion are labeled.

Metropolitan Havana showing places mentioned frequently in the text, with the names they bore at the time.

Introduction

Un tipo muy popular

Near the docks and custom house of Old Havana, in front of the meticulously restored basilica of the convent of San Francisco de Asís, stands the life-size bronze statue of a figure with long, flowing hair and beard, wrapped in a D'Artagnan-style cape which seems to drift in the wind as he walks. This statue is one of the very few erected in Havana since the revolution of 1959. It does not portray a rebel hero, a patriotic general, a famous writer, a great architect, or the composer of some unforgettable song dedicated to this city on the bay. Rather, it is the statue of the Parisian Gentleman, El Caballero de París.

The French themselves would have called him a *clochard*, a vagabond. From the 1920s to the 1970s he slept where he could, on one corner or another as he moved about the city, feeding himself on what he found or was offered by street vendors or passers-by, holding up his pants with a rope belt from which dangled pencils secured by strings. Yet, dressed in his signature cape over a tattered set of tails, the self-styled Parisian Gentleman projected an aura of dignity and majesty. The European aristocrat washed up on the shores of this New World—or so he presented himself—made speeches to the crowds in seventeenth-century Spanish or busied himself arranging his mysterious bags and bundles and masses of newspapers and magazines.

He was, by most accounts, a Spanish immigrant who had come to Cuba as a teenager and found work in Havana's sophisticated stores and hotels. Some said he had gone crazy for love, while others said he'd been jailed for a murder or a robbery he did not commit. Over the course of decades, he became an institution. Ageless, capable of appearing at any hour of day or night, attached to no neighborhood in particular, white but poor, both comic and tragic, he became a sort of essential citizen of Havana, to whom the city's residents have dedicated songs, poems, memoirs, imagined biographies, and plays. "*Un tipo muy popular*," one such song calls him—which suggests "popular" and "of the people" all at once.

The Caballero died in 1985 and was buried in an obscure grave on the city's outskirts. When the ruined colonial church and convent of San Francisco (turned to civilian uses since the mid-nineteenth century) was restored in the year 2001, the city historian requested the transfer of the Caballero's ashes to that sanctuary beside the city's earliest marketplace. The reception this vagabond received sums up the spirit of his adopted city; throughout his lifetime on the streets, even those who laughed at him protected him. They conversed with him and accepted the quill pens and colored papers he gave out as gifts to those who offered him alms. He once buttonholed a Cardinal, who listened politely as the Caballero explained that the church should sell all its goods and distribute the proceeds among the poor. By the 1940s, he was such an institution that he was interviewed in the press. In the 1950s, he appeared on television alongside two similar itinerant characters, La Marquesa and Bigote de Gato. In the 1960s, he was afforded carte-blanche for free food from the kitchens of the newly state-run restaurants.

The courtesy and protection afforded to the Caballero testifies to something about Havana that every visitor notes—this city is the most welcoming place. The people of Havana welcomed the Caballero as they welcome almost everyone, with hospitality and compassion. It doesn't take much to strike up a conversation, even if you are a stranger, or strange.

We believe this characteristic stems from the city's origins. Havana began as a port and a crossroads, and it has been that way ever since—a melting pot of transients and immigrants and refugees, of slaves and freedmen and freedwomen, as well as conquistadors and plutocrats, a confluence of the four points of the compass, of Spain, Africa, China, and the Levant, of the Caribbean islands and the Americas on both sides of the Rio Grande. The name of the city, La Habana or La Havana, comes from Spanish transcriptions of an indigenous word. But in ensuing years many came to believe that the name derived from haven and harbor, which the city has always been in both a physical and a social sense. Exiles adding to city's mix in various eras have included Irish Catholics, French Protestants and Bonapartists, South American royalists and revolutionaries, Haitian ex-planters and ex-canecutters, Indonesian communists and South African guerrillas, and American fugitives ranging from Black Panthers to gangsters and millionaires. Through it all, Havana has been a city that takes what comes—and assimilates it. Comparisons of the Cuban capital to the French one have been frequent, and will appear in what follows, but what made El Caballero de París beloved was that he was quintessentially Havana—and being quintessentially Havana did not rule out naming himself after someplace else.

At the same time, the Caballero's popularity had to do with the way he spoke out for his city. We will come, eventually, to the story of the Caballero's arrest for defaming a president, part of a long tradition of protest against endemic corruption and graft. For now, we note that mixing defense with hospitality is another characteristic of Havana. The narrow neck of the bay that welcomed so many immigrants and visitors was closed up every night in the seventeenth and eighteenth centuries by a chain of logs pulled tight between its two flanking fortresses, at the same nine o'clock hour as a cannon shot was fired and the gates of the city's walls were shut tight. In the tense days of May and June of 1586, when the threatening fleet of the privateer Francis Drake tacked back and forth along the coastline, citizens and subjects from the city and surrounding farms gathered to keep watch and drill with the scarce arms available to them. In 1762, when British forces besieged Havana from the land, local guerrillas attacked behind their lines. In 1961 and 1962, when an invasion from the north was—with reason—expected at any moment, the seaside Malecón drive filled with sandbag barriers, cannons, militia men and women, and antiaircraft guns.

We have opened this book with the Caballero for one more reason. We, just like him, have adopted the city and have been adopted by it. Both of us have been its residents without having been bred there, and in this we are hardly unique. A popular joke in Havana in the 1990s involved Fidel Castro seeking advice about the perennial issue of the capital's overcrowding. For counsel about this vexing problem, he summoned Pepito, the proverbial bad boy of generations of Cuban jokes. "No problem, *comandante*," Pepito replied. He advised the President to line up twenty *camellos* (camels), the popular name for the giant, crowded, lurching, two-humped tractor-trailer buses invented to cope with the transport

crisis that ballooned in those years. "Twenty *camellos*," repeated
Pepito, "and one Mercedes-Benz." He said to fill up the buses with
recent migrants from Oriente—the island's easternmost region—
and send them back where they belong. "Very good, Pepito,"
answered the President, a graduate of the University of Havana but
originally an immigrant from Oriente himself. "I think I'll do that,
send them back as you say. I can provide the twenty buses. But why
do we need the Mercedes-Benz?" "*Comandante*," Pepito demanded,
"You're not planning to ride in one of those *camellos* yourself?!" It is
partly because neither of us is any more indigenous than the
commander-in-chief that we believe our viewpoints can help North
American readers see this crossroads as it needs to be seen, from
both within and without. Having lived its daily life (one as temporary resident and the other as permanent) we see it in a way that
travel writers, chroniclers, and tourists of past and present centuries do not. Having lived outside, we perhaps have a better sense
of what makes it special than do those who have always lived
within. Thus we are as Havanan, and as foreign, as tens of thousands of others who live there today or who were born there and
have held onto its memory while living in other parts.

Further, we have tried to use our double authorship to offer U.S.
readers a binocular, three-dimensional account. In the late
nineteenth century and the first half of the twentieth, panoramic
views of Havana were a staple not just of American picture postcards but of three-dimensional double-image devices from the
Stereopticon to the Viewmaster. In the years since, visions of the
Cuban capital have often been one-sided, monocular, for political
reasons above all. In the course of writing this book we have
argued with each other and learned from our arguments. At the
same time, we have often let the impressions of our two distinct
viewpoints stand side by side, not saying a given moment was
solely fish or solely fowl, or its most representative figure was
solely *fulano* or *mengano*, Peter or Paul.

The *yanquí* in our authorial pair first saw Havana in the predawn
light of late November, 1969, through the windows of a Hungarian
bus carrying him from the José Martí International Airport to a
cane-cutting camp in the countryside to the east. He had come to
check out the new postrevolutionary Cuba, and at that moment a
mammoth sugar harvest was where the action was. Over the next
few months, the capital loomed tantalizingly in the distance, tasted
in the small bites of weekend visits and above all in the stories of

the Cubans with whom he worked in those fields, almost all of them from Havana. Then and in subsequent visits in the 1970s and the 1980s, he took in distinct spots and routes that did not yet add up to a coherent map—eating rabbit at the restaurant across from where he would later live, getting eyeglasses at the ophthalmological hospital across from where he would later teach, taking buses that by the time he returned had ceased to run—all the while hearing stories and more stories from old and new friends and random residents on the street. He finally got the chance to live and work in Havana over a four-year period in the 1990s, during which he explored the city by foot, bicycle, bus, and very occasionally by car. One day early in his stay a friend-to-be said, on their first meeting, "Are you sure you're a North American? You listen too well." He does not believe his fellow Americans are incapable of listening, but he took the warning to heart. He goes back whenever he can, asks a lot of questions, and listens to the rhythms of Havana's never-silent citizens. He realizes that never-silent is an exaggeration. Unlike his countrymen and women, most residents of Havana keep quiet while they eat.

The Cuban of our pair was born in the capital but grew up in a town in the center of the island. His first conscious impression of Havana was thus a product of his imagination, engendered by an uncle who worked in a toy store on the Calle Galiano and would arrive in the provincial town laden with gifts and fabulous tales. He discovered the capital for real in December of 1961, descending from a train full of literacy teachers returning from the mountains, to take up residence as a boarding student in junior high. His first dorm was a sumptuous abandoned mansion in the former Country Club district. He studied in the cavernous ex-parochial schools of La Vibora and El Vedado, from which he emerged on the weekends to explore the city's night life and beaches. In the later 1960s, as a university student and fledgling writer, he shared the excitement of the city's literary and theatrical scenes, stood guard as member of a militia unit, and cut cane (him too) along with hundreds of thousands of other Havanans. When his daughter was born he was living in a tenement on Callejon del Chorro, around the corner from the Plaza de la Catedral, where she took her first steps.

He was later a neighbor of the baseball stadium of Cerro and the Cemetery of Colón—and all of these places will figure in the pages to follow—but where he has most enjoyed living is by the sea. He had this pleasure first in Miramar and now a few steps from the old

fort called El Castillo de La Chorrera, which is approximately
where the first European settlers of Havana built their huts. When
he wants to show the city to special visitors, he always takes them
walking along the nearby Malecón, where he has spent so many
years reading, conversing, watching the sunsets, making big decisions, falling in love, and above all watching his fellow residents go
by. From this perch he feels a mysterious pleasure in their coexistence, in knowing them, imagining their thoughts, yet seeing them
with the new eyes of a visitor all the same.

Having introduced the city and ourselves, we need to say just a
few words about what we have been able to fit into this book and
what we have left out. "Havana is Cuba," goes a saying popular in
the capital. "All the rest is landscape." It's a quip in the typical style
of Cuban humor—ironic, self-referential, evidently not true, but
with an assertion that the teller refuses to let go of. The capital has
always had strong links with the interior, which has supplied
everything from the yucca roots out of which to make the *casabe*
bread that nourished the earliest settlers, to sugar profits in later
times, to the proceeds from beach resorts or nickel mines. Yet
Havana has maintained equally strong links with the exterior, and
a sense of itself as distinct for being uniquely in touch with both.
The terms used are testimony to this viewpoint. The long, skinny
island of Cuba contains thousands of miles of seacoast, and no
place on the island is more than fifty miles from the sea. Yet the
term for all this territory when viewed from Havana is "interior"
just the same.

So there's a dilemma in trying to tell the history of the city, especially to readers for whom the history of the island is not well
known. We are not trying to write a history of Cuba, but we cannot
write a history of its capital without doing some of that. Likewise in
a book of some three hundred pages, we cannot provide an ency-
clopedic history of the capital. In Spanish, the word *historia* means
both history and story. Writers of history, like writers of fiction, pick
and choose among many real-life ingredients to get at their version
of an inner truth. We have tried to select ingredients that are
representative—places, moments, characters, and stories representative of the capital and its eras—and to make a similar selection,
smaller but necessary, of such elements representative of the larger
national history. In telling the story of the capital, we have not ig-
nored its architecture, its famous buildings, its urban planning or

the lack of it, and its geographic spread. But primarily we've tried to tell the story of its people, at all rungs of society, including those who have left many records and monuments behind them and those who have left almost none.

Finally, a note about our research and another about language.

While we have gone directly to some archival sources to settle doubts and fill holes, we have largely relied on the dedicated work of many researchers who went there before us. For the most part we have used published works—oral histories, travel reports, literature, journalism, and scholarly work by researchers and writers from both our countries. In a bibliographic essay (p. 279) we note some of the scholars to whom we owe our greatest debts. For the period beginning in the 1920s, we have supplemented these sources by taking oral histories of families who illustrate what we see as being the most important events, backgrounds, and trends. We have chosen these families, also, because they cross what is often seen as a high, even impenetrable wall dividing post-1959 Cuba from some other Cuba "before." Cuban history is marked by ruptures, most notably those caused by revolutions: the revolutions against Spain in the nineteenth century and the one against the Batista government and (as things developed) the United States in 1959 and the years after. These ruptures changed Havana in ways that allowed no going back. But in the lives of cities as in other lives, continuities are always as important as ruptures. There is no going forward, either, without them. In this history of Havana we have also looked for and found the things that remain the same.

In what follows, translations from Cuban Spanish are almost always our own. We've kept Spanish words and Havana slang to a minimum, but at times they are essential to flavor the stew, and we hope readers will learn some of them. In the process we have grappled with what to do about an adjective missing from the English language, whose job would be to accurately describe things from or pertaining to the United States. José Martí used the term "Our America" to describe the many American nations south of the Rio Grande, but what do we call the influential residents and products and colloquial language of the nation that lies to the north? Even in Spanish, the adjective *estadounidense* (United-States-ian), though it exists, is rarely used. Cubans often say *norteamericano*, but Canadians and Mexicans rightly point out that they are North Americans too. So we have reluctantly gone with the usage

"American," even though Brazilians are American people, Chilean wines are American products, and Mexican speech is American language too.

Whatever word we use, we have called attention to the ways that New York, Tampa, Miami, and other U.S. cities have influenced Havana since at least the eighteenth century, and have made some mention of Havana's considerable influence on them. We hope that recognition of these cultural ties will contribute to a long-delayed restoration of unhindered contact between U.S. cities and Cuban ones, especially the capital, in a climate of equality and mutual respect.

Dick Cluster and Rafael Hernández,
Cambridge, Massachusetts and Havana, Cuba, 2006.

1

Key to the Indies

When Christopher Columbus explored the northern coast of Cuba on his first voyage to America, he mistook the territory for a peninsula extending from the mainland of China, inhabited by subjects of the Great Khan. After the inhabitants convinced him—temporarily—that this was not so, he turned back, eastward toward home. Thus he missed his chance to lay eyes on the dramatic break in Cuba's coastline that would become Havana: the high cliff, narrow channel, protected bay, and sweeping oceanfront where the city would later rise. Yet this part of the island did not altogether escape his notice. In his letter to the Spanish sovereigns who had sponsored his voyage, he reported, "There are in the western part of the island two provinces which I did not visit; one of these is called by the Indians 'Avan,' and its inhabitants are born with tails."

Born with tails? The Admiral's letter and journals are full of half-truths, lies, delusions, wishful thinking, and mysteries. On his second voyage, a native chief told him (as best as he could make out) that Cuba was "an island without end." Centuries later, his bones finally made it to the fabled Avan, to be buried in the city's new cathedral—or so everyone believed, but now it appears that they may have been his brother's remains, by mistake. So let us just note that even before the city was settled, foreign sensibilities found in it the stuff of fantasies—the unknown, the exaggerated, and a whiff of the devil as well.

When Spanish soldier-settlers finally reached and conquered the western part of the island some twenty-five years after Columbus's voyage, they were still calling it "La Avana" or "La Abana," a name which they took from a word often repeated by the inhabitants, a word recorded by the Spaniards as Havaguanex or Habaguanex, which they thought to be the name of a local chief. In 1515 or 1516 they founded a town on the southern coast in an ill-chosen, swampy, mosquito-ridden spot with a poor harbor. This town they named in honor of St. Christopher (and perhaps also the Admiral) as San Cristóbal de La Habana. The blending of Habaguanex and St. Christopher established another precedent. In Havana, distinct cultures and creeds would always cross and mix.

Geographically, however, a better site already beckoned: the fine bay on the north coast that Columbus had not seen, but Sebastian de Ocampo had. Ocampo was a veteran of Columbus's second voyage, dispatched later by the Spanish crown to establish Cuba's true shape once and for all. Circumnavigating that long thin body of land, he concluded it was an island indeed. In the course of this circumnavigation he landed his two ships in a bay he called Carenas, where he stopped for the process called "careening," or scraping the hulls and recoating them with natural tar or pitch which he found oozing in abundance from the rocks.

Sometime thereafter the place was visited by Father Bartolomé de las Casas, who had already participated in the conquests of Hispaniola and eastern Cuba as military officer, chaplain, settler, landowner, and master of indigenous serfs or slaves. The horrors he had observed—the decimation of the native population by massacre, disease, and forced labor panning local streams for scant quantities of gold—would later be recorded in his justly famous Brief History of the Destruction of the Indies, and in the petitions for an end to Indian slavery that he filed with the King. Of the Bay of Carenas, he wrote prophetically, "There are few harbors in Spain, and perhaps not in any other parts of the world, that may equal it." Thus he too predicted the future of Havana. For five centuries it would be a strategic location and an international port.

It took one more ingredient, though, to bring this about. Venturing to the New World in search of a short route to China and India, the Spaniards stumbled instead on a new continent, with civilizations possessed of more silver and gold than they had ever before seen. These civilizations, as Columbus had noted, "have no iron or steel or weapons," and a small number of Spanish troops "would suffice to destroy all that land." The first to find and conquer such riches was Hernán Cortés, a Spanish law school dropout turned military adventurer, briefly deputy governor of Cuba, who in 1519 slipped out of Santiago de Cuba in defiance of the governor's orders with eleven ships under his own command. He picked up some additional recruits from among the disgruntled settlers of the original San Cristóbal de La Habana, and soon made landfall in Veracruz to begin the conquest of Mexico. When he sent a ship full of Aztec gold to the King, his emissaries sailed along Cuba's north coast and stopped for provisions in the Bay of Carenas or someplace nearby. It soon became clear that the harbor offered an ideal spot for assembling and provisioning the treasure fleets returning to Spain, from which they could take advantage of the Gulf Stream and the Bahama Channel for a speedy voyage to Seville.

In the meantime, refugees from the original San Cristóbal de La Habana settled here. They did not choose the shore of the bay at first, but rather the mouth of a river some four miles to the west, which the native inhabitants called Casiguaguas and the Spaniards called La Chorrera, the spout. This spot is now well within metropolitan Havana, the mouth of the river today called the Almendares. During intervening years it would be the site of bombardment and landing by British invaders in the eighteenth century, and the terminus of a train line to the secluded bathing and vacation spots of Vedado in the nineteenth. In the twentieth century a Secretary of Public Works would use the fruits of corruption to build his pleasure dome there, complete with bronze lions and live ones—an estate later to be sacked by a crowd celebrating a Cuban revolution that nearly triumphed when Fidel Castro was only five years old. Today that estate is a restaurant and night club frequented mostly by foreign tourists, and the nearby end of Havana's seawall a gathering point for Cuban youth. But in 1518 the settlement was just a small gathering of *bohíos*, the thatch-roof huts of palm leaves, mud, and branches that the settlers copied from the native Taino Indians—a settlement which most of the Spaniards soon abandoned, yet again, for new quarters on the bay.

There is no historical record of exactly when they moved, or how they marked the city's third founding, if at all. But modern Havana takes it as an article of faith that on St. Christopher's Day of 1519, those Spaniards celebrated this third and final move with a town council meeting followed by a mass, both held in the open air under a towering ceiba tree close by the shore of the bay. The roots of this legend are so deep that already in 1754, when the allegedly historic tree died, governor Francisco Cagigal de la Vega ordered the carving of a commemorative column to be placed at its foot. "Stop here, passerby," his inscribed proclamation commanded in Latin, a language which very few of the residents of the city could read. He enjoined future pilgrims to imagine "a tree, a leafy ceiba, or shall I say a memorable sign of the prudence and the ancient religion of the young city." He ordered a new tree planted from a cutting of the old.

The column is still there, at the edge of Old Havana's Plaza de Armas, standing before a small commemorative neoclassical temple built in 1828. But it's the tree, not the column or the temple, that forms a strand of the web of popular culture in Havana. Ceibas are powerful trees in Cuban lore, which draws from the traditions of both Africa and Spain. When the Virgin came to the palm tree, one myth has it, the tree would not step aside, and so it was condemned to absorb the full rays of the sun. The ceiba, which did not make the same mistake, was blessed with the spreading foliage that crowns its tall, bulbous, elephant-leg trunk. For the Africans brought to Cuba as slaves the ceiba took the place of a species of baobab, and so became the deity Iroko, uniter of heaven and earth, and the dwelling place of many more deities. When Chinese traditions were added to the Yoruba-Catholic mix, the ceiba tree also became the body of Sanfán Kon, now identified with the *orisha* Changó and his alter ego, Santa Bárbara. Every November 16, hundreds of *habaneros* come to circle the ceiba, three times, in silence. On each circuit they make a wish.

We do not know what the founders wished for, this small group of Spaniards, all or almost all of them men, seeking their fortunes in the Indies far from home. We do know something of what they did. Once again, they built bohíos, which they laid out along a few crooked dirt lanes. Some waited for their chance to join other expeditions to the American mainland. When Cuban governor Hernando de Soto set sail from Havana for Florida in 1538 with a flotilla of ships and a thousand troops to pursue the chimeras of the Fountain of Youth and the Seven Cities of Cibola made of solid gold, he took most of the town's citizens with him. He left his wife Doña Isabel de Bobadilla behind in at least nominal command. Four years later, a few survivors of his expedition brought news of his death on the shores of the Mississippi, the great river he had found. Meanwhile, in Havana, others had set out to make a living by provisioning the passing ships and fleets.

The ships needed fresh water, which was brought in small boats from La Chorrera. They needed dried meat and leather, both secured from livestock raised on the settlers' land grants on the city's outskirts, and they needed durable wood for repairs, which could be felled from the forests of caoba, mahogany, cedar, and ebony that surrounded the city on all landward sides. But most of all, they needed bread. If Cuba was no place for growing wheat, making do without wheat flour was something else the Spaniards had learned from the native inhabitants before they disappeared. The root of a plant the Tainos called *yucay* could be ground into a kind of flour, which in turn could be baked into a dry round bread called *casabe*, with the texture of a thin cracker, which could be sold to the passing crews. The surviving Indians were put to work cultivating this food in the settlers' land grants. Soon, this labor passed to small numbers of newly imported African slaves.

Casabe is now rare in Havana, though it can still be found on the eastern part of the island, but yucca, boiled and then drenched in garlic sauce, remains a staple with pride of place on the dinner table. In the meantime, the native word for the substitute bread found its way into Spanish and then French, so that the European colonizers, by the time they took the yucca plant to Africa, called it "cassava." But the problem for Havana's handful of landowning citizens was how to capitalize on it. Though the prices of *casabe* and dried meat doubled or even tripled when significant numbers of ships were in port, still Havana was a poor place at best. In the 1550s, when the imports of gold and silver from the Americas reached the unprecedented level of 2 million ducats a year (the equivalent of some 16,000 pounds of gold), Havana could boast only fifty landowners, four streets with scattered lots and houses of boards and thatch, an adobe church with a small, half-completed bell tower, and a ruined earthenwork fort that De Soto had left behind. The total population of the town and surrounding area was probably well under a thousand, perhaps half Spaniards and the rest Indians, Africans, mestizos, and mulattos, some slave and some free. The grandest house—belonging to the farmer, real estate developer, butcher-shop owner, and public official Juan de Rojas—was the only two-story building and one of the few to boast masonry rather than bare cedar boards and palm thatch.

The threat of piracy, more than the sale of *casabe*, led to the town's first real spurt of growth. As a safe port en route to and from

Spain's New World empire, Havana developed a unique strategic position. By the end of the sixteenth century, Havana would acquire the honorific title "Key to the Indies," primarily because rival empires were intent on picking the Spanish lock. French pirates and privateers were the first to begin menacing Spanish shipping, not only in European waters, but in the seas of the American colonies (the so-called Spanish Main). They picked off isolated ships on the high seas, and they set out to attack the poorly defended ports.

In 1537, a French pirate exacted 700 ducats in gold as his price for not putting Havana to the torch. The residents paid, but when three ships opportunely arrived from Mexico after the Frenchmen left, the local authorities ordered them to deposit their gold and silver ashore, and give chase. The pirates captured the Spanish pursuers, returned to Havana, and confiscated the town's replenished stock of treasure. In 1555, another Frenchman, the privateer Jacques de Sores, approached at the head of a fleet of four ships. De Sores had already raided Santiago de Cuba, kidnapping the archbishop and leading citizens, whom he freed for a ransom of eighty thousand pesos and the silver ornaments of the church. Guided by a Portuguese pilot who had once lived in Havana, he proceeded to that harbor where he expected to find valuable cargoes at the docks.

When there turned out to be no treasure ships, de Sores and his crew occupied the town for nearly a month, during which the pirate used Juan de Rojas's two-story house as his fortress, repelled an attack by a hastily gathered militia, and demanded a ransom of hidden gold and silver plus *casabe* and meat. When the residents couldn't or wouldn't comply, he ordered the buildings smeared with pitch (the same local natural substance that had so entranced Sebastian de Ocampo) and set afire. All told, seventeen of Havana's fifty-one landowners and an unknown number of other Spaniards, Africans, and native inhabitants lost their lives in battle or reprisals. In a final act of farewell de Sores raided the surrounding farms, taking further prisoners whom he held for ransom; six male slaves whose masters did not pay up were hanged.

The town council, reporting to the King, insisted that de Sores was "a terrible Lutheran heretic, as were all of those who came with him," as could be seen from their words and deeds. "His Divine Majesty" must have had a reason for chastising the city, the local authorities concluded sorrowfully, but the King, unconvinced, decided to take action. Faced not only with the French threat but with the beginnings of a still more dangerous English one, the Spanish court had decided that the American trade needed protection. Thenceforth, the vital cargoes would not travel in small groups but in great convoys, accompanied by warships. From the 1560s on, two fleets left Seville each year, one in April or May for the Caribbean islands and Mexico, one in August for Cartagena and Panama. The following spring both return fleets would assemble, bit by bit, in Havana. There the treasure ships of Spanish America gathered, assembling gold and silver, pearls and plumage, precious hardwoods and hardy potatoes, the astonishing flavors of pineapple and chocolate—and there, too, the ceramics and silks and spices that came across the Pacific in special galleons from Manila to Acapulco, crossed Mexico overland, and again were loaded onto ships in Veracruz.

In Havana assembled, in short, everything worth shipping back to fill the coffers of Spain and its legion of creditors. In Havana, too, the armed galleons of the Spanish military fleet would await this treasure, availing themselves of services of refitting and repair, while their crews took shore leave in the town. So for weeks and often months, as the fleet gathered, Havana would become home to galleons, cargo ships, merchants, soldiers, sailors, commanders, and crews—most of them with considerable money to spend.

To protect the newly strategic town, a permanent military garrison was established. On the high cliff or *morro* on the east side of Havana Bay, a tall stone watchtower was built, from which sentinels could watch for hostile ships and warn the town. In the town itself rose a solid stone fortress, a four-pointed star designed to withstand a lengthy siege, with drawbridge, moat, high parapets, and walls fifteen feet thick. The Castillo de La Real Fuerza, completed in 1577 a stone's throw from the famous ceiba, is the oldest construction that still stands in Havana today. Its rough utilitarian walls contrast with the elegant portals and colonnades of two centuries later, but its strategic location and design can still be appreciated at a glance. The Real Fuerza's cannon commanded a new town square, the Plaza de Armas, as well as the waters of the port. There were seven cannon to begin with, a quantity soon doubled by purchases from passing warships, though this did not keep governors and fort commanders from begging Madrid for more and better ones.

La Fuerza proved only a beginning. Despite the new fortification, in 1586 Havana received a visit from the English archprivateer

Francis Drake. On previous expeditions, Drake's ships had rav-
ished the sea lanes and coasts of the Caribbean and South America,
and even made their way into the Pacific, capturing rich prizes of
the coasts of Peru. In this new incursion, they had already attacked
Santo Domingo and Cartagena de Indias. In May, Drake's armada
was observed rounding Cape San Antonio on Cuba's western tip,
where it stopped to take on water and firewood. Now lookouts
were posted along the seafront from La Chorrera to the village of
Cojímar far to the east of the bay, and the town council assembled
all available Spanish settlers from the countryside around Havana
and put them to work, along with slaves, free blacks, and Indians,
digging trenches and manning observation posts.

After five days of tacking back and forth along the coastline, Drake
turned northward to raze the Spanish settlement at St. Augustine, in
Florida, instead. That Havana escaped English attack this time, however, did not ease the fear of future attempts. A new governor, the
field marshal Juan de Tejada, and an Italian military engineer,
Giovanni Battista Antonelli, were dispatched to Havana to render
the port invulnerable. Antonelli had been in Spanish service for
many years, and this was his second American journey, although all
we know of the first is that it got him as far as the Straits of Magellan,
from which he had returned "naked and poor" and inclined to enter
a monastery until this new commission beckoned him westward
once again. His charge was to construct a pair of forts at the mouth of
the bay, as well as a canal to bring the fresh water of the Chorrera to
the harbor where it could safely supply ships.

The canal opened first, in 1592, discharging its current "as wide
as the body of an ox" in the area then known as the Plaza of the
Swamp and two other waterfront sites. It was called the Royal
Ditch (*zanja*), and a part of its route is still followed by the street
called Zanja that passes through Central Havana and Chinatown.
The ditch's terminus is marked today by the half-block Callejón del
Chorro that leads from the Plaza de la Catedral to the artists' print-
making cooperative at its end. "The Field Marshall Jvan de Texada
brought this water in 1592" reads a very old inscription above an
old spout-hole in a seashell design, while a few blocks south, near
the Plaza Vieja, recent restoration efforts have exposed a section of
the ditch itself, revealing the combination of rock and coral out of
which it was laboriously built by slaves.

On the flat western shore of the bay's narrow neck, north of the
town itself, meanwhile, gradually rose the Castillo de San Salvador

de la Punta, today a maritime museum, which forms the starting point of the modern Malecón. On the great cliff opposite, Antonelli laid out the fortress that has become the backdrop for every foreign newscaster reporting from Havana, and the site, over the years, of garrisons, battles, and dungeons, book fairs, art expositions, and more: el Castillo de los Tres Reyes del Morro, the Morro Castle, its walls and turrets rising directly out of the rock, connected on the landward side by a flying bridge, topped by a lighthouse (then a tall tower with a signal fire) whose beam can be seen from the hills and rooftops of Havana and from miles out to sea. Across the slim channel between the forts was strung a chain of wood and iron, anchored to a buried cannon at either end, that could be drawn up at night or in the face of attacking ships. Thus ships in the harbor were protected not only by the artillery of the forts but by this physical barrier as well.

It took forty years to complete both fortresses, financed like the Real Fuerza by taxes on shipping and sales in Havana and by a series of subsidies from the viceroyalty of New Spain (Mexico), for which the fleets continued to be a lifeline. When these immense construction projects were finally complete, Havana became, by royal Spanish decree, a city, "the key to the New World and bulwark of the Indies," soon to be granted an official seal bearing the likeness of the three forts, as silver towers in a blue field, ranged around a golden key. Between 1575 and 1650, shipments of gold and silver alone from Spain's American colonies averaged an incredible 6 million ducats a year. As guardian of this trade, Havana became a city still rude but at the same time cosmopolitan, a city of wharves and warehouses and all manner of nautical workshops for repairing or manufacturing ships' equipment, instruments, supplies, and maps. It was a city where viceroys in transit rubbed shoulders with itinerant vendors, priests with prostitutes, Andalusian soldiers and sailors with Chinese traders and African slaves.

On the one hand, a sixteenth-century governor, sounding rather like Columbus, wrote with true or mock horror of his new post, "All the criminals banished from Peru and New Spain and other parts, those sent back to Spain for failing to fetch their wives, the bankrupt merchants, the wives fleeing their husbands—all come in the fleets, as do to friars in lay clothes and vagabonds and rascals and sailors jumping ship, all of whom roam through the citizens' properties and fear neither royal justice nor God." On the other hand, we can only guess what excitement must have been provoked when Havana received its most exotic visitor of these years, the samurai Hasekura Tsunenaga, the first Japanese emissary to cross the Pacific. He arrived from Mexico in 1614 with thirty retainers and a Dominican priest en route to Madrid and Rome on a secret mission to establish direct trade between Japan and the Spanish Empire. His global trade mission failed when the Tokugawa shogunate decided to close Japan to outside influence, but Tsunenaga returned to Havana quite recently, at the beginning of the twenty-first century, in the form of a life-sized statue, a gift from his native province of Sendai, in a small Japanese garden halfway between the Real Fuerza and La Punta flanked by two rows of tall, sinuous royal palms.

Noble visitors and nascent industries aside, however, Havana's residents lived chiefly off of what supports most shipping towns and military ports: supplying drink, cheap lodging, food, gambling and sex. And customs duties and their attendant corruption and slavery, though of a type significantly different from the later plantation sort.

In 1594, Governor Juan de Maldonado decreed closure of any tavern that refused to make a forced loan for the completion of the two new forts—and he counted eighty that *did* contribute, in a city whose irregular populated streets could not have equaled more than thirty square blocks. This number, he added "would not be a small one, even in Madrid." The town council, some three decades before, had estimated total annual sales at fifty-two barrels of wine a year, approximately twenty thousand bottles of modern size. To keep down "disorder" (and probably to limit competition), an early regulation limited tavern keepers to one open barrel at a time, and stated they could not be resupplied until they displayed the disassembled staves of the previous barrel in their yards. The wine, of course, had to be imported just like its consumers. Principally from the Canary Islands, it came in the outbound ships, so the town's legion of tavern operators were operating on slender margins between what they bought and what they sold. Most of them operated out of their own houses, where many also sold lodging (with or without hammocks or beds) and prepared food. Others sold food on the streets, either prepared dishes or fruits picked from trees within the town or carried in from the outlying farms.

In all of these trades, Africans and mulattos were active as well as Spaniards, and possibly more so, though they were always subject to regulations to keep their competition down:

> Because many black women and other persons go about on the streets selling sausage and pastries of yucca flour and ground corn without authorization . . . it is ordered that sausages shall be sold only at a price of one *real* for the length of one yard and a half, and all the other goods should not be sold unless the *regidor* or his deputy should declare a price for it.
>
> Because many black slave women of this town have taken up the business of having a house in which to sell lodging or wine or tobacco at much prejudice to the public good, it is proclaimed that from today on no black slave woman shall dare live in a house of her own nor have a tavern nor sell tobacco on the pain of fifty lashes for any of said black women who act to the contrary, and any owner who allows this shall incur a fine of two pesos.

At the same time, larger business in the wine trade was done from the top, and like other opportunities for economic favoritism, it engendered constant feuds. Fort commander Diego Fernandes de Quiñones, in 1584, accused the current governor and his wife of profiteering on wine and oils, buying them directly from incoming ships at pretax prices, restricting the supply available to others, and operating their own taverns that sold drink at twice the normal rate.

As for bulk food supplies, *casabe* still fed the soldiers of the forts, but the ships often took on sea turtle, butchered on the outskirts of the town and cut into long thin slices, salted, and hung in the sun and wind to dry. "And so it serveth the mariners in all their voyage to Spain," wrote Thomas Gage, who sailed back to Europe from Havana in 1637, "which they eat boiled with a little garlic, and I have heard them say that to them it tasted as well as any veal." Being a ship's passenger rather than a sailor, he dined on chickens and pigs that were taken on board live, and slaughtered en route.

Rivaling provision of drink, food, and lodging were the industries of gambling and prostitution, in which the military garrisons, among others, were intimately involved. Gambling was not only permitted but officially authorized, with the governor, fort commanders, and other officials running games in their houses, from which they extracted a sizable take. One governor's attempt—sincere or not—to outlaw games of chance failed because, as he informed the King, he had jurisdiction over the games in Havana

citizens' houses but not the areas under control of the most important figures, the generals of the fleets. The crown responded by
conceding the right to run gaming inside the forts to an official
called the sergeant major, who surely appreciated the monopoly, to
the extent to which it endured. Fernandes de Quiñones, quoted
above, boasted to the King of his own efforts regulating gambling:
he prohibited cursing during the games, set a penalty for interfer-
ing with the roll of the dice or the deal of cards, and barred the
soldiers from betting the uniforms off their backs.

Francisco de Calona, master of public works, was accused by
four of his Spanish stonecutters of gambling "day and night" and
owing more than his entire salary of 800 ducats a year. Gambling
bred robbery. Practically all the white males of the city went into
the streets armed with sword or dagger, though such weapons
were prohibited for those of darker skin. Don Martín Calvo de la
Puerta, town counselor and court official, obtained a royal decree
authorizing him to carry a small arsenal of two swords, two dag-
gers, and a musket when he ventured onto the streets. His servants,
"to protect their persons," were authorized to go about similarly
armed to the teeth. One way or another, the city was hard to
govern—there were too many characters in the drama, with too
many sources of power, and it has been that way ever since.

Prostitution was of course a major industry in a city whose economy was based on periodic protracted stays by transient men, and
a relative shortage of women as well. Cuban historian Manuel
Moreno Fraginals has pointed out how the city's sexual slang
developed a strongly maritime flavor: the streetwalker was called a
fletera, derived from the term for rented ships or cargo space, and
the term for coitus became *singar* (to row with a single oar protrud-
ing from the stern). Other such maritime sex slang was later
displaced by slang derived from the processing of sugar.

Given the shortage of free white women (and their resultant
value in the marriage market), prostitution was closely bound up
with slavery, as well. Aside from a few mines and the military construction projects, in which the slaves were royal property imported for the purposes, slavery in Cuba's first two centuries was a
small-scale affair. Havana's wealthier citizens owned a few slaves
who acted as household servants, worked on the owners' small
farms or ranches on the outskirts of the city, or were hired out as
day laborers in construction and other trades. When masters
assigned their slaves to work as day laborers, they often provided

incentive for them to develop new (more profitable) skills or to work hard without much supervision, by allowing them to keep part of the daily pay. The luckier male slaves were apprenticed to skilled craftsmen, and often succeeded in eventually buying their freedom. The unlucky were rented for the crueler work of laboring on the huge forts, alongside the slaves belonging to the crown.

Females often ran small eateries for sailors, as noted above, but especially were earmarked for sexual services. Governor Juan de Salamanca, in 1658, suggested that it might be advisable "to require the owners of black women and mulattas to keep them within their houses and not give them permission to live outside nor to go to the mills and corrals . . . because these slaves thus earn for their owners wages much greater than those that are [otherwise] earned," but he did not find that such a prohibition had much effect.

It was common for soldiers in the forts to buy one or two female slaves, and supplement their military earnings (generally delayed) with their earnings as pimps. "Andrea, twenty-five, of the Mandinga nation" was sold by a local citizen to an artilleryman in 1588 for 250 ducats, far more than a soldier could normally afford. That same year, the royal notary Melchor Casas bought the slaves Juan and Esperanza for 500 ducats, then shortly resold Esperanza, a twenty-year-old Biafran, to Pedro de Campos, "a soldier of the fort" for a sum not recorded, of which 140 ducats was a loan which Campos would later pay back.

This practice was not limited to soldiers. A contract from 1579 has a Spaniard renting his female slave to Alonso Rodriguez, *moreno* (black), for a year at a price of five ducats a month, with the stipulation that, while the fleet was in port, the renter had to pay to the owner "what other women of the town would bring in during this time." Churchmen were also involved in the traffic in one way or another, if another section of Governor Salamanca's report to the crown is to be believed:

I have found many [of these women] who maintain friendship with clergy, and in God's service I have tried to banish some for their dissolute behavior and require others to abstain from illicit friendships, but I had to stop because the clergy began to mutiny under protection of a judge . . . When the bishop Don Juan de Montiel received notice of such things, and began to visit his subjects, he died most rapidly and, according to the rabble (as perhaps Your Majesty may

have heard by other means), his dying was assisted, as often happens
in these Indies.

The use of urban slaves as day laborers who could buy their freedom was rooted in part in the scarcity of white wage workers, and
in part in medieval Spanish legal codes from a time when slaves
were more likely to be Moors than Africans. In any case it contributed to the growth in Havana's numbers of free mulattoes and
blacks. So too did the gender imbalance among Spanish settlers,
which resulted in the male settlers coupling first with indigenous
women, and then with African slaves.

Generally speaking, the offspring of the Spanish-Indian unions
were legitimized, and frequently they were *blanqueado* (bleached).
The classic example is the progeny of one Anton Recio, whose
slaves raised cattle in various locations in the outskirts of the city
and who owned some urban lots as well. In 1567 he bought for
800 ducats the office of depository general, otherwise known as
"keeper of the box with three keys." The office charged him with
safekeeping of the funds from tax collections and from the estates
of those who died without heirs on this side of the sea, for which
service he was rewarded not only with a commission of 2.5 percent
but also with the privilege of investing the funds in enterprises of
his choosing. His will listed items valued at 20,000 ducats, including assets in livestock, land, buildings, and slaves, a gold-handled
sword and dagger, and a set of silver tableware. His son Juan, by
his Indian mistress, inherited his estate and—despite a protest by
the rival landowners and officeholders of the de Rojas family—the
job of keeper of escrow funds as well.

The offspring of African-Spanish unions, often the only children
of their fathers, were frequently granted their freedom, or allowed
to buy it at least. Of Havana slaves who obtained their freedom at
young age in this period, the records show a majority being described as mulatto. One Spaniard who purchased the freedom of a
mulatto slave in 1604 said he did so to serve God and because the
slave's father was "an honorable man and my friend." This seems
to have been particularly true of girls. A survey of documents from
the seventeenth and early eighteenth centuries shows that female
slaves were more likely to be granted their freedom either for services rendered or at the time of the owner's death. The survey also
shows that slave women were more likely than men to buy their
freedom, and generally this too at an earlier age.

One way or another, by the seventeenth century, the free blacks and mulattos began to be of considerable numbers, and they—some of them owning a few slaves themselves—worked not only as laborers, laundresses, prostitutes, and street vendors, but also as skilled artisans, small merchants, and operators of established inns and taverns. They had their own religious fraternities that marched in the city's religious processions, and as of 1638 they had a church, the Church of the Holy Spirit, which (after much remodeling) is the oldest in Havana today. Town council minutes began to complain of blacks and mulatos dressing in vibrant colors too rich for their station and blood.

One further testimony to their rise, dating from the end of this period, is the will of Doña Lorenza de Carvajal, who in 1700 left her single-story adobe house facing the moat of the Real Fuerza to her former house slave, the mulatta Juana Carvajal "for the care and friendship with which she has attended me." Juana had already been granted her freedom under the condition that she should continue in service until her mistress's death. She inherited enough money from Doña Lorenza that she soon set about improving the house, where she lived for the next thirty-three years, remodeling it and adding a second story much as white families were starting to do to theirs. She in turn left the house to her two nieces, Margarita and Mónica de Ribera, one of whom lived in a smaller building next door, while a mulatto carpenter named Lúcas Gómez lived on the other side. The nieces sold Juana's house, presumably at some profit, to Don Pedro José Calvo de la Puerta, who was buying up property on the block. Don Pedro was the great-grandson of the Don Martín Calvo of two-sword, two-dagger, and musket fame.

All the same, city ordinances continued the longstanding practice of listing separate penalties according to race. Where a white resident might have to pay a fine, those from "other spheres" received physical punishment: lashes, confinement in stocks, or worse. Colored bakers of *casabe* could have their earthenware grilles smashed or confiscated if they could not name a white landowner they had bought the yucca from.

Across the moat from Juana Carvajal, at the pinnacle of Havana society, the governors enjoyed the distinction, views, and breezes of Real Fuerza's upper story. They were transients in Havana, generally career Spanish military men awarded the post as a plum. Pedro de Valdés, governor and captain general[1] from 1602 to 1607, was a former naval commander who had led several Indies fleets and skippered a prominent warship in the ill-fated Spanish Armada of 1588. He'd been captured in the English Channel by Francis Drake, of whom Valdés later testified that his "valour and felicity was so great that Mars and Neptune seemed to attend him in his attempts." Ransomed from his English captivity, Valdés returned to the King's service and was later awarded the Cuban governorship, which came with attendant luxuries: a budget of 3000 gold pesos for wardrobe, other personal effects, and tableware, plus three house slaves and fourteen paid servant staff. Those 3000 pesos would have bought the captain-general more than his share of the silks and velvets, the fine linens and taffetas, the contrasting emerald greens, blacks, pinks, and yellows preferred by the upper crust. No wonder that an early visitor wrote of the "birds of brilliant plumage" who emerged from the city's "rudely crafted nests."

Valdés left ample record of the rivalries for social position that grew up between governors, fort commanders, and local officials. At the base of such disputes was always money: who had the authority to inspect incoming ships for both taxable goods and contraband, with the opportunities for control of public funds and private payoffs that this implied. The conflict flared most visibly, however, over small symbols of precedence such as who sat where in ceremonial occasions, or who got to ease his bones with a pillow while sitting on the hard benches or sarcophagi in the church. As this old sea dog reported to the King:

> I ordered a velvet cushion taken away from Juan de Villaverde, captain of the Morro, and it came about in this way: Villaverde decided to carry publicly and in my presence a formal staff with insignia of general, the same as I carry in this city in your name. Besides, he took to carrying a velvet cushion into church and sat at my side with both staff and cushion as if there were no difference between us. Though I warned him not to do this, so as not to fall into an act of rebellion, he did it again and so I had the cushion taken from him.

In another letter to the King, Valdés spoke about his own unpopularity with the colonists. He attributed that problem to his insistence that the *naturales* (natives) treat him with the deference that his superior standing deserved. This is the first instance in the Archives of the Indies in which a Spanish official uses such a term to apply to Cubans of European origin. It was a sign of a gap that would loom larger and larger from then on.

Meanwhile, the city grew slowly, and began to cover its rough-ness with some signs of its later grace. Where Valdés had needed to parade in his finery on horseback or slave-carried sedan chair over the muddy streets, in the 1620s governor Lorenzo de Cabrera lurched through the streets in the city's first carriage, along with his relative Don Juan de Benavides, a general of the fleet. Atop the Real Fuerza, ten years later, was built a slender and largely ornamental watchtower, giving the utilitarian fort a fairy-tale castle touch. The tower was topped by a weathervane cast in bronze, the nearly life-sized figure of a woman holding the military cross of Calatrava in one hand and an olive branch in the other and gazing (when the wind was right) out to sea. This figure became known as La Giraldilla, the little sister to the larger-than-life female figure which topped La Giralda, the 300 foot high bell tower of the Cathedral of Seville. But once again differences between Spaniards and *naturales* appeared. La Giralda's weathervane is a representation of the Catholic faith, a demure if triumphant figure, standing straight up-right, decorously cloaked, with bowed head. La Giraldilla stands with her hand on her hip, right knee bent as if in motion, her skirt hiked halfway up her right thigh and, in counterpoint, flying in the breeze behind her left foot. She wears a form-fitting top, she is crowned with a tiara, and her chin tilts proudly up into the air. La Giraldilla became and remains as much a symbol of Havana as the Morro Castle. Whatever the intent of her sculptor (a local craftsman by the name of Martín de Pinzón) Havana legend soon had her de-picting Doña Isabel de Bobadilla, the wife and deputy of Hernando de Soto, gazing seaward for a glimpse of his long-delayed return.

Little by little, Havana and its environs began to produce more than victuals for troops and passing ships. Cannons for the forts were cast in a short-lived foundry alongside the bay, between La Punta and the town, where now stands a children's playground be-hind Tsunenaga's monument, called "La Maestranza" (armory) in recognition of that fact. In the wake of the foundry came shipyards, further south along the bay near the Alameda de Paula, which used Cuban hardwoods to turn out frigates and galleons and cargo ships for the protection of the coasts, the pursuit of pirates and smug-glers, and the annual Indies fleet. The forest of ebony, mahogany, cedar, and oak that had surrounded the city disappeared into ships and the holds of ships, until there were no trees fit for cutting within a twelve mile radius of the city, and the shipbuilders began to feud with the cattle ranchers over who had the right to exploit the forests further out. Tobacco cultivation began (adopted from the native Tainos and Sibonneys) as did construction of small mills to grind the dried tobacco into snuff. Production of sugar began in a minor way, encouraged in part by construction of the *zanja*, whose current south and west of the city was enough to power primitive mills. Among the first in the sugar business were the Recio family, the descendants of Antón, who established their small plantation in the town of Regla across the bay.

Though Havana would never be a city of great cathedrals, ten churches and convents had been built or begun by the end of the seventeenth century. The pealing of their bells now added to the chants of stevedores and food vendors, the appeals of streetwalkers and taunts of sailors, the rolling of dice and drilling of troops and the signal cannon shots from the Morro to announce the comings and goings of ships. Two hospitals (one of them for soldiers) also operated under the auspices of the church.

Religious festivals, royal births, and other important occasions were marked with processions and masquerades, parades including candles and lanterns, artillery barrages from ships and shore, floats with music and dancing, jousting, and running of bulls. Town council records detail spending for "inventions" for such celebrations, which include giants, dragons, monkeys, midgets, and Moors, and complain of women mixing too freely in processions and entertainments of this type. Of popular music in the city at this date, nothing reliable is known. Still, it must have been sometime in these first centuries that Spanish ballads and guitar strings learned to live in creative tension with African drums and call-and-response, and that Havana made its first great contribution to Cuba's polyrhythmic, Afro-Euro-Caribbean musical instrumentation: the *claves*, the rhythm sticks derived from the pegs of wooden sailing ships.

The city suffered the growing pangs of all early modern cities: A fire of 1622 destroyed nearly a hundred houses, and a plague that lasted from May to October of 1649, probably yellow fever, carried off as many as one third of the residents, according to one report. The population in 1660, according to a census, totaled 8000, which was one third of that of the island as a whole. In the 1670s began the last of the military constructions of this period, the construction of a wall around the landward boundaries of the city. Every night and every morning, a cannon blast from one of the warships in the harbor signaled the closing and opening of the gates, and the drawing up or lowering down of the chain strung between the forts at the neck of the bay.

The Italian traveler Giovanni Gemelli Careri, in the chronicle of his round the world voyage, has left the first extensive description of the Cuban capital, where he stayed for two-and-a-half months during the winter of 1698, waiting for a fleet to leave in the spring. He describes a compact, round, walled city a mile and a half in circumference, of mostly single-story houses, populated by "beautiful women and agreeable looking men." He reports a high cost of living, especially when the fleets are in, with wheat bread available for those who can pay the high price of imported flour, and *casabe* eaten not only by the poor, but also by the "extensive families" among the well to do. The workforce is, to his eye, entirely slave, rented out at four reales a day, or six when the fleet is in, and he is interested by a large group of blacks and mulattos preparing for a procession in carnival.

Gemelli Careri's social visits while in Havana are mostly with travelers—Flemish noblewomen returning home from South America as rich widows, university graduates from Peru looking to buy themselves royal posts in Madrid. By contrast, what interests him in Havana itself (devoid, still, of university or nobility) are the tropical fruits brought in from outlying farms—he encounters, for the first time, the guanabana and the caimito—and the exotic birds that may be hunted or collected, from parrots to hummingbirds, as well as a shipload of cardinals which has just arrived from Florida. He notes how the sailors of the fleet, who have just been paid their back salaries, rush to invest in these strange red birds.

When the fleet finally sails, Gemelli Careri travels on the lead galleon, which fires six ceremonial cannonades when it passes the Real Fuerza, which are answered by the guns of the fort, and six more when it passes the Morro, answered the same way. After the warship clears the channel, there is a surprising discovery on board—a woman dressed as a man. As it is too late to turn back, she is lodged among the women, whoever she is, and Havana, whyever she is leaving it, is left behind. But not all the travelers have departed. Despite stern commands that all members of the fleet must leave with their ships, on pain of death, a sizeable number of sailors are missing, having jumped ship after receiving their pay. The Key to the Indies must be more attractive to them than Spain.

2

The Hour of the Mameys

About 1740, Brook Watson, a fourteen-year-old orphan apprenticed to a Boston merchant, had the luck or misfortune to descend from his ship for a swim in Havana Bay to escape the oppressive and unaccustomed heat while accompanying some cargo of his master's. There he was attacked by a shark, which took off his leg before he could be rescued. Years later, as a successful London businessman, he told the story to the American portraitist John Singleton Copley. The painter responded with the first famous American vision of Havana. In Copley's canvas *Watson and the Shark*, the shores of the bay are framed by tall convent towers and the unmistakable bulk of the Morro Castle, and ringed by a forest of three-masted ships. At the center of the painting a naked, pale-skinned youth flails on his back among wind-whipped green swells, while an immense open-jawed shark twice his size, staring out of one cold baleful eye, closes in for the kill. A white officer in knee-britches jabs a spear in the shark's direction. A black sailor, next to him, tosses the desperate youth a rope.

Copley had never seen Havana (or, quite possibly, a shark) but by this time engravings of the city were in wide circulation in England and its trading partners, because in 1762–63, between the moment of Watson's boyhood adventure and Copley's stay in London during the American Revolution, there passed a ten-month period when Havana was a British possession. The Taking of Havana by the English, as this event is always called in Cuba, provided Anglo-Saxon eyes and boots with their first large-scale exposure to a city that would continue to draw them forever more. Equally important, it provided Havana with new realities and new myths that would define Cuban nationality and set a contradictory pattern for relations with foreign powers and foreign peoples in the times to come.

The reasons for the British attack, in the last year of the great-power conflict known as the Seven Years' War, were mixed. Above all, to British imperial and military planners in London, Havana was still the center of Spanish military control in the Caribbean and by extension in Spain's entire American realm. The English were increasingly disputing control of the Caribbean, undermining Spain's monopoly on settlement and trade. In the seventeenth century, Britain had begun colonizing small islands unoccupied by the Spanish, and a British naval expedition had succeeded in wresting Jamaica from Spain. But Havana, boasting at least thirty thousand residents, remained the most important port in the Americas, ranking in both population and riches behind only Lima and Mexico. In 1762 it was significantly larger than Philadelphia and about three times the size of New York. Besides strategic goals, the lure of booty from the city and its transient cargoes beckoned the British military as strongly as it had tempted Francis Drake.

To merchants in England and its North American colonies, meanwhile, Havana meant a market in which to sell slaves, textiles, and machinery, and from which to buy the products of industries still in their infancy in Cuba, but of growing importance to European and colonial tastes. Molasses refined from West Indian sugar cane was crucial to the rum distilleries of New England, and the outskirts of Havana by now contained about a hundred small plantations with primitive mills. Tobacco was likewise being produced and ground into snuff, but its export from Cuba was strictly controlled by a royal monopoly conceded only to merchants of the port of Cádiz in Spain. Contraband trade between Cuba and the British empire was an established tradition, but it was mostly limited to remote coastal areas of the countryside, outside of strict Spanish control. Regla, the small harbor across the bay from Havana that housed the patron saint of sailors, also had a longstanding reputation as a smuggler's haven. Perhaps the ship carrying Brook Watson had been making a quiet visit there.

For both strategic and commercial reasons, then, in 1762 secret plans were drawn up for a naval force of unprecedented size— some two hundred ships and twenty thousand men—to converge on Havana from Britain, Jamaica, and New England. A seventeen-year-old Connecticut volunteer named Levi Redfield enlisted with the hopes of defending his homeland from the French, and of marching through Vermont to Lake Champlain "over a fertile country, the whole of which I had long wished to view." He found instead that he had "left the peaceful abode of my childhood, and commenced a scene of troubles that I had never anticipated." He was shipped to New York, where the troops were confined to their ships for fear of desertion until the fleet set sail for Havana. Though weather, sea battles, and the grounding of some ships delayed the arrival of Redfield and the 4000 regular and provincial troops departing from New York, still on June 6, 1762, the rest of the invasion fleet of 50 warships, 100 or more transports, and 15,000 soldiers, sailors, and slave laborers appeared off Havana, to the consternation of the Spanish governor who had scoffed at rumors of their approach.

Rather than attempt to force entrance to the harbor past the cannons of the Morro and Punta and through their connecting barrier chain, the British chose to land thousands of their troops some miles to the east of the bay, just beyond the fortress at the outlying harbor of Cojímar, which they bombarded until its defenders fled. Cojímar was the same small anchorage where an American writer would two centuries later moor his motor launch, drink, talk with Cuban fishermen, and set his last novel, *The Old Man and the Sea*.

The invading troops encamped on the empty stretch of coast beyond Cojímar, where residents of the housing development of Alamar (to which we will return in the 1970s) today go to swim. Then they made their way overland to the heights of La Cabaña, a ridge overlooking the bay which governor and captain-general Juan de Prado Portocarrero had begun to fortify too late. On these heights the English set up a gun battery to threaten the Morro Castle from the landward side.

There followed two months of siege, cannon duels from ships and shore, and bloody skirmishes bringing heavy loss of life on both sides. A British cannonball exploded alongside a powder magazine near where the art-deco Bacardi building stands today. By some miracle the powder depot did not ignite, but the street was called for many years Calle de la Bomba in commemoration of this narrow escape (it is now the western end of Calle San Juan de Dios), and a nearby market was called The Powderhouse (El Polvorín). Thousands of civilians, including the nuns from the convents and many other women, were evacuated from the city; so were great quantities of the prominent families' cash. Male slaves, on the other hand, were brought in from surrounding farms and mills to participate in the defense.

The British made a second landing, to the west of the city at the mouth of La Chorrera, after cannonading the squat, square fortress there into submission, and occupied the rugged coral seacoast between La Chorrera and the city. Inland, they diverted the waters of the Royal Ditch into the Bay and attempted to cut the walled city off from the countryside, reinforcements, and supplies.

Responsibility for feeding the beleaguered populace fell to the city's hereditary chief magistrate, Pedro José Calvo de la Puerta, whose townhouse was the former dwelling of the ex-slave Juana de Carvajal, now much expanded by combination with other properties on the same block. Don Pedro's office carried the duty of regulating the slaughterhouse and meat distribution, previously a lucrative task compensated with a fee called the "right of the knife-thrust," three silver *reales* for every slaughtered cow. As the siege tightened, food became scarce. Spanish authorities issued an order instructing citizens to throw all their dogs into the sea, so as not to compete for scarce supplies.

While the British overwhelmed Spanish troops and the local white, mulatto, and black militia units in conventional fighting, some of the militias turned to guerrilla warfare under independently operating chiefs, in the same spirit that had animated the settlers who counterattacked the French pirate occupiers of two centuries before. These guerrillas inflicted new casualties, took prisoners, and threatened the supply lines of British forward troops. The most famous was the group from Guanabacoa led by the mayor of that village, José Antonio Gómez de Boullones. Relieved of his command and confined to the defensive encampment on the hill of Jesús del Monte by a jealous Spanish colonel, Gómez de Boullones died before the end of the siege. Some versions have him perishing of apoplexy, others of melancholy, others of exhaustion after his feats. All record that he became a hero, the nascent nation's very first one, who has passed into Havana legend under his nickname Pepe Antonio, no last name required.[1]

Still more damaging to the English were the effects of another native enemy—tropical fevers. Given the exposure to midday sun and evening mosquitoes, the lack of fresh water in the trenches, and the effect of guerrilla action on food supplies, illness took such a toll that the majority of the besieging troops were out of action much of the time. The result of the massive expedition hung in doubt.

Finally, the New England contingent arrived, including both the regular army units and the 2000 provincial volunteers from New York, Rhode Island, Connecticut, and New Jersey, including Levi Redfield, the seventeen-year-old who had hoped to march through Vermont toward Canada and fight against the French. These reinforcements, coupled with the efforts of sappers who at last succeeded in blowing up a section of the Morro's seaward wall, allowed the English to storm the castle. They were then able to reduce La Punta fortress to submission with the Morro's guns. Twelve days later, Spanish authorities surrendered the city, and the British occupiers marched in. The prize yielded the victors a booty of some 3 million British pounds in funds from the royal treasury, goods and cargoes belonging to Spanish merchants, Spanish naval ships and supplies, and reparation levies extracted from the civilian elite and the church. Terms of the capitulation allowed Spanish troops to be repatriated and city authorities to administer local affairs after swearing loyalty to George III. Local residents had four years to decide whether they would become British subjects or would emigrate to Spain.

"I walked over the hill a way to see the fighting and there was a very grand affair to be seen," reports the journal of Roswell Park of Preston, Connecticut, who like Redfield arrived in the siege's final days. "The city of Hivanna with all its fine buildings, churches, nunneries, the great battery, the governor's fort in town, the many batteries round the famous place for to bait the bull for diversion. There was the finest land to look to I ever saw. Coconut trees, cabbage trees [palms], canaries, grapes, the cattle, the ass, the mule." He did not get to see much more. On August 13 he records the capitulation, and on August 16 his journal ends. He took sick, his wife's postscript to his diary says, and "was buried at the Havannah where they made a burying place to bury those who died there." Deaths on the Spanish side may have reached 2000, though some reports say less. British losses totaled about 5000, the great majority from disease.

There are few surviving testimonies from Havana residents, but what there are show how the defense, capture, and occupation of the city heightened the distinction between Spaniards and *naturales*. Only eleven days after the English victory appeared a memorandum, addressed to the Spanish king Carlos III, signed by the *"señoras de La Habana."* In this letter, the ladies of Havana's aristocracy recount the events of the attack and siege, accusing the captain-general and his top aides of having intended the city's surrender all along. They cite the Spanish commanders' refusal to use guerrilla tactics to stop the British advance through unfamiliar territory; their having failed to either fortify La Cabaña hill or clear it of anything providing shelter for the English; their abandoning that height without an organized defense; their sinking three warships in the mouth of the harbor to prevent a British entry, at the cost keeping all the rest of the King's navy bottled up inside; their holing up within the walls of the city rather than risking their lives in an attempt to relieve the Morro; their failing to recognize the importance of the English preparations to mine the castle; and, finally, their deciding on the capitulation of the city without consulting the city council, citizens, or bishop.

In contrast, the letter lauds guerrilla leader Pepe Antonio and also Luis de Aguiar, a city councilor who defended La Chorrera fortress and harried the English gun emplacements and supply lines thereafter. It takes pains, more surprisingly, to remember "a large number of slaves, released by us their owners" who mounted cannon and other defenses, as well the members of a free mulatto militia unit who, without pay, did attempt to fortify La Cabaña, and a contingent of twenty black militiamen who sallied forth from the Morro to attack the British with machetes in hand. It further takes to task, in a generalized denunciation, the "despotism of the governors of these parts of the Indies who, when any of your vassals take the legitimate measure of complaining to your Majesty or making you aware of any important news, trample upon them and close all doors by use of the word *sedition.*"

Most historians attribute the composition of this remarkable letter—indeed seditious of contemporary authority and ideology, if brimming with declared loyalty to the King—to the Marquesa Beatriz de Jústiz y Zayas, then twenty-nine years old. The marquesa's family was typical of Havana's new aristocracy. Her mother came from a landed Cuban family, while her father was a Spanish colonel and former fort commander. She had married a Havana-born city councilor, treasury official, and possessor of one of the first titles of nobility to be sold to rich Cubans by the Spanish crown. The Jústiz house was one of the city's finest, representative of its growing prosperity as its production of ships, sugar, and tobacco slowly increased. Close to the sea by the Plaza de Armas, the mansion boasted a Moorish-style watchtower that rose four stories above the street. Not limiting herself to the Memorial, the Marquesa de Jústiz wrote and published (again anonymously) a poem likewise addressed to the King. "A Sorrowful Metrical Expression of the Siege and Surrender of Havana" echoes many of the same criticisms and praises, while glossing them with biblical references, baroque verbal dexterity, and lamentations as to the fate of city and its ships. In particular, Jústiz y Zayas singles out the valor of the *paysanage* (native-born civilians) "who drew their first breath in this land, and gave it their last." She contrasts them with the "hardened commanders" who "closed their ears" to all entreaty for action. The poem also sets a pattern for later patriotic images of a female Havana or Cuba resisting a male threat from the north.

> If to close the port
> they sacrificed those ships
> that was no difficult birth
> but miscarriage and mistake.
> For it left the passage open,
> that trinity poorly placed,
> and brought insult to the Port
> whose splendor feels with deep pain
> the danger of being forced.

One of the first acts of the new English governor Lord Albemarle (or "*el Milor*" as he was styled by the Havanans in one of their earliest adoptions of English words) was to invite the ladies of the aristocracy to a series of dances, "but the majority replied that they had not shed tears to then entertain themselves in diversions, and few attended." So reported a Jesuit priest in a letter to his superior in Seville, one of the few surviving views of the occupation from the Havana side. The priest added that the governor "repeated his invitation for a second night, extending the invitation and his compliments in visits to their houses, so that many attended, not being able to excuse themselves, but their displeasure could be read in their faces and the invitations ceased." In the meantime, according to popular tradition, during the first days the humbler classes took their revenge by selling the occupiers a lethal combination of bananas (previously unknown to the English) and the rough cane liquor called aguardiente, which made them heavily sick. *Habaneros* lampooned the British troops, who patrolled the city in their red uniform coats and black pants, by calling them *mameyes*, after that favorite Cuban fruit with its bright red pulp and long black seed.

The disdain was apparently mutual in those early days. "The better sort of people," haughtily observed Joseph Gorham, a regular-duty officer from Cape Cod, "[are] courteous and civil, but seemingly indolent, fond of rich and gaudy furniture and apparel. The common people are a low, cunning, deceitful, false and thieving set, the Spanish joined indiscriminately in marriage with Negroes, mulattos, etc., which produces as bad a mongrel crew, perhaps as any on Earth." The mixing of races got a more bemused—if confused—response from Levi Redfield. He reported that the Hispanic whites were themselves "of tawny complexion," that the free white and black inhabitants "enjoy the same liberty and equality" and that "many white gentlemen, of considerable respectability among the Spaniards, are seen to walk the streets with their sweet black wenches by their sides, perhaps each leading a lusty copper colored infant *sans culotte* by the hand."

Be that as it may, the confusion surrounding the city's capitulation was the signal for numbers of enslaved Africans to escape to the countryside—fleeing their old masters or the threat of worse treatment by the occupiers, or both. The city council promptly commissioned nineteen entrepreneurs "able, of good reputation, and white," to hunt them down, along with any livestock that they had taken, for a fee of ten pesos per slave and five per mule or horse. The council specified that those to be retrieved did not include the hundred or so who had been promised freedom during the siege by then-governor Prado for taking up arms against the English, an action which Prado told the king he had taken to prevent the English from making the same promise first. In fact, some of the newly appointed slave hunters did set about capturing and selling free blacks, while others of the hunters were themselves taken prisoner by Spanish authorities in parts of the island outside English jurisdiction, who accused them of having collaborated with the enemy.

As time wore on, relations between English and Cubans seem to have changed. The city remained under occupation, with cannon removed from ships and batteries commanding the streets and squares, but the majority of troops from both sides boarded ships for home. If some among the elite retired to their country estates, others who had evacuated the city returned, and they brought their hidden cash.

Two members of the local aristocracy—both of them sugar planters and city officials—served as lieutenant governors under Lord Albemarle. One was Sebastian de Peñalver, descended from a royal treasurer and tax collector, who had recently added a gracious arcaded gallery to provide relief from the sun outside his mansion on what was then still the Plaza of the Swamp, terminus of the Royal Ditch. (Under the name Palacio de los Marqueses de Aguas Claras, housing the restaurant El Patio, it now looks out on the Plaza de la Catedral.) The other was Gonzalo Recio de Oquendo, great-great-great-great-grandson of an indigenous woman and Anton Recio, the "keeper of the box with three keys." Peñalver acquired the nickname *el inglesito* for his alleged subservience to Albemarle, but he was not alone in seeing what opportunities this new fleet and garrison might offer. As in times past, repeated prohibitions (from both local authorities and *el Milor*) on sales of wine or aguardiente to the British troops by tavern keepers or itinerant vendors testify to a practice that must have been widespread. Social barriers broke down too. Two young women who defied their fathers and sought to elope with English soldiers were discovered hiding in empty barrels onboard departing ships, giving rise to a ditty, probably invented by Spanish sailors, that said:

> The girls of Havana
> have lost the fear of God,
> for they go off with the English
> in casks for salt cod.[2]

Cuban scholar Luisa Campuzano has observed that such couplets may have been a form of Spanish revenge on the female authors of the critical memorandum and the "Metrical Expression" for their temerity. That the blame for fraternization was unfairly placed on women, however, does not mean the fraternization wasn't real. The Jesuit (who, being of Irish origin, had his own bones to pick with the English) complained in his letter about the familiarity and courtesy offered to the English officers in many houses, including houses of some distinction, adding "I don't know where this would have led if our captivity had lasted some years more."

Some of that temptation to mix with the English must have had to do with novelty, with Havana's eternal port-town capacity to investigate and assimilate the new. More important were the economic opportunities, as the Jesuit's letter also maintains:

> Though in the beginning there were many who wanted to be the first to embark themselves and their goods back to Spain, and it seemed that many reams would be needed for the paperwork, I believe that after four years a handful of sheets would have sufficed—not owing to the attraction of English customs, but for the quantities of food, clothing, economic opportunities and other goods that from these countries flow.

Concretely, the Spanish monopolies were eliminated at a single stroke, as were the high taxes levied in Spain on goods headed for Havana. So too, at least by the *Milor*'s official edict, was the past practice of bribing local officials as a regular cost of doing business. Trade with England, the British West Indies, and North America opened wide. Reports from the time claim that close to a thousand commercial trading ships entered or left the port of Havana during the ten months of British control, when the quantity previously arriving for the purpose of trade with Cuba itself had been ten or twelve a year at most. Allowing for some exaggeration, and the fact that many ships came primarily to remove troops and captured supplies, still the change is evident.

Merchants descended on Havana from London, Liverpool, Kingston, New York, Boston, and Philadelphia. "Ourselves have great reason to rejoice," exulted the preacher Samuel Frink of Shrewsbury, Massachusetts, in a sermon of thanksgiving when news of the opening of Havana arrived. "That Englishmen should some time or other walk as freely about the city as Spaniards," he said, was an old prophecy fulfilled. "In every street, two or more warehouses have sprung up," wrote the Marqués de Jústiz y Santa Ana, husband of the poet, in a letter to the Spanish ex-governor (with whom he seems to have been on more cordial terms than the marquesa was). His family had limited itself to buying some ceramics, he claimed, but the English had "infested us with all of their clothing and other goods." Grains, flour, wool, linen, and machinery all came in the holds of the merchant vessels.

"There was sufficient demand for everything brought to market from Europe or America," Albemarle later claimed, "the Spaniards [Havanans] having been glad to buy the goods as fast as they could, finding them much cheaper" than before. Some other testimonies disagree, claiming that Havana did not yet have sufficient purchasing power to buy everything that came. Lt. Governor Peñalver, among others, was involved in a scheme to reexport English goods to Veracruz. It was during the occupation or shortly after that Pedro José Calvo de la Puerta hired a muralist to decorate the walls of his house, a fashion that spread as the wealth of the city's aristocracy grew. The unknown artist, probably self-trained, painted colorful images of Havana—complete with aristocrats, house slaves, and English soldiers—as well as European cities and country scenes. Archeologists date the mural to the time of the occupation both from their study of the materials used and from the breadth of information the artist apparently had access to.

In exchange for what they sold in Havana, the English and North American merchants took out cash, sugar, tobacco, and IOUs—the last of which would give them trading privileges even after the occupation came to an end. *Habaneros* voyaged to North American ports with some of these cargoes, establishing new commercial relationships that would last, and glimpsing markets that could be theirs to enjoy.

Historians argue as to whether in this ten-month period there was a boom in sugar production, or merely an image of what that boom might be. They agree, however, that the opportunity for trade with England and its possessions brought Cuban sugar planters what they most urgently needed if they were to expand production to compete with the large estates of the French and British islands which had dominated the market so far. Planters needed modern machinery, and they needed many more laborers to feed that machinery with firewood and sugar cane. The British commerce brought the machinery, but most especially and tragically, it brought slaves.

The chief merchant accompanying and supplying the English fleet was also a leading slaver, Thomas Kennion of Jamaica and Liverpool. Kennion brought in shiploads of Africans himself and also acted as authorized reseller for others in the trade. Thousands of Africans were brought in chains from Jamaica, Africa itself, and possibly the Carolinas. More entered in this brief period—and were sold at lower prices—than in the previous several years or even decade of Spanish rule. The English began to import the flood of slaves that the Spanish monopoly had been unable or afraid to introduce.

Writing thirty years later, Francisco de Arango y Parreño, the foremost Cuban economist and planter-ideologue of his day, declared the period of British domination "the true epoch of the resurrection of Havana." Arango, an in-law of the Calvos de la Puerta and the great-grandson of yet another Spaniard who had arrived as tax collector for the King, was born two years after the occupation but wrote about it as if he had been there. "The tragic event of its surrender to the English," he declared, "gave [the city] life in two ways: the first was the considerable riches, with the great proportion of Negroes, machinery, and textiles which one year of commerce with Great Britain rained down; the second was demonstrating to our court [in Spain] the importance of this city and calling forth all its attention and care."

All its attention and care, because Havana did not remain English for long. On the worldwide chessboard of imperial conflict that reached from Manila to the Mississippi, the Cuban capital turned out to be a pawn. In December of 1762, Benjamin Franklin opined, "The taking of the Havannah is a conquest of the greatest importance and will doubtless contribute a due share of weight in procuring us a reasonable terms of peace, if John Bull does not get drunk with victory, double his fists, and bid all the world kiss his Arse." Though a faction in the British Parliament and in North America wanted to hold onto Havana, majority opinion in both places had other priorities—as did sugar planters in the British West Indies, who didn't want another English sugar island competing with them. The Treaty of Paris that ended the Seven-Years' War gave Britain dominion over Canada and Florida, new navigation rights in the Caribbean, and new territories in India, Africa, and the Mediterranean. Havana went back to Spain, and with it came Louisiana (as compensation for other losses) from France.

But Spain relaxed its grip on Cuban commerce, preferring to lighten some regulations, especially on the slave trade, and to tax the increased proceeds instead. Over the next thirty-five years, 100,000 slaves entered the country, as compared to an estimated 60,000 between 1512 and 1763. In the three quarters of a century thereafter—between 1790 and 1865—something like 600,000 more Africans were brought to Cuba in chains. The sugar boom transformed the countryside and the capital, making the one a living hell for hundreds of thousands of enslaved men and women, and the other a magnet for all the riches they produced. Two external events gave impetus to that transformation.

The first was the American Revolution, for as Franklin's remarks suggest, the divisions between colonials and the mother country in the north were growing even more rapidly than those between Havana and Madrid. Of the "English" who conquered Havana, Joseph Gorham of Cape Cod would fight for England and then emigrate to Canada; Levi Redfield of Connecticut would fight for the Thirteen Colonies and then settle down as a music teacher in Brattleboro, Vermont. Two future generals were also among the expeditionary force: Col. William Howe and Col. Israel Putnam, who thirteen years later commanded the two opposing forces at the Battle of Bunker Hill. When this new conflict came, Spain again joined France in opposing England, throwing Havana open to unrestricted trade with the Thirteen Colonies and allowing the rebel navy and privateers to make use of the port.

Though support for the rebels was tentative in Spain, it was enthusiastic in Cuba—both for commercial reasons and to wipe out the taste of the English conquest. The Havana merchant and smuggler Juan de Miralles, who had been involved in the American trade since the English occupation if not before, became Spain's secret and then official ambassador to the Continental Congress. Traveling to the Carolinas, Virginia, Philadelphia, and George Washington's headquarters in New Jersey, he promoted export from Havana of sugar, hides, coffee, and munitions, and imports from the colonies of meat, fish, lumber, flour, and rice. Later European wars and treaties led Madrid to turn the legal trade between North America and Cuba on and off like a faucet over the next decades, but the process now under way could not be stopped. In 1798, for a prophetic moment, total trade between Cuba and the United States exceeded that between Cuba and Spain.

Though Juan de Miralles died at Washington's headquarters in 1780, he had created the network that made possible a crucial if forgotten Cuban aid to the American revolt: a loan of 1.8 million pesos by Havana bankers, planters, and merchants to the Spanish crown to supply the Continental Army on the eve of the Battle of Yorktown, when the troops had gone for months without pay or supplies. When the French ship that was to carry the money docked in Havana in August of 1781, not all of the promised sum had been assembled. Once more "las señoras de La Habana" played their part in Anglo-Spanish-Cuban relations, at least according to a pamphlet published soon afterward by an officer in the French fleet. *Les dames d'Havane*, he says, put their jewels in pawn to contribute to the loan.

Finally, when Spain formally entered the war and recaptured Florida from British hands, battalions of Havana's black and

mulatto militia were sent as part of an expeditionary force to capture the Bahamas under Captain-General Juan Manuel de
Cagigal—son of the previous governor Cagigal, who had erected
the pillar to mark the site of the famous ceiba where the city had
begun. Among those who served in that expedition (accompanied
by a squadron of South Carolina privateers) was another Pepe
Antonio, a woodworker by the name of José Antonio Aponte, who
lived in the working-class barrios that sprang up outside Old
Havana's walls. We will meet Aponte again twenty years later—at
the head of an islandwide abolitionist conspiracy involving free
coloreds, whites, and slaves.

Aponte's place in history leads us to the other event that would,
paradoxically, make nineteenth-century Havana the capital of the
richest sugar plantation economy on the globe: the slave rebellion
in the world's largest sugar producer of the late eighteenth century,
the French colony of St. Domingue (Haiti). The Haitian slaves' 1791
revolt against the inhuman French yoke, and the ten years of bitter
warfare that followed, destroyed that island's sugar plantations
and left a vacuum that Cuban producers quickly filled.

In the two centuries to follow, relations between Havana and its
neighbors to the north would go through changes that would con-
sign the events of 1762–63 to a very distant past. *El Milor* would
vanish from the capital's vocabulary, to be replaced by *el beisbol,
el yanqui, la mafia, el high-laif, el bisnes, el Ford, el sánwich*, and *el show*.
The pattern of the brief period of British influence—reinforcement
of Cuban identity in contrast to that of Spaniard, resisting domination by a new foreign power yet welcoming what the foreigners
might have to offer—would likewise reappear in bigger and more
complex ways. But one linguistic residue has persisted from the
time the Redcoats appeared outside Havana's walls and across its
bay. To express "when push comes to shove," a Cuban will say *"a la
hora de los mameyes"*—in the hour of the mameys.

3

Paris of The Antilles

In the Plaza de Armas, midway through March of 1828, the flower of Havana's society recelebrated the city's founding in a new era. Seventy-four years had passed since Captain-General Cagigal erected his commemorative pillar and replanted the ceiba tree. This time the celebration featured colorful banners, bunting, lanterns, and even a hot air balloon, but its centerpiece was a work of art. For the three hundred and ninth anniversary of the settlement alongside the Bay of Carenas, Spanish authorities had appropriated 10,000 pesos, and ended up spending twice that amount, for a small Grecian temple adorned inside with murals by the French-born painter Jean-Baptiste Vermay.

The painter was himself a sign of the times. Formerly of the court of Napoleon Bonaparte, the Frenchman had transplanted himself to Havana after Napoleon's fall, by way of Germany, Italy, and the United States. As Juan Bautista Vermay, he established the city's first art school, the Academia de San Alejandro, which still exists and is turning out world-class artists today. He established a theater, the Diorama, so called because it doubled as a gallery displaying art works in a new, back-lit form. Inside El Templete, the commemorative memorial, he painted two side murals depicting the legendary first mass and first council meeting. Then he painted a central one depicting the inauguration ceremony itself.

In the painting, sober dress has replaced the "birds of brilliant plumage" of earlier times. Spanish officers in black boots, skintight white leggings, black coats, and gold braid stand on a carpet laid in front of the new monument, while their wives and daughters in black dresses and white lace mantillas sit on cushions, all observing the white-robed priests officiating a memorial mass. In the background, a mixed crowd including some blacks and mulattos press forward for a look—some in dark frock coats, others just a sea of faces behind a fence. Vermay's wife is accompanied by a young slave nearly as well dressed as she. This is not the rough city of the treasure fleets. It's the rich and bustling commercial center of the nineteenth-century sugar boom.

By 1828, the painter's adopted home had literally burst through its walls. Half the 130,000 inhabitants now lived in new neighborhoods outside the old earth-and-stonework defensive barrier, into which more and more gates had been punched to make way for the flow of goods from interior plantations and mills. At the gates, gangs of slaves, still mostly African born, hefted hundred-pound boxes and three-hundred pound casks of sugar and molasses, transferring them from ox-drawn wagons to smaller mule-drawn carts that could negotiate the clogged, narrow streets, muddy or dusty as the season decreed. Not only sugar passed through, but also cured tobacco in great pressed sheaves wrapped in cowhide, and coffee in forty-pound bags. All of it was bound for storerooms in the city and then for the holds of the thousands of ships that dropped anchor in Havana Bay every year. Through the seven gates (soon to be nine) the cart-drivers also brought fruits from the countryside and meats from the slaughterhouse to feed the city's population, and load after load of green fodder to feed the oxen, mules, and horses that pulled not only the freight carts but the passenger chaises of the upper crust.

By the 1860s, the wall would be deemed an impediment to commerce. It and the adjacent land would be subdivided and put up for sale. Those who bought the parcels had to demolish each section of the wall at their own expense, and then they could build newer, and still more imposing buildings, to live in or to rent out. These buildings featured still more stories, columns, arcades, grand wooden doors, and wrought iron balconies. Some of them may be seen along the Paseo del Prado today.

Wall or no, the city did not cease to be a military stronghold. After recovering Havana from the British, Madrid had invested millions in new fortifications: La Cabaña, immense and sprawling, on the ridge across the bay; Atarés, on the hill commanding the southern end of the harbor; and El Príncipe, on another hill far to the west overlooking the Royal Ditch. Spain faced a new threat, however, when its American colonies began rebelling on their own. Between 1810 and 1824, most of the Spanish empire in the New World crumbled. In the latter year, high in the Peruvian Andes, the battle of Ayacucho brought to a close a cycle of continental independence struggles that established new nations from Tierra del Fuego to the Isthmus of Panama and in Mexico as well. In the face of such reverses, Havana became the stronghold from which the Cuban countryside and Puerto Rico could be kept secure, and the lost possessions might still be recovered via expeditions then being prepared.

The Spanish garrisons in Havana totaled 20,000 to 40,000 men during much of the nineteenth century. The inscribed bronze plaque mounted on the pediment of the commemorative Templete called the city, "Most Loyal Havana, Religious and Peaceful." Captain-General Francisco Dionisio Vives and Bishop Juan José Díaz Espada presided over El Templete's inauguration. *Fidelísima, religiosa, y pacífica* was certainly their wish. Of Vives, whose name happened to mean "you live," it was said in Havana, "*Vives como Vives, y vivirás*. Live like Vives, and you'll be living well."

Economically as well as militarily, Havana's importance grew. After the Haitian revolution, Cuba replaced Haiti as the world's top producer of tropical products, sugar above all. Cuba likewise became the importer of everything that, in its fever to produce sugar, it could not or would not produce itself—from lumber to locomotives to salt beef and cod, from cobblestones that came as ballast from New England to slaves from the Yoruba, Carabalí, Congo, Arará and other nations of Africa. The great bulk of this commerce went through Havana, whose resident Spanish officials and merchants exacted their profit tax by tax, ship by ship, and bribe by bribe.

Over the years since the English occupation, the Plaza de Armas that El Templete now faced had been transformed. In place of the humble city church rose the Palace of the Captains-General, an imposing structure of the porous local sea-formed limestone, plastered and painted, with an entranceway of imported Italian marble, nine archways facing the plaza to form a long shaded arcade, and rows of open windows guarded by ironwork imported from Bilbao.

At right angles to it stood the army and financial headquarters, topped with a terrace and tower a stone's throw from La Giraldilla, the insouciant *habanera* crowning the Real Fuerza, who no longer dominated the skyline quite as much as she had before. On the third side of the square, equally palatial but lighter in design and bulk and color, stood the arcaded home and business headquarters of the Count of Santovenia, a recently ennobled Cuban-born sugar planter, which is typical of the mansions erected in these boom years by the elite.

Titles of nobility, indeed, were to be found everywhere, sold to shore up the failing Spanish treasury and to buy Cuban planters' loyalty at the same time. Some resident Spaniards derided these native-born oligarchs as "sugar nobles," as if their titles might melt. But they could not deny that the Calvos de la Puerta had become the Counts of Buenavista, and the Peñalvers and the Recios, despite collaborating with the English, had become the Marqueses of Casa Peñalver (granted to *el inglesito*'s son), the Counts of Arcos (to his nephew), and the Counts of the Royal Proclamation (to Gonzalo Recio de Oquendo himself). The mansions of such sugar planters, imperial officials, and *nouveau riche* Spanish merchants combined aristocratic luxury with the new niches in global commerce that made it possible. Built around enclosed courtyards in the style inherited from Andalusia, they used much of the ground floor space as storehouses for products destined for the ships in the harbor or recently unloaded from them, though the ground floor might also house a billiard room, library, office space, or sitting room. Atop a large marble staircase, high-ceilinged galleries provided common space and opened onto function rooms up to forty feet long and private chambers beyond. Stained glass transoms, often in the shape of half-moons called *mediopuntos* divided into fan-shaped windows of rainbow colors, protected the occupants from the direct rays of the sun. Halfway up, a low mezzanine housed the domestic slaves, if they did not live in smaller, darker quarters crowded in an attic or hidden toward the back of the house.

"The construction of houses in Havana is very peculiar, and one must get accustomed to them to like it," reported Danish novelist Frederika Bremer, one the most astute of the many foreign visitors who have left us accounts of nineteenth-century Havana. She was writing about the smaller, but still comfortable, single-story home of a British businessman and family in which she stayed during her visit of 1851. "Everything is arranged so as to produce as much air

and as much circulation as possible. Long galleries, with wide
semicircular arcades, open into the court (this house has them on
all four sides): in these galleries the whole household may be
found, all busy, and leading a sort of public life; here dinner is
eaten, visits are received, the lady of the house sews surrounded by
her female slaves."

Indeed, most visitors, while complaining of the heat, smells,
noise, dirty streets, and lack of sidewalks, were charmed by the
appearance of the old city, low to the ground compared to others of
Europe or North America. Nearly all the houses and shops were
painted in pastel colors of yellow, orange, green, or blue to soften
the reflection of the sun which, as an American visitor said, "makes
each individual building and object stand out in its clear, liquid
light." The fondest such description comes from the pen of María
Mercedes de Santa Cruz y Montalvo, a daughter of the sugarocracy
who had left the country as a teenager, married into the French nobility, and returned to visit in 1840 as the Countess of Merlín. In her
first reencounter with her birthplace, Merlín outdoes Vermay by
concisely taking note of all the classes that contribute to the city and
its wealth, even as she idealizes the scene:

Here comes the city, here it is, with its balconies, awnings, and
rooftops, the delightful single-story houses of the middle class, the
doors wide enough to admit a carriage and the tall grated windows,
but everything open, everything open, so that one can see at a glance
the details of domestic life—the patio strewn with flowers, the little
girl's bed with crinoline curtains tied with pink-colored bows . . . Now
we reach the docks, populated by a mixed multitude of mulattos and
blacks, some in white pants, white jacket, and great straw hats, others
in torn short trousers and a bright colored bandanna tied around their
heads, others still with gray felt hats pulled down over their eyes and
a red sash tied around the ribs, all of them sweating in the heat . . . We
see an infinity of barrels, boxes, bundles, carried in wagons pulled by
mules and guided negligently by a black man in shirtsleeves.
Everywhere signs that proclaim coffee, sugar, vanilla, indigo, cam-
phor, and cacao, and the unceasing songs and shouts of those poor
blacks who can work only to that rhythm. Everyone in motion, stirring, no one stops. The clarity of the air lends itself to this racket, as
does the brightness of the day, something sharp, that penetrates the
pores and makes one shiver. Everything here is life, lively and fiery,
like the sun showering its rays upon our heads.

Behind the growth and animation of the city lay the spiraling production of the plantations. This production moved farther from Havana, as the lands of the first boom wore out and turned into towns and suburbs, but the new concentration in Matanzas province was still relatively nearby. Havana continued to be the primary residence of the mill and plantation owners, who left day-to-day management to overseers or relatives, and it was still the primary port. Sugar exports had risen from 10,000 tons a year in the 1770s to 30,000 by the turn of the century, 300,000 in 1850, and over 700,000 by 1868. Cuba's first railroad connected Havana to the plantation zones of Bejucal and Guines in 1837 and 1838, making Havana the first city in the Spanish-speaking world to enjoy rail transportation, and one of only a handful on the entire globe. When Spain's first seventeen miles of railway opened in Barcelona, a decade later, Cuba had twenty-two times that much. Havana was already linked with the new sugar boom lands of interior Matanzas by steel and by steam.

Equally worthy of notice is the destination of what was shipped out. By the late 1840s, the primary consumers of Cuban exports were first the United States, then England, and then Spain. By the end of the next decade, the value of exports to the United States more than tripled that of exports to Spain, and imports from the United States had surpassed those from Spain as well. The first railroads were built under Cuban ownership and direction, with English investment capital, and equipment and engineering from the United States. Other technologies did not linger. The first steamboat docked in 1819, just twelve years after Robert Fulton's invention made its Hudson River debut, and regular service between Havana and Matanzas began that same year. The first steam-powered sugar mill went into operation then as well.

Gas lighting arrived inside the walls in 1844. It soon extended to the outer zones. A Cape Cod tourist better disposed than Maj. Gorham described his late afternoon walk peeking into the brilliantly lit luxury homes of El Cerro, where "flowers spread a sweet perfume through the rooms, and gas flames make each face visible, even from the street, and every detail, every adornment stand out." The upper class had begun building these neoclassical suburban villas, which showed more American and French than Spanish influence, in the first third of the century to get away from the noise and dirt and disease of the old city. This migration accentuated after the cholera epidemic of 1833, which carried off some nine thousand residents including Juan Bautista Vermay. The Cuban families in El Cerro (those of the Count of Santovenia among them) were joined by English, Americans, and Germans as well.

Meanwhile the working class, especially free colored people, had been building small wood-and-thatch cabins, or stucco and tile-roof cottages if they could afford it, closer in to the walls. These barrios—Jesús María, La Salud, Guadalupe, El Horcón, San Lázaro, and Colón—sprang up in what is today Centro Habana and a part of Habana Vieja, on lots sold off by landed families including the Peñalvers and Recios, land where some of the earliest sugar cane had been grown. Late in the century, as urbanization and disease encroached on Cerro, the elite began to move again. They built new villas, with seaside vistas and breezes, on the hill sloping upward from the oceanfront between the inner suburbs and the Almendares River, as the stream formerly known as La Chorrera began to be called, more mellifluously, in honor of a departed bishop (actually named Almendariz).

This new luxury district took shape in the area long called El Vedado ("prohibited") because cutting its trees had been banned in early centuries to make it harder for invaders to attack the city from the west. In 1859 a horse-drawn streetcar line was established along what is today the busy Calle Línea. The streetcar ran from the broad new Paseo del Prado[1] outside the walls to an isolated restaurant and swimming facilities by the old Chorrera fort. In 1872 a short-line railway took its place. This railway featured a contraption generally called the Cucharadita (little cockroach) or the Maquinita de Vapor (little steam engine), a single car combining steam engine and passengers benches all in one. Slowly the development of El Vedado progressed. At the top of its slope, in the 1870s, the church, crown, and municipal government followed suit by developing a vast city of the dead, named after Columbus although the Admiral's supposed bones continued to rest in the Cathedral downtown. (They had been evacuated from Santo Domingo to Havana in 1795—and would be evacuated again, to Spain, in 1898.) The new "Necropolis de Colón," laid out along a quadrilateral grid of streets roughly a half mile on each side, gradually filled with sumptuous family vaults and mausoleums holding the remains of the rich, and common repositories in which were assembled those of the poor. The living population of the city and its suburbs, meanwhile, had reached 200,000.

In short, a new Havana emerged, less centralized and more polarized, but exaggerating two tendencies already long in evidence: it was an even richer city, and an even more cosmopolitan one. A visit to Havana's museum of urban archeology—in the restored dwelling of Juana de Carvajal and Pedro Calvo de la Puerta, where the recently rediscovered murals may also be seen—reveals what the city's middle and upper classes consumed. The collections, dug up in the recent process of rehabilitating the old city, include roof tiles from France and Italy, glass beads from Venice, Dutch gin bottles, Leipzig perfumes, English cherry toothpaste and ivory toothbrushes. Equally telling, there is an overwhelming variety of day-to-day personal care products from the United States. Scott's Emulsion, Swain's Panacea, Phillips Milk of Magnesia, and a Bakelite syringe by Goodyear for the cleaning of the ears only begin the list. Singer sewing machines began to be imported in the 1860s, and Remington typewriters in the 1880s.

Increasingly, travel between Havana and U.S. cities grew easier, while direct links with the mother country grew less. New Orleans was only two days away by steamship, and New York five. By mid-century there was also twice-weekly steamship service to Philadelphia, twice monthly to Baltimore, and more. "The civilization of Havana and Cuba in general is a mixture imported from the

Steamboat from the U.S. entering Havana Bay, early 19th century, between fortresses of El Morro (left background), La Cabaña (right background), and La Punta (right foreground).

neighboring country," the Colombian exile entrepreneur Nicolás Tanco noted in 1853. "This mixture is one of the most surprising things here, this contrast between the Spanish civilization that is disappearing little by little, and the modern American one that irresistibly invades." Tanco himself was in Havana to arrange the importation of Chinese contract laborers for railroads and plantations, which would eventually add another strain to Havana's bubbling mix. Excavations show that there were already shops run by Chinese and Arabic merchants, and the museum collection includes Chinese porcelains and stoneware with the preserved pits of imported peaches from centuries ago.

At the Café Dominica at the corner of O'Reilly and Mercaderes, close by the Plaza de Armas and famed for its marble fountain, iced drinks, and fruit desserts equal to the best in Paris, the menu proudly proclaimed that English, French, and German were all spoken within. On the other side of town, men of affairs and the intelligentsia gathered for cigars and conversation at a café on the Prado pointedly named the "Louvre." The Café Louvre also offered an elegant attached bathhouse where they might soak. Havana became an obligatory stop for tourists and businessmen bound from Europe to either North or South America, from one America to the other, or en route to California or the Far East. Modern hotels sprang up to house them—the Inglaterra (England) on the Prado next to the Café Louvre, and Telégrafo, founded in 1860 on the Calle Amistad and relocated to the corner of Prado and Neptuno in 1888.

Even the former palace of the Counts of Santovenia on the Plaza de Armas was rented in the 1860s to a Col. Louis Lay of New Orleans, who turned it into the luxurious Santa Isabel Hotel. Among other illustrious guests it housed the German archeologist Hermann Schliemann, discoverer of the buried ruins of Troy. In 1880, the Catalán businessman Ventura Trotcha built a restaurant-theater in the far-off, nearly empty, and bucolic Vedado. The luxurious salon featured *mediopunto* windows and wrought-iron balconies, on top of which he added, ten years later, two stories of hotel rooms and suites. Legend places a famous affair between the actress Sara Bernhardt and a Spanish bullfighter in a room on the top floor of Trotcha's hideaway.

So it was that the capital of "The Pearl of the Antilles" gained a reputation as the "Paris of the Americas" too. The ladies of the aristocracy organized philharmonic societies, importing the leading musicians, ballet dancers, and opera companies of Europe on tour.

By the 1830s and 1840s the Opera House on the waterfront and the Tacón Theater inland offered opera, dramatic, and dance performances a minimum of four times a week; Vermay's Diorama operated under new auspices as well. Don Francisco Marty, the proprietor of the Tacón, was a horse of a different color—a Catalán ex-pirate, slave trader, and (thanks to his friendship with governor Miguel de Tacón, Vives's iron-fisted successor after whom the theater was named) monopoly owner of the city's fish market and wharves. His theater, on the other side of the Café Louvre from where the Inglaterra would be built, held upwards of two thousand spectators and was famous for its wide stage and its immense chandelier, a modern gaslit spider imported from the United States. Visitors frequently compared the Tacón (today the Sala García Lorca) to the leading theaters of Paris or London, or even to La Scala in Milan.

The Parque Central, with Tacón Theater at left and Hotel Inglaterra at right. This postcard was mailed in 1911 (the inscription points to "my room" in the hotel), but the view appears to be earlier. The statue in right foreground is either that of Queen Isabella (removed in 1899) or the short-lived imitation of the Statue of Liberty (see chapter 7) not the later statue of José Martí.

Havana provided enough work, audience, and remuneration that some Italian singing stars settled in this welcoming environment once they had reached the twilight of their careers. Stars in their prime, meanwhile, added Havana to the itinerary of their American tours. In 1851, P.T. Barnum brought international sensation Jenny Lind to sing in Havana after her New Orleans appearance, and Lind was still there, completing her run of performances, when her friend Frederika Bremer arrived. The "Swedish Nightingale" took the Danish writer for a drive along the length of the Paseos Prado and Tacón. As Bremer described it:

> The magnificent promenade extends for certainly upward of three English miles between broad avenues of palm and other tropical trees, beds of flowers, marble statues and fountains, the finest promenade anyone can image, to say nothing of its being under the clear heaven of Cuba. The moon was in her first quarter, and floated like a little boat above the western horizon. The entire circle of the moon appeared unusually clear.

Said the well-traveled Nicolás Tanco, the promenades of Havana "can well compete with the Champs Elysees or Bois de Boulogne."

These Paseos were the showplaces of white Havana society. Parading along them in a horse-drawn *volanta* (two-wheeled carriage) was a nightly rite for the titled aristocracy, the officialdom, and anyone else who could afford it, and a weekend necessity for all who had some pretension to status in the middle class. This ritual caught visitors' attention for two reasons: the carriages themselves (which occasioned as much comment and wonder as the 1950s American cars do today) and their role in the restricted lives of white females, especially those of marriageable age, as we shall see.

"A sort of large insect, with immense hind legs and a long proboscis [like] some queer kind of daddy-long-legs," Frederika Bremer said of this uniquely Cuban invention, designed to avoid getting stuck in the mud of Old Havana's streets or the potholes, ditches and rocks of the roads beyond. The *volanta* had only two wheels, but these were immense, six or seven feet in diameter, and placed behind the body of the open, single-seat carriage itself. The carriage in turn rested on two long, springy iron shafts, attached at one end to the axle housing, and at the other to the harness of the horse or mule. This made the vehicles feel "so light and springy that they would scarcely crush the legs of a fly if their wheels passed over him," said an English traveler. They were driven by a uniformed black driver in high leather boots or gaiters, a bright red jacket, and long spurs, who rode mounted on the horse. The *volantas* for hire were not ornamented, but in the case of private ones, the richer the owner, the more likely the carriage, harness, and driver to be ornamented with silver fittings, silver spurs and buckles, and gold thread, often to the value of thousands of dollars worth. In the streets of the old city, reported Richard Henry Dana, "in most *volantas* a gentleman is reclining, cigar in mouth; while in others, is a great puff of blue or pink muslin or cambric, extending over the sides to the shafts, topped off by a fan, with signs of a face behind it."

On the Paseos, however, the women were not hidden, but on display. Visitors were struck, there, by the *habaneras'* bare heads, arms, and hands, open necklines, adornment with flowers, and readiness to flirt. "A girl whose family can afford a *volanta* would rather stop eating than fail to show off her charms," Nicolás Tanco wrote, "and the concurrence at the six p.m. promenade surprises every foreigner, the whole length of four to six miles filled by a continuous belt of carriages and spectators on foot . . . When they must stop to avoid accidents, which is often, the line of onlookers gets a chance to direct their compliments to the young ladies, which are answered with gracious smiles or the electric telegraph of the fans." The Cuban women handled these fans with such dexterity, observed the English visitor Matilda Charlotte Houstoun acerbically, "that this seems to be one of the principal employments of their lives." The evening promenade in the *volanta*, she added, "is the grand event of every day; gossip then goes on at a great rate, every passer-by is scanned and scrutinized, appointments are made, and reputations are sneered away."

The flip side of this display of white *habaneras* on the marriage market was their restriction in other public spheres. They were not seen on foot or in stores, and in very few cafés. They traveled only in their *volantas* or smaller carriages called *quitrines*, sending their slaves into shops and cafés to make purchases, or to summon clerks or waiters out to deliver housewares or fruit juices or ice cream while the carriage blocked traffic on the street. Said a South Carolina doctor, "The custom of appearing in public only in a volanta is so general that some of my fellow-boarders, American ladies, who ventured to do their shopping on foot were greeted in their progress by the half suppressed exclamations of the astonished Habaneros, who seemed as much surprised to see a lady walk through their streets, as a Persian would be to see one unveiled in his."

LADIES ON THE PARQUE DE ISABEL II.

The promenade: Society women in *volanta*, coachman, mounted Spanish officer, and Cuban gentlemen on foot. In background is the statue of the symbolic Indian woman "Havana," at the inland end of the Paseo del Prado.

Mujeres públicas (public women) was a polite term for prostitutes; decent women stayed in the private sphere. Literacy rates among Cuban women were low even in the upper classes, and females were not allowed to enroll in either of the city's universities (the more prestigious of which was a seminary, though it gave degrees in law and philosophy as well). For middle-and-upper class white women who wished to escape from these rigid formulas, especially as the women's rights movement made headway in the United States in the course of the century, the best hope was to be educated in the North as their brothers increasingly were.

Shortly after the Civil War, New York artist Samuel Hazard claimed to have been asked by a "young innocent" whether women, as well as Negro slaves, were now free in his country. When he replied that they were, she said, "It is not so here." Writer Anselmo Suárez Romero (a reformer on other issues) warned parents in 1860 not to send their daughters abroad for education for fear that they would acquire customs "diametrically opposed to those of the land of their birth." It would be, educator Carlos Saladrigas argued twenty years later, "an act against nature," doing harm to the principles "of concord and stability so essential to the defense and perpetuation of the family." Travel chronicles by Cuban female visitors to the North make frequent reference to women's greater mobility and access to the public sphere: "How often, in the midst of such gatherings, do I rue the sad and monotonous life of the girls of Cuba, always enclosed within the walls of their houses, with no more distraction than the wearisome motion of their rocking chairs." So reported a correspondent of the magazine *La Habana Elegante* who wrote under the pen name of Elga Adman.

The paradox is evident. The females who were free to move about the streets of Havana were overwhelmingly free colored women or slaves. Whether vendors, laundresses, midwives, cooks, or housewives, whether working for themselves or their owners or something of both, they went about their difficult business free of the restrictions imposed on whites. The lives of the black women and mulattas of Havana barely make it into most travel memoirs, but they figure at the center of the most famous portrait of life in the nineteenth-century capital, the one painted in loving and sometimes horrified detail by Cuban novelist Cirilo Villaverde in his classic work *Cecilia Valdés*.

We will come to Cecilia herself in a moment, but we will start with another of the novel's characters, Genoveva Santa Cruz, who walks every morning from her cottage outside the walls to the Plaza Vieja, where the arcades and front rooms of the mansions are rented out to dozens of Spanish immigrant shopkeepers, while vendors of less resources fill the open square with their stalls selling green vegetables, fruits, root vegetables, live chickens, dead game animals, songbirds in cages, dried beans, and fish fresh from the river or sea. The makeshift shops are "all without cover or awning," Villaverde tells us, "nor a single respectable face; peasants and blacks, some poorly dressed and the others barely dressed at all." All filled with noise and smells and motion, below a sharp blue sky dotted with occasional passing clouds "like transparent silk or invisible angels' wings."

Genoveva takes her surname from the Santa Cruz y Montalvo family, her former owners, whose townhouse—the Palace of the Counts of Jaruco—was one of the arcaded mansions, "perhaps the haughtiest in the city," incongruously ringing the tumultuous market square. (This building is today the gallery and headquarters of the arts organization Fondo de Bienes Culturales.) She owes her freedom to her former fellow-slave Dolores Santa Cruz. "Dolores sold meat, sold fruit, sold everything, and Dolores bought her freedom. Then she got me out of the slave barracks, bought a shack, and I sold meats, sold sweets, sold everything for her. I worked and worked and I bought my freedom too. Now I sell meat, lard, eggs, fruit, whatever I can." She lives with her husband, the water vendor Trebusio Polanca, although, as was most common among the working class of the city, "we aren't married in the church." The day we meet her, she leaves the Plaza with a tray of pork, lard, and eggs balanced deftly on her head, and she navigates the clogged streets of Old Havana crying out, "Housewives! Won't you buy something from me today?" Her husband must follow the same itinerary, because the water vendors fill their barrels from the fountain in the middle of Plaza Vieja (from its "cloudy and greasy" spout, says the author Villaverde), and transport them through the streets in carts to sell for half a silver *real* each.

Curiously, Genoveva Santa Cruz's former owners were, precisely, the family of María Mercedes Santa Cruz y Montalvo, the Countess of Merlín. In her travel memoir, Merlín describes women like Genoveva with a certain blend of envy and distaste: "Ladies are seen little in public. Only the black women parade through all the streets, with their shoulders and chests exposed, a cigar in the mouth, emitting great clouds of smoke . . . These *negras* show off, rocking their hips in the middle of street, with their kerchiefs on their heads, their bracelets, and the cigar." Frederika Bremer, without the superior air of Merlín, compares what she sees in Havana to what she has just seen in the United States: "Certain it is that one here sees negroes and mulattoes much more frequently engaged in trade than there, and their wives are commonly very well, nay, even splendidly dressed. It is not unusual to see mulatto women, with flowers in their hair, walking with their families on the principal promenades in a manner which denotes freedom and prosperity."

The explanation of this paradox lies in the gender balance of Havana and in the continued growth of its precarious colored middle class. White women were in short supply, because new Spanish immigration was almost exclusively male: soldiers, sailors, officials on temporary postings, defeated royalist refugees from the continent, and increasing waves of young men who came from Spain, unaccompanied, to "do America" like the shopkeepers ringing the Plaza Vieja—to go from rags to riches as best they could. According to a detailed Havana census taken in 1861, among the white population, men outnumbered women by nearly two to one. Among free people of color, on the other hand, the ratio was approximately equal, both for mulattos and for blacks. Though male slaves vastly outnumbered female slaves in the countryside, in the city itself the numbers were probably equal as well. The results were threefold: For the slaveowning aristocracy, white women became the symbol of exclusivity, superiority, and purity, so that their restricted sphere served, says historian Luis Martínez-Fernández "as a constant visual reminder of the separation between elite white society and the people of color they ruled." Especially, they needed to be kept at a remove from nonwhite men. On the other hand, for white men in general, colored women were either the only option or a constant temptation—as informal partners, mistresses, slaves forced into sexual services, or wives. "Necessity gives birth to mulattos," goes an old Cuban proverb, and necessity did. Finally, given the toeholds they had established in the centuries when Havana was a stopover and Spanish immigration sparser, free blacks and mulattos (or slaves doing day work) filled the working-class positions—not just street vendors but tailors, cooks, silversmiths, musicians, stevedores, decorators, midwives—that upper-class whites found demeaning, and lower-class whites were unable or unwilling to assume.

As a result of all three factors, Havana's cosmopolitan character did not just involve the blended cultures of Spain, northern Europe, and the United States. Havana stirred African traditions and African blood into the mix. The result can be seen and heard in everything from speech to stride to family history. Today's Havanans of all classes and races swallow syllables and consonants and blur the distinctions between their *r*s and *l*s and even *d*s in a way most reminiscent of the pronunciation Villaverde attributes to Genoveva Santa Cruz. Linguists trace this characteristic accent to the Andalusian Spanish of the original settlers as modified by the difference between the consonant sounds of West African languages and Romance ones. By the twentieth century, when any Havana family would claim a purely European ancestry, the satirical response was, "And your grandmother, where are you hiding her?"

All of this mixing of genes and cultures lies as the heart of Cirilo Villaverde's novel. *Cecilia Valdés, or the Hill of the Angel* is Cuba's *Uncle Tom's Cabin, Sister Carrie*, and *Portrait of a Lady* rolled into one. It seems to traverse every plaza and barrio of the city it celebrates, as does its heroine. Everyone in modern Havana knows Cecilia, whose story has been made into both a famous operetta and a film. They know her better in most cases than they know any actual historical figure of her era, and historians turn to the novel for its photographic descriptions of the life and customs of the time. *Cecilia Valdés* is a classic melodrama, firmly against slavery while often profoundly racist, but eloquent about the degree to which black and white Havana society coexisted, touched, and mixed. A closer look at *Cecilia* will lead us into a deeper look at Havana's mixture, mobility, and barriers of race and class.

4

Cecilia, Cabildos, and Contradance

In Villaverde's novel, we first see the heroine as an eleven or twelve year old "blowing through the streets night and day," mischievously pocketing mangos, raisins, fritters, and bananas from the trays of vendors and shopkeepers. Like most Valdés's of nineteenth-century Havana, Cecilia owes her surname to the Casa de Cuna (cradle house), the orphanage at the corner of Muralla and Oficios founded by Bishop Gerónimo Valdés, which featured a revolving compartment in the front door in which mothers, fathers, or servants could deposit newborn children they did not want or could not afford. Some of these babies, like Cecilia, were the fruit of affairs between rich white businessmen and colored mistresses. Cecila's secret father is Cándido Gamboa, whose name means pure or naive but who is actually anything but. A Spanish immigrant who started out as a building-supplies contractor and rose to the position of slave merchant, he has married into a landed Cuban family and is anxiously awaiting the title of nobility due to arrive any day from Madrid.

The tragedy of the novel is a new affair in the next generation. Cecilia grows into a dazzling young light-skinned woman, and unknowingly falls in love with her half-brother Leonardo Gamboa.

When Leonardo gets Cecilia pregnant, he sets her up in a rented house to keep her as his mistress, an arrangement he plans to continue after his marriage to the landed heiress selected for him. But Cecilia wants him to marry her, love her, and also allow her and especially her child to pass into white society. "He promised and he'll keep his word," she insists to her best friend, "or else I wouldn't love him the way I do." At the same time she admits her ambitions: "Yes, it's true that I like white men better than black ones. I couldn't show my face for shame if I had *un hijo saltoatrás*." (*Saltoatrás*, literally jumping backward, is slang for a child darker than its parent.) Cecilia is in turn hopelessly loved by José Dolores Pimienta— journeyman tailor, clarinetist, and composer—who has always hoped to marry her someday.

That José Dolores is a musician is no accident, for the precarious coexistence of black and white was intimately mixed with music and dance. We first see Leonardo and Cecilia's budding romance at a dance, a semipublic party in a private house. Such parties were thrown by all levels of Havana society—by some estimates fifty per night during the many saints days, holy weeks, and other festivals which gave religious cover to the revelry—in tiny homes and grand ones, in dance halls of varying reputation, in the Philharmonic Society, and even in the Teatro Tacón, where a raised dance floor could be installed in place of the orchestra seats. Most of these parties also featured gambling, especially the card game called *monte*. Bettors would surround long narrow gaming tables, placing bets from piles of silver and gold coins, while onlookers surrounded the bettors, their emotions riding on every card. These parties paid for themselves through the house's take from the gaming, the sale of drinks, or both. The twin passion for dancing and gambling, said Nicolás Tanco, helped account for the city's reputation as the Paris of the Americas, "a very gay city, where every man of means enjoys himself, where the people are constantly at play."

The party where we meet Leonardo and Cecilia is a *baile de cuna*, a popular fiesta in a poor district squeezed up against the city wall, "open to individuals of both sexes of the colored classes, yet not closed to those young white men who tended to honor them with their presence . . . some out of pure appreciation, others for motives not so pure." For entertainment, the party-giver has hired a seven-piece band of strings, drums, flutes, and clarinet. The band's leader and clarinetist is Cecilia's admirer José Dolores, composer of "The Candy Seller," the hit of that season's parties and the next, dedicated to Cecilia herself. Like many later hit songs such as *El manisero* (the peanut vendor), José Dolores's creation derives from the *pregones* or chants of vendors like Genoveva Santa Cruz and Trebusio Polanca.

Both the music of José Dolores's group and the "furious" dance to its beat are what Cubans of the era called *contradanza* or simply *danza*. The word derived from the English "country dance" and came into Spanish by way of French. Originally it referred to European folk dancing, but Cuban sensibility and African rhythms gave it a new twist. The *danza cubana*, Villaverde tells us, is "such a special and far-traveled modification of the Spanish *danza* that its origin can barely be seen." Villaverde seems conflicted in his description of the *danza*: moaning and intoxicating, sad and stirring, spicy and graceful, carnal and emotional, deep and piercing, monotonous and melodious. His description of the music seems closest in spirit to North American jazz (by most accounts not yet invented, though New Orleans and Havana were closely linked by travel and trade): "The violinists tightened their bows, the flutists pierced the air with the high, sharp sounds of their instruments, the drummer's racing rhythm was an exquisite invention, and the bassist made a bow of his own body and drew the deepest notes imaginable, while the clarinet executed the most difficult and melodious variations . . . The clarinet cried out, 'Candy here, I'm selling candy,' while the violin and the bass repeated this in another tone, and the drums formed a clamorous chorus behind the melancholy voice of the vendor of the sweets."

What is true at the *baile de cuna* is true also at the height of native-born Cuban society—the fancy ball given on a different night at the Philharmonic, to which Leonardo arrives late after searching in vain for Cecilia at the house parties on the Hill of the Angel. "The most illustrious Cuban youth of both sexes surrendered, at least for the moment, to their favorite diversion, by the dazzling light of the crystal chandeliers [in an] intimate conversation of lovers, the caresses of souls who are mutually attracted, but whom time, space, circumstance, and custom have kept apart." In both locales, *danza* was played with European instruments, without the conga drums, gourds, rhythm sticks, cow bells, and other African borrowings or Cuban inventions that would enliven later genres. Yet the first time he notes the "moaning" character of the music, Villaverde declares that "it comes from the heart of a people enslaved."

In the end of the novel, Leonardo's selfishness, the duplicity of his and Cecilia's mutual father, Cecilia's romantic infatuation and

José Dolores's despair eventually prove the undoing of virtually everyone. Some months after the birth of his and Cecilia's daughter, Leonardo and his well-born bride-to-be Isabel Ilincheta climb the steps from the Calle Compostela to the candle-lit church of San Ángel Custodio, atop the Hill of the Angel, where they will be married as befits their class. In the soft November twilight, José Dolores Pimienta, his hat pulled low over his eyes, brushes past Leonardo. "The young man brought his hand to left side of his chest, groaned softly, tried to support himself on the arm of his bride, then fell at her feet, splashing her brilliant white silk dress with blood. Brushing his arm at the level of his chest, knife had penetrated directly to his heart."

The plot of *Cecilia Valdés* focuses on black desires to whiten or assimilate, to rise out of colored society or into its Europeanized *petit bourgeoisie*. The *baile de cuna* copies Cuban high society, opening with a minuet. Another dance Cecilia attends, limited to the elite of colored society, not only features European dancing but requires European fancy dress in the form of coats and tails from the men.

In fact, real-life violinists of color like Claudio Brindis de Salas and Ulpiano Estrada, who put in cameo appearances at this fictional dance, excelled in both popular genres and classical ones. They gave lessons to the children of the aristocracy and were hired to play in church, for the dances of the Philharmonic and to serenade the *paseos*, as well as to entertain the parties of their own class. Brindis de Salas scrimped and saved to send his son, a child genius also named Claudio, to study in Paris. The junior Brindis had a distinguished career as a classical concert violinist, touring Italy (where he was hailed as "the black Paganini"), Germany, Russia, England, Venezuela, Argentina, Mexico, and Cuba. He settled in Germany, marrying into the nobility, but died finally in Buenos Aires, of tuberculosis, old and poor, in 1911.

Also named as a guest at the novel's select colored party is the poet Gabriel de la Concepción Valdés, better known by his pen name of Plácido. Like Cecilia, the real-life Plácido was a Valdés of the Cradle House, sent there to hide his white parentage and then reclaimed. In Plácido's case, his father was a black barber (indebted by gambling, some sources say) and his mother a Spanish dancer in the company of the Opera House. Brought up by his paternal grandfather, he later married María Gila Morales, daughter of the well-known midwife María del Pilar Poveda, who catered to

Havana families rich and poor, white and black, and to some of the leading families of Matanzas as well.

Plácido worked over the years in Havana, Matanzas, and elsewhere on the island as a printer, comb-maker, silversmith, and carpenter. He also, however, managed to publish his poetry, and Villaverde called him "the most inspired poet that Cuba has seen." His sonnets, *letrillas*, and other classic forms were drawn from the Spanish romantic tradition but often adapted to Cuban nature and, sometimes, to thinly disguised appeals for freedom from tyranny.

In the earliest years of the century, colored school teachers taught both white and black students in the city's small number of elementary schools. Lorenzo Melendez and Mariano Moya won a prize sponsored by a local Spanish treasury official for the teachers who could present the most outstanding students—in their case, six whites and four colored. In this same period, Juana Pastor, a free mulatta from Jesús María, and Matías Velazco, the mulatto son of a white priest, also became highly regarded teachers of whites. From 1816 on, however, educational reformers pushed for more segregation, and by 1846 a detailed census of occupations showed no Cuban teachers of color anywhere.

In humbler but sometimes more lucrative trades, on the other hand, the 1846 records show that, in all of Cuba, free blacks and mulattos made up 99 percent of wage-earning cooks and coachmen, 75 percent of midwives, 72 percent of tailors, 69 percent of wet nurses, 63 percent of builders and masons, 60 percent of shoemakers; they also made up 38 percent of seamstresses, 34 percent of hat makers, and 26 percent of tobacconists and cigar makers. These figures don't take slaves into account, and newspaper advertisements, for instance, reveal a common practice of selling as wet nurses mothers who had recently given birth; they were generally offered "without infant" in the ads. Still, for those blacks and mulattos who did have their freedom, all these trades offered room to move up. Francisco Uribe appears in *Cecilia* as the employer of José Dolores Pimienta and tailor to Leonardo Gamboa and many others of his ilk. Uribe did in fact exercise this profession, working from 1833 in a rented shop on Calle Muralla, under a sign advertising himself as "tailor of fashion." At the time of his death he owned two adjoining houses in Jesús María, with wooden walls and tile roofs, and twelve slaves, most of whom worked in his shop as washerwomen and ironers, some of them in the process of buying their freedom, to judge from papers dating from that time.

As for real-life cases embodying Cecilia's goal, examples of mistresses marrying into the oligarchy are hard to find. A more common case might be represented by a woman named Petrona Izquierdo, whose story is known through the property records of one of her sons. Born into slavery around 1835 in rural Alquízar to parents who were both Cuban-born slaves, Petrona was of a color between black and mulatta, "commonly called 'Chinese' or 'earth.' " Somehow she passed into the possession of a Don Jacinto Durán, of Casablanca, the fishing and maritime village tucked just below La Cabaña, separated from Old Havana by the narrow neck of the bay. Starting at the age of fifteen, Petrona Izquierdo had three children, each by "father unknown," each with a white godfather, and each given liberty at birth by Don Jacinto, who legally owned them. When Don Jacinto died in 1864, he left a will giving Petrona her freedom and a house in Casablanca. The will also officially recognized the last-born son, José Dolores Abraham, as his own. José Dolores inherited from his father four more houses on the same street.

Formal marriage between whites and people of color was barred by Spanish imperial laws, though there were two ways around this ban. One was to have the colored party, if lightskinned enough, declared white, often by way of a false certificate of baptism obtained through a bribe—or, occasionally, as a result of having emerged from the Cradle House with parentage unknown. The other was to petition for an exception to the law, granted only to couples involving a white man and a colored woman, and only if the white man was of equal or lower economic class. So the painter Don Simón de Jesús Barcañela appeared before city authorities in 1823, seeking permission to marry the mulatta Feliciana Pascuala Tolet y Cargnes, "whom he has made pregnant under promise." Permission was granted because Barcañela's parents were both tailors, a trade infrequent among whites. So, too, the sailor Don Manuel de León, immigrant from Canary Islands, was allowed to marry the mulatta Rafaela Pérez, with whom he had been living in Jesús María for thirty years. In the same neighborhood, the Galician Don Luis Luaces petitioned to marry the mulatta María de La Luz García, because, he said, "her parents, besides being honorable and of good behavior, own real estate which her father has pledged to make available to the petitioner for a workshop in which to roll cigars."

This far, *Cecilia Valdés* can serve us as a window into nineteenth-century Havana's intersection of black and white cultures. What

Villaverde chose not to see, however, was the survival of true African culture within this mix. Especially, Africa stayed alive in the dozens of colored societies called *cabildos de nación*, which don't appear in his classic portrait of nineteenth-century Havana at all. As Villaverde's fellow novelist Félix Tanco lamented in a private letter of 1837, "Who fails to see, in the movements of our boys and girls in their contradances and waltzes, an imitation of the miming carried on by the blacks in their *cabildos*? Who doesn't know that bass viol of the *danza* is the echo of [their] drums?"

The *cabildos de nación* (ethnic councils) were originally created by Spanish authorities on the model of similar societies for Africans, gypsies, and other "lower races" in Seville. The authorities' goal was social control, to be achieved by splintering African-born free laborers and urban slaves according to their native nations, languages, and localities. The cabildo system also created a semifeudal structure under which these societies' "kings" or "captains" represented their members in formal dealings with the government and could be held responsible for their crimes or fines. The cabildos however, simultaneously provided a space for traditional rituals, for mutual aid, and even for political organizing against slavery and Spanish rule.

By the nineteenth century, when the authorities were evidently worried about the cabildos proving a double-edged sword, new laws required them to be located only in the poor black neighborhoods outside the old city's walls. The Carabalí Apapá, the Lucumí Yesa, the Congo Real, and the Congo Modongo, among many others, owned or rented houses for their cabildos in the barrio of Jesús María, to the west of the shipyard (now the central train station). Though officially limited to African-born free blacks, Havana's cabildos also included African-born slaves and Cuban-born blacks and mulattos, sometimes in leadership positions.

The cabildos collected dues, lent money at interest (often as mortgages), and collected the money or property of members who died without heirs. Like other mutual aid societies, they used their funds to pay for members' medical care or funerals. They used them, too, to buy members, their lost children, or their spouses out of slavery. Cabildos also developed economic power in other ways. The Carabalí societies came to be, in effect, the hiring hall for longshore workers and foremen on Havana's docks. Many of the cabildos' prominent members, usually successful tradesmen, bought themselves commissions in the black or mulatto militia, which brought prestige and some degree of protection from arbitrary legal penalties such as whippings or fines. The captain of the cabildo of the Carabalí Ososo, Francisco Barroso, owned a funeral parlor and was first sergeant of a mulatto battalion. Dock foremen Marcelino Gamarra and Augustín Ceballos were lieutenant and sergeant in a black and mulatto battalion, respectively.

Juan Bertault and Genoveva Morejón, both brought to Cuba as slaves, had gained their freedom and saved about 1500 pesos by the time they married in Havana in 1840 or 1841. Bertault listed his occupation as upholsterer but also owned several wagons and mules, so he may have run a freight business. The couple bought a house in Jesús María at the time of their marriage and soon owned part of another building in the old city, near where the Calle de la Bomba met the wall, a block beyond the fictional tailor-clarinetist and his sister in *Cecilia Valdés*. They bought these rooms from the captain of one of the Carabalí cabildos, of which Bertault became captain in turn. Around mid-century Bertault began to flourish as a moneylender and mortgager, his fortune growing through inheritance of property left by three men and two women of the cabildo. By the time of Morejón's death in 1870, the couple owned seven houses, mostly in Jesús María, and a vacant lot repossessed from a Catalán shopkeeper there as well. The legal record contains a suggestion that Bertault may have misused his position in the cabildo for personal gain, but in any case his story shows the economic power that could reside there.

Cabildos had female officials (*matronas* or "queens"), as well, who also acquired considerable power and prestige. Maria de Regla Fajardo, ex-*matrona* of the Ugri Cabildo, took advantage of a debt of 1700 pesos that this cabildo owed to her son. She insisted her friend Inés de Flores be elected *matrona* upon her own death, in partial forgiveness of the loan. Shoring up their status, cabildo officials dressed in a style borrowed from colonial military dignitaries: starched shirts, embroidered jackets, bright sashes, silver headed canes. The *matronas*, while retaining African head scarves, wore gowns covered with Valencian silk, embroidered sashes with precious stones, and gold scepters and earrings. At the same time, the cabildos all preserved traditional language, religion, music, and dance. In some societies, the votes for captains and *matronas* were collected inside a *güira* or gourd that served as voting urn. The same *güira* served as a percussion instrument, the one still seen in Cuban bands today.

Music and dance were an integral part of all the West African and Central African religions that the slaves brought with them. They were employed to erase boundaries between the religious and secular, between worship and enjoyment, and between living beings, deities, and the dead. On Sundays and feast days, the cabildos were permitted to hold such *toques* for their members. Some of them also offered curious onlookers the chance to watch, generally for a fee that subsidized the house, the altars and effigies within in it, and the treasury that paid for funerals, purchases of liberty, and other member needs. Frederika Bremer, once again, noted carefully what she saw:

I found a large room, very like those of public houses among us, in which I saw these naked to the waist, wild, energetic figures and countenances, who were beating drums with energetic animation. These drums were hollowed trees stems over the opening of which was stretched a parchment skin, on which the negroes drummed, in part with sticks and in part with their hands, with their thumbs, with their fists, with wonderful agility and skill . . . The time and measure, which sometimes varied, was exquisitely true; no one can imagine a more natural, perfect, and lively precision in that irregularly regular time.

She also saw dances by couples, not contradances but what would later be called *rumba*, stylized courtship between "ladies of various shades of color, dressed in ragged finery; men without any finery, almost without any attire at all on the upper part of the body . . . these African dances, with their peculiar wild life, at the same time so irregular and yet so rhythmical." She calls the dance an "artistic performance" and then checks herself, her racial blinders clicking in: "or shall I say a perfected natural art—they drummed as bees hum and beavers build."

Generally speaking the ceremonies held inside the *casas de cabildo* invoked the African deities (*orishas* to the Yoruba) in their original forms. They used statues or dolls representing the Lucumí Changó and Yemayá and others, or the Carabalí Okún and Okandé. They practiced systems of foretelling the future, prescribing behavior, and influencing events through the use of shells, roots, smoke, food and drink, animals and other means. But images of the original deities were not allowed in outdoor processions (except for one day of the year), so the cabildos learned to cloak them in the form of

Catholic saints: Changó and Okún became Santa Bárbara, Yemayá and Okandé became the Virgin of Regla, Ochún became the Virgin of Charity who would later be recognized as Cuba's patron saint. *Bailes de cuna* like the one in Cecilia Valdés were often thrown in honor of the host's adopted saint. The long process that led to modern-day *santería*, a religion that mixes African and Christian traditions, had begun.

Similarly, the cabildos developed bilingual ways to refer to their officials and themselves. The Congo, for instance, joined the other cabildos in calling their officials *capataces* (overseers) in their dealings with Spanish authorities, but among themselves they called the captain a *sali*, a term of respect. As pressures for conformity mounted, the societies began adopting Christian names for themselves. So the Carabalí Iziegue y Izuama took the name Immaculate Conception, the Congo Real became the society of the Magi king Melchor, and the Carabalí Ososo became Our Lady of the Light. The fusion took place in other ways too, such that it is often hard to tell in hindsight who was fooling whom. The names for the nations were often derived from those in use among the slave traders: Lucumí for those in West Africa who mostly called themselves Yoruba, Carabalí (from the slave port of Calabar on the river of the same name) for the Ibo, Ibibio, and Ekoi, yet they had or took on a life of their own. Lucumí apparently derived from a Yoruba greeting meaning "friend." A male hoopskirted figure wearing a horned crown become known by Havana's onlookers as La Culona (big-assed woman) but this name apparently hid a Malinke and Mandingo word meaning "wise" or "educated" that described the wearer of the ritual skirt.

The most famous of all the "Negro dances" took place once a year, on the Feast of Epiphany, January 6, also known as the Day of the Magi, or El Día de Reyes, the Day of Kings. On this date only, slaves were given the day off from work. Members of the cabildos were allowed to parade through the streets to dance, drum, chant in their languages of origin, and openly invoke their gods whose effigies they brought out from their cabildo houses and bore aloft on poles. They danced in lines, in circles, and in couples. Some wore traditional masks and hoods, face paints, animal skins, and straw skirts, as well as beads, mirrors, rattles, and glitter of all sorts. Some wore Spanish fancy dress—top hats, large cravats, breast pins, swordbelts and cutlasses, cuff links, sashes, shawls, tassels, fans, ribbons, and cardboard gilt crowns—whether in emulation or in parody it was difficult to tell. (The closest U.S. comparison would be the Congo Square dances of pre-Civil War New Orleans, a tradition that later flowed into the Mardi Gras as those of El Día de Reyes would enliven Carnival.)

From all points in the city, the celebrants converged on the Plaza de Armas, under the official pretense that they were celebrating the Three Kings, though they were honoring their own kings and queens as well. "This negro," wrote a bemused Frenchman in the mid-1850s, "who was enormously tall, and had a tolerably good-looking head, gave his hands gravely to a sort of feminine black-amoor who represented some queen or other. He walked with a deliberate majestic step, never laughed, and seemed to be reflecting deeply on the grandeur of his mission to the world." Jugglers and tumblers, meanwhile, extended their hats to onlooking whites, asking for an *aguinaldo* (tip or bonus), a practice borrowed from Catholic saints-day festivals. Costumed stilt dancers took advantage of their height to appeal for *aguinaldos* to patricians watching the spectacle from upper balconies and galleries. Once gathered in the Plazas, the cabildos one by one entered into the courtyard of the captain-general's palace, paying allegiance and collecting tips. "The old negro women, the most expressive or the most nervous, were the ones who most shook on high their hollow gourd rattles covered in netting, almost delirious in asking God to watch over and preserve the health of His Excellency the Governor General," read a report in a Cuban magazine toward the end of the century. This is most likely not what they were doing at all.

Indeed, accounts by Spaniards, Cuban whites, and foreign visitors all describe the Day of Kings with terms like discordant, outlandish, barbaric, dreadful, feverish, contorted, lascivious, grotesque, ridiculous, wild, savage, foolish, monstrous, and obscene. At best, a local journalist in the 1840s wrote of "the veneer of religious solemnity they give to these profane acts," but the most common adjectives were "devilish" and "diabolical." This characterization stemmed from fear of Africa and Africans, and from familiarity with Spanish festival traditions in which masked devils did play a part. White chroniclers called any costumed ritual figure in the Day of Kings processions a *"diablito"* or little devil, even though it more likely represented a god incarnate or an honored ancestor revived. The figure seen as the epitome of the *diablito* was the Abakuá *ireme*, a costumed creature known for his full mask and conical hood, checkerboard-patterned like the rest of his outfit, and his fringes and cuffs of palm

fiber which, like his bells, were set in motion by the angular movements of his dance to the beat of the sacred ekué drum. However, this
official or respectable discourse which saw the African influences as
diabolic grew increasingly at odds with popular feelings. The
Abakuá offer an early example of this change.

Popularly called *ñáñigos*, the Abakuá were not so much a separate religion as a secret society of male initiates, whose rituals probably derived from an Ekoi leopard society. First established in the
Havana port barrio of Regla in the 1830s, ñáñigo societies took root
among the free workers of the port cities, especially longshoremen
and construction workers. Their secular functions included mutual
defense and avenging of wrongs. Devils or no, on Christmas Eve of
1863, on the Calzada Ancha del Norte (now Calle San Lázaro in
Centro Habana) a group of white men formed the first of many
white Abakuá *ponencias* (chapters), the Akanarán Efó Muñón
Ekobio Mukarará. Versions of the origins of this "reformation"
vary widely, but all agree that it was work of a mulatto ñáñigo
named Andrés Petit, often known as "the gentleman of color."
Petit, probably a dockworker in Regla, was also an initiate of a
Congo religious society and of a lay Catholic order, and the founder
of a new syncretic sect of his own.

Petit either gave or sold the secret Abakuá rites (some versions
say he sold them for gold to be used in buying slaves their freedom)
to the whites, who were either young aristocrats in search of identity and reputation, or dock and cigar and slaughterhouse workers
who labored alongside black ñáñigos, or both. Be that as it may,
after some years of resistance, the Abakuá network recognized the
right of white chapters to participate as equals and brothers—and
Spanish colonial authorities tried assiduously to suppress them
both. This in turn opened the door to incorporation of mostly (but
not exclusively) lower class whites into other religious societies
and practices of African origin. Afro-Cuban religions, taken as a
whole, came finally to outdistance orthodox Catholicism as the
most popular religious faith in Havana and other cities. As journalist, fiction writer and researcher Tata Quiñones, himself a declared
Abakuá, argues in a recent essay, "The 'reformation' begun by
Andrés Facundo Cristo de los Dolores Petit played its part in the
arduous and complex process of forming the Cuban nation, by
linking blacks, whites, and mulattos in a single network of beliefs,
interests, and solidarity. Ñáñiguismo, up to then a 'black thing,'
became what it has been since: Cuban."

When the Día de Reyes celebrations were finally suppressed, late in the century after the official abolition of slavery, their traditions flowed into that of the pre-Lenten Spanish carnival, which had previously been a more sedate procession of carriages and floats. Similarly, if you go today to the anniversary of a *santero*'s orisha, where friends, relatives, and extended family crowd into the celebrant's home to eat, drink, dance, and pay homage to the altar of the saint, you may find yourself in the presence of a *toque de violín* in which a multiracial trio of violin, accordion, and conga drum plays a version of a Spanish sailor song in honor of Yemayá or Changó. It is one more example of the coexistence of creeds in Havana—and in the crowd at this *cumpleaños de santo* may be fervent communists, black-market capitalists, or people who are a bit of both.

Something of this characteristic of coexistence and contradiction was glimpsed by the foreign visitors of the nineteenth century. They were continually surprised at how all the contending segments of Havana society lived jumbled together, how divisions of race and class were social but not strictly physical, and how, in addition, the new always existed alongside ruin and decay. Late twentieth and early twenty-first century visitors have tended to think that they are finding this for the first time, but that is not so.

"There is no 'West End' in Havana," nineteenth-century travel writers repeat over and over, implicitly comparing Havana to London with a regularity that suggests each is plagiarizing from the one before. "The stately mansion of the millionaire is often in juxtaposition with the magazine [warehouse] of *tasajo*, jerked beef, with its sign of a large slice swinging over its door . . . There is no *select* residential quarter of the city, the best family houses being scattered about among the business premises, and often adjoining very objectionable neighbours . . . [In the heights of Cerro] are where the aristocracy of the city reside, and where is found grandeur and squalid poverty intermingled to the greatest extent we ever beheld."

Trying to sum up the whole city, Frederica Bremer wrote that it showed:

> a great mixture of regularity and irregularity, of old and new, of the splendid and the dilapidated. Close beside the elegant arched arcade, with its gayly painted walls, stands a half-ruinous wall, the fresco paintings of which are half obliterated or have peeled off with

the mortar. And this old wall is not repaired, nor the old painting restored. All this—the countenances and life of the colored population;
the silent, wedgelike way in which the volantas insinuate themselves between the rows of houses, give to Havana a peculiar character, and a romantic life which is unlike that of any other city which
I have seen, and especially unlike those of England and North
America.

This sensation of mixture is deepened by the fact that, due to both
climate and the city's peculiarities, life has always been lived so
much out of doors. In the nineteenth century, at festival times the
indoor parties were supplemented by stands set up the street, selling drinks and all manner of food. On the Hill of the Angel, the specialty was golden buttered corn tortillas cooked on clay discs as the
Tainos had cooked *casabe*. The area around the church of La
Merced, near where the *baile de cuna* in *Cecilia Valdés* takes place,

Meat wagon in front of one of the many colonnaded arcades of Old
Havana mansions, whose street levels were often warehouses.
Photo: Library of Congress.

was known for its pies and sugar drops, roasted nuts, and sweet drinks flavored with cinnamon and cloves. Outside the walls, by the Teatro Tacón, were stands selling coffee and fruits and anything that might be cooked, as the German visitor Edward Otto wrote. It was pleasant, he said, to emerge from a crowded dance in the theater, "breathe in the cool air and palms and orange trees and refresh oneself with the coffee and fruits on sale in the plazas; everywhere were lights and fires for boiling and roasting. It was pleasant, those thousands of men wandering in the night."

The other side of this life in the street was the noise that came with it. "For sleeping, I might as well have been stretched on the bass drum," complained Richard Henry Dana about a band playing outside his window, "and the servants in the court of the hall seem to be tending at tables of quarrelling men" who kept him up till five a.m. And then, "as the maskers go home from their reels at this hideous hour of Sunday morning [and] the servants ceased their noises, the cocks began to crow and the bells to chime, the trumpets began to bray, and the cries of the streets broke in before dawn."

Some of the "thousands of men," of course, had more than eating or sleeping on their minds. The port city had not abandoned its old trade of selling sex, only added new strata to the industry. "The priestesses of Venus," Otto claimed, "have permission to live on any street, and so, in general, they choose the best streets and rent a room next to the first house of the city . . . and cultivate the same habits as the distinguished ladies . . . peek[ing] out the bars of the high windows at nightfall, with a lit cigarette in their mouths."

Though still relying in part on rented slave women and on free women of color, the sex trade also increasingly attracted immigrants from Europe and the United States. In 1853, Otto's countrywoman Luisa Bonetti (apparently of Italian background, but born in Germany) was repeatedly arrested for "creating a public scandal." She was placed in the Casa de Recogidas, a special detention center for unmarried girls on the loose, unmarried or separated women deemed "scandalous and incorrigible," and women convicted of crimes. "Harlots" (*meretrices*), "public women," and "prostitutes" were in fact registered, taxed, and allowed to practice their trade within certain limits. Bonetti's crime seems not to have been prostitution as such but rather her public denunciations, at late hours and at the top of her lungs, of a certain Dr. Nicolás Manzini. In these tirades and her later letters of protest from the Casa de

Recogidas, she charged that Manzini had encouraged her to deposit her earnings with him for safekeeping, and then kept them "for himself, his house, and luxuries that he never had before." Bonetti, who was literate and had a daughter attending a private school, was finally deported without a trial.

In the 1860s, the American Samuel Hazard professed shock at finding that "plenty of our countrywomen, in the interest of making a lot of money in their relations with rich Spaniards, come here to join this unfortunate class." Historian Louis Pérez notes that such "rich Spaniards" were not their only customers, because there were by the mid-nineteenth century already brothels "operated by North Americans principally for North Americans"—business travelers, tourists, railroad workers, and the crews of the great number of merchant ships. He cites among American prostitutes Ellen N. King of New London, who went to work in a Havana brothel after losing her job on a Cienfuegos plantation, and actress Adah Isaacs Menken, abandoned by her lover in Havana in 1853 and seeking to earn passage back to the United States. Fragmentary statistics suggest that in the 1860s and 1870s the majority of prostitutes were probably immigrants from Spain and the Canary Islands. In the 1880s and 1890s, as the economic situation deteriorated, they were joined by increasing numbers of Cuban-born women, the majority of them white.

So Havana became the Paris of the Americas in terms of high art, café society, popular entertainment, gambling, and sex. However, Paris itself in those years saw revolution and counterrevolution. So did Havana. If Cuba was the ever-faithful isle, remaining under Spanish rule long past other American colonies, it did not do so in a fashion either enthusiastic or simple. Alongside luxury, poverty, coexistence, and cultural fusion, Havana was a site of rebellion, repression, and assertion of a new Cuban nationhood. So we have to retrace our steps through a less exotic and more politicized nineteenth-century Havana, starting with the "Conspiracy of Aponte" in the year 1812.

5

Stirrings of Nationhood

Today, the street called Belascoaín is a major north-south axis running through the heart of the city. It starts from the seafront Malecón, alongside the equestrian statue of Antonio Maceo and the sky-scraping Amejeiras Brothers Hospital, which looks like a bank tower because that's what it was designed to be. It traverses Centro Habana from north to south and ends at the big, busy farmers' market of Cuatro Caminos, below the old Spanish fortress of Atarés.

For most of the nineteenth century, however, Belascoaín marked the western edge of the city—the limit of the barrios that had sprung up outside the walls. Bordering it at the ocean end was an orphanage, followed by an insane asylum, a cemetery, and further inland a bull ring—all institutions requiring either distance from dwellings, or a lot of space, or both. The only neighborhood on the far side of Belascoaín was called, aptly enough, Pueblo Nuevo. Sometime before the year 1811, the carpenter and woodcarver José Antonio Aponte y Ulabarra built himself a cottage in Pueblo Nuevo, of wooden planks and palm thatch. It stood on a primitive lane, predecessor of the street that later came to be called Jesús Peregrino, a name that would obliquely memorialize Aponte himself. For Aponte would soon become a revolutionary, long before his successors Antonio Maceo or the Amejeiras brothers were born.

Aponte was a free black man who built his house thanks to a loan or a gift of 300 pesos from his mother Mariana Poveda, a free black woman likewise born in Cuba whose occupation is unknown. In this cottage Aponte lived with his wife, his youngest son Juan de Paula, and at least one stepdaughter, María Josefa Valdés. Here he maintained his workshop, which consisted of a carpenter's bench and a box of tools. More unusual was his small library—Aponte could read and he did. His collection ranged from world history to natural history, from architecture to military matters to a guide to Cuba for foreigners, from a manual on crafting letters to *Don Quijote de la Mancha* and biographies of famous men.

By 1811, Aponte was somewhere over fifty years old. He had been, as we have mentioned earlier, a corporal in Havana's black militia battalion, having served overseas during the campaigns related to the American Revolution in Florida and probably in the capture of Nassau. Official orders detailing the privileges conferred by this service hung on his wall. His father, of Yoruba origin, was a member of the prestigious secret society called the Ogboni, said to be descendants of the *orisha* Changó, and passed this membership on to his son. José Antonio was himself the head of a small Lucumí cabildo, the Cabildo Changó-Teddún, of which his house-workshop was the seat. This adherence to African religion did not preclude his accepting a commission, in 1811, to carve and paint a Virgin of Guadalupe for a nearby parish church. The walls of his house bore portraits of Christian saints, and he had built an effigy on his front door or an altar within (reports differ) depicting Jesus as a pilgrim, from which the later name of his street derived. He appeared to be a model citizen (though as a black man he had no political rights), but in the same year that he carved the Virgin of Guadalupe he sent his wife and his son, an eighteen-year-old tailor, to live across the bay in Guanabacoa for their own safety. He was about to embark on a conspiracy to overthrow slavery and Spanish rule.

The plan did not arise in isolation. Napoleon's armies had invaded Spain, producing a political vacuum in the mother country that ignited independence actions from the River Plate (today Argentina) to Mexico. In 1810, a wealthy white Cuban, Gen. Luis Francisco Bassave y Cardenas, conspired with a group of fellow freemasons to overthrow the government with the help of the colored militias. The plot was discovered, and Bassave was sent to Spain for trial. Meanwhile, unfolding events in Spain gave the

American colonies their first representation in the Cortes, the Spanish parliament. A Mexican delegate introduced a measure to outlaw the slave trade and gradually eliminate slavery itself.

In this climate, Aponte began spreading word that slavery might indeed be abolished—and perhaps already had been, but colonial officials and Cuban planters (both of whom vociferously opposed the Mexican resolution) had suppressed the news. He also made contact, through a Catalán merchant of republican sentiments, with Cuban-born whites who had been connected with the conspiracy of the year before. Under cover of cabildo meetings he began to recruit followers, not just among the Lucumí but among most of the African ethnic groups. He made contact with important figures such as Salvador Ternero, long-time *capataz* of a Mina society, who lived in the neighboring barrio of La Salud by the bridge where the Calle Manrique crossed the Royal Ditch. Ternero began to hold meetings in his house too. Attendees at the meetings in La Salud and Pueblo Nuevo included shoe, furniture, charcoal, and saddle makers, oxcart drivers and porters of cane and fodder, teachers, carpenters, bell-ringers, and probably more. The conspirators made contact with the officers of a black Spanish regiment, raised in Santo Domingo, which happened to be returning from Central America by way of Havana. Since these officers had first-hand experience with the rebellion in Haiti, Spanish authorities were keeping them sequestered in barracks in Casablanca. Nonetheless, Aponte, Ternero, and a third ally found a pretext to talk to them, and made a request for arms and leadership to be provided once an insurrection was launched.

Throughout 1811, plans for this insurrection spread across the island. Aponte and others set up links with free blacks and slaves in Puerto Príncipe (now Camagüey) and Bayamo in the East. In meetings and by word of mouth, they discussed slavery's abolition in Haiti, and they envisioned a Cuban regime that would be free of slavery, Spain, and discrimination by race. The plan was to foment uprisings on plantations both in the East and in the environs of Havana, putting fields and mills to the torch, and setting diversionary fires in Havana's suburbs. In the confusion, the conspirators (many with first-hand knowledge from service in the militia) would seize several barracks and arms depots in the outer barrios of the city, principally the Dragoon Barracks in La Salud and the Castillo de Atarés just south of Jesús María. They would distribute to the population of color all the weapons they could seize.

Antislavery handbills started to appear, including one posted on the back wall of the captain-general's palace, where the coachmen gathered and coaches were kept. Three free black women, María de la Luz Sánchez, Patria de la Espinosa, and María de los Dolores, also held meetings and spread word of the impending rebellion to female slaves on the Trinidad plantation and mill in Guanabacoa. Secretly, a date for the uprising was set: January 5, 1811, the eve of the Day of Kings. In a coded message they alerted potential white supporters to be prepared, because "a column is about to fall" and "the hymn of celebration will be sung before the time of the mass."

When word of a conspiracy in the East leaked out to Spanish officials, the date for the uprising in the capital was postponed. After some debate, Aponte convinced his Havana allies to go forward. On March 15, three of the free blacks who had met in Aponte's house joined with slaves of the plantation Peñas Altas, in Guanabo along the coast east of Havana, to begin the revolt. They succeeded in taking the mill after a brief but bloody assault in which the owner's son was killed. They put the mill to the torch and spread out to hide or to distribute the news. An attempt to repeat the plan at the nearby plantation La Trinidad failed, however, and unbeknownst to Aponte three plotters within the walls of Old Havana (two coachmen and a shoemaker, all slaves) had been discovered and imprisoned. Then word reached the captain-general that mysterious meetings had taken place in Salvador Ternero's house, and a neighbor admitted that after the uprising in Guanabo he had been invited to join the insurrection. A few hours later, before Aponte could raise above his house the white flag with the image of Our Lady of Remedios that was supposed to signal the time for the assault on the barracks, he and most of his network were arrested. They were soon brought to La Cabaña for interrogation. Among the evidence presented against them were African religious objects and a fleur-de-lis seal used as a countersign on documents, found in Ternero's house. In Aponte's, authorities confiscated a large scrapbook of paintings and drawings, including a map of the city and its environs, portraits of Toussaint L'Ouvertoure and George Washington, and depictions of victorious black troops and black priests.

On March 9, 1812, Aponte and his fellow conspirators were hanged from gallows erected just inside the walls, in the Plaza de Las Ursulinas at the end of Calle Sol. The captain-general ordered that their heads be cut off and displayed in "the most appropriate public places as a warning to others." José Antonio Aponte's severed head was placed inside an iron cage and hung at the border of the city near his house, right where the headquarters of the Masonic Lodges of Cuba stands today, at the busy corner of Carlos III and Belascoaín. The first attempt to end slavery and Spanish rule had failed. *Más malo que Aponte* ("more evil than Aponte") entered the vocabulary of conservative Havana, but Aponte's name lived on in its popular memory. The street where he lived took its name from the altar or effigy he had built. In *Cecilia Valdés*, when María de Regla tries to remember when she was assigned as wet nurse to the newborn Cecilia, she fixes it as "the year they sent Aponte to the hangman," which was the beginning of many troubles for her as well.

The Conspiracy of Aponte (like the contemporary slave revolts planned by Gabriel Prosser and Nat Turner in Virginia, Denmark Vesey in South Carolina, and others in Jamaica, Barbados, and Antigua) conjured up the fear among slaveowners that the history of Haiti could repeat itself. After Aponte, Spanish authorities clamped down on their colored militias, arresting any member who showed signs of holding meetings, teaching reading skills, or other "subversive activities" in his home. Even individual public expressions of pride were viewed with suspicion. In 1826, a mulatto painter and ex-sergeant named Pedro Cortés protested being refused seating in a whites-only restaurant. Cortés, rebuked by a white patron for demanding a seat, declared that "the Spanish are shameless and stubborn." He was arrested and questioned, and released only after apologizing for his "extremely bad behavior that day." The restaurant in question, court records tell us, was in the Plaza del Vapor—the new indoor market, said to be one of the world's biggest, recently built outside the old walls. This was presumably the restaurant owned by Pancho Marty, the ex-pirate and soon-to-be developer of the Teatro Tacón, who decorated it with a large painting of Havana's first steamship (*vapor*) that gave the market its name.

Pedro Cortés's infraction, and all others like it, were brought before a new Military Commission established by Captain-General Vives to try cases of subversion, whether by independence-minded whites or antislavery and equality-minded blacks. When Vives returned to Madrid in 1832 at the end of his nine-year Cuban tour of duty, he testified that, "The existence of free blacks and mulattos in the middle of the enslavement of their comrades is an example that will be very prejudicial some day, if effective measures are not taken in order to prevent [the slaves'] constant and natural tendency toward emancipation, in which case they may attempt by themselves or with outside help to prevail over the white population." He proposed the deportation of all free people of color, but recognized that any such attempt would produce the disease it attempted to cure, for its injustice "would awaken discontent and produce unfailingly the ruin of the country."

Vives' fear was well founded. Many free blacks and mulattos were themselves ex-slaves or the children of slaves, and they were always subject to the racial barriers that slave society required. Even when they owned slaves themselves, they seem to have made it possible for these to purchase their freedom, by paying a slight salary for domestic or business tasks, or by renting them out as a source of income for both master and slave. Plots similar to Aponte's continued to surface. Plantation slaves continued to stage isolated revolts, and far off in the mountainous interior numerous communities of runaways struggled to survive.[1]

Vives's successor, Miguel de Tacón, figures in the architectural history of Havana for his improvements of the regal *paseos* and for lending his name to the theater built by his friend Marty. He was also a law-and-order governor to the extreme. Tacón clamped down further on any hint of subversion, tightened press censorship, instituted nightly patrols to cut down on theft and assault, made some attempt to limit public gambling, and built a sinister monument to Spanish power that would last a hundred years, forty more than Spanish rule. At the seaward end of the Paseo del Prado, just before the Castillo de la Punta and across from where the barracks for newly imported slaves had until recently stood, he ordered the construction of an immense new jail. This yellow limestone colossus measured two hundred by nearly four hundred feet, with two stories each twenty-four feet high, and held more than two thousand inmates—political prisoners, common criminals, and those somewhere in between. These chain gangs may be thanked for the extension and leveling of the city's boulevards and the quarrying of the stone from which its new mansions were built.

One travel writer, citing a local census, claimed that there were a thousand prisoners working in chain gangs in 1841. Richard Henry Dana, walking near the jail in 1859, heard a sound like soldiers marching, banging their sabers against the paving stones, which in fact was the work gangs forming ranks. "Poor wretches!" he wrote.

"Each man has an iron band riveted round his ankle, and another around his waist, and the chain is a fastened, one end into each of these bands, and dangles between them, clanking with every movement." Prisoners wore these chains working or eating or sleeping, day and night. Common prisoners in the jail were kept in wards with stone floors and no beds if Dana is to believed, though those who could afford to pay some of their upkeep were assigned to better-equipped "wards of distinction." The New Jail also held 1200 troops with separate pavilions for their commanders and officers. From the sea, it towered over the Castillo de la Punta, momentarily distracting shipboard arrivals from the older monuments and striking natural setting of the bay. "Among the objects which caught my sight were the fortress where the state prisoners are kept, a second prison, and—a gallows," Frederika Bremer remarked. "But those beautiful waving palms and those verdant hills enchanted my eyes."

Beyond the verdant hills, in 1843 and 1844, a string of slave rebellions in the rich cane lands of Matanzas filled Cuba's jails with the victims of Tacón's successor, Captain-General Leopoldo O'Donnell, in what historians later called "The Ladder" or "The Year of the Lash." Reacting to the rebellions in Matanzas, O'Donnell claimed to have uncovered a vast conspiracy involving British abolitionists, free Cubans of color, members of the Cuban sugarocracy, and bloodthirsty slaves. Historians have not been able to determine the truth of this claim. Britain was by this time committed to wage labor and the suppression of the slave trade. The British consul and others had held tentative talks with planters about ending the importation of new slaves, and with potential leaders among free Cubans of color as well. However, a conspiracy uniting all factions and opposing interests, such as O'Donnell claimed to have uncovered, is unlikely. Most of the evidence gathered by the Military Commissions was extracted by torture carried out in the prisons of Matanzas and Havana: specifically, by tying the suspect to a ladder, and whipping him or her until he or she confessed and implicated others, or died. O'Donnell and his allies probably took advantage of whatever conspiracy existed to teach a lesson to all potential forces for change.

As a result of the first confessions, thousands more blacks and mulattos, slave and free, were sent to be tortured on the ladder. Unknown numbers, certainly in the hundreds, died. In the capital, the brunt of the punishment fell on the free people of color, especially those with some status or some modest wealth. In fact, much of what we know about the life histories of prominent Havana free blacks and mulattos, recounted in the previous chapter, comes from the court records of La Escalera. The poet Plácido, singled out by O'Donnell as a chief conspirator, was executed by firing squad in Matanzas; his last poem was a farewell to the mother who had given him up to the Cradle House. His mother-in-law María del Pilar Poveda, in Havana, was stripped of her mid-wife's license and sentenced to a year's forced labor. The tailor Francisco Uribe, arrested and awaiting the ladder, committed suicide to escape that fate. The musician Claudio Brindis de Salas the elder was exiled, as were many more. In three months in the spring of 1844, seven hundred Cubans of color left the island, the majority going to Mexico, and smaller numbers to Africa, the United States, Jamaica, Brazil, and Europe. Augustín Ceballos, dock gang captain, militia sublieutenant, and one of the richest Havanans of color, was sent to prison in Cárdenas to waste away and die. Several more "ungrateful" dock captains were charged with involvement in the conspiracy. "Given the influence they must enjoy and have enjoyed because of their knowledge and resources," the Military Commission judged, "it is evident they were in the first ranks of the conspiracy hatched by those of their color."

Under pressure from Spanish interrogators, those tied to the ladder or threatened with execution implicated white Cuban-born aristocrats in the real or alleged plot. Jailed, held incommunicado, and interrogated many times before being sent to the firing squad, Plácido claimed (according to his interrogator) that Domingo Del Monte had attempted to recruit him into the plot. Del Monte was Havana's most prominent liberal intellectual, and its richest as well. Lawyer, arts patron, literary critic, formative promoter of Cuban literature, he had married into a mega-rich planter family and resided in the grandest and newest mansion of which the capital could yet boast. He serves as an example of the trap in which the liberal wing of the sugarocracy found themselves. They aspired toward independence and even an end to slavery, but could not lead the country to either one.

Born in Venezuela, Del Monte came to Havana with his parents as a child and entered the Seminary of San Carlos (alma mater of Leonardo Gamboa) at the age of only twelve. He moved on to the University of Havana at fifteen. In the 1820s, he became the trusted associate of a prominent but nearly blind Havana lawyer, who soon financed a voyage to the United States and Europe for this brilliant young member of his firm. On his return to Cuba he participated in the founding of several literary magazines and societies and joined the prestigious Economic Society of the Country's Friends, the intellectual inner circle of the native-born planter elite, publishers of the first significant Cuban newspaper, the *Papel Periódico de La Habana.* Steeped in European culture, with a mastery of Latin, Italian, Portuguese, French, and English, Del Monte began to patronize and promote young Cuban writers. His position as intellectual spokesperson and cultural arbiter was solidified by his match with Rosa Aldama, to whom he proposed marriage at a Philharmonic Society fancy ball. Rosa's father, also named Domingo, was among the most prominent importers of slaves in the early years of the century, and he had invested his gains in Matanzas plantations. By 1836, a survey of wealthy Cubans ranked Domingo de Aldama y Arechaga as the twelfth richest in the land. After a stay in Matanzas, the young couple established themselves in Havana, first at a sumptuous old house in the old city, and finally, just before La Escalera, in the new "Palace of Aldama" outside the walls at the beginning of the Paseo de Tacón.

The Palacio de Aldama, which now houses the Cuban Institute of History, was actually two houses in one, linked by a colonnaded gallery which ran for an entire city block along Calle Amistad across from the military parade ground. An immense stone edifice with staircases of Italian marble and ceilings carved and painted in precious woods, the Palacio housed the senior Aldama and his unmarried children in one unit, and Domingo and Rosa in the other. Of neoclassical style, it broke with the Andalusian and baroque traditions of the old city. It embraced all that was modern, including a library for Del Monte's collection of science and literature, bedrooms facing the street rather than the courtyard, cement tiles imitating stone in the patios, and a flush toilet—something even the Spanish royal family did not have. One member of the family wrote a letter to relatives living in Paris itself, describing to them the details of this invention which they had not yet seen.

In all of the several Havana locations where Domingo Del Monte lived in the late 1830s and early 1840s, his house formed the center of the country's intellectual life. Besides promoting literature and learning, he criticized the woeful state of education under Spanish rule. His report on the near-total lack of public primary education was suppressed by the colonial government, and his request for the establishment of a department of Humanities at the university was deemed too dangerous, and denied. Politically, Del Monte argued for greater Cuban autonomy within the empire. He set about provoking a debate about the slave trade and the future of slavery itself.

The status of the slave trade requires a few words of explanation. Britain, converted to free labor by the necessities of the industrial revolution and the demands of abolitionists, outlawed the Atlantic slave trade in 1807 and abolished slavery in its Caribbean colonies in 1833–39. The United States agreed to ban the import of new slaves in 1808, and a decade later Spain agreed as well, in return for an English payoff of 10 million pesetas. However, dependent as they were on the profits from Cuba's slave-based sugar industry, neither Madrid nor its representatives made any serious attempt to enforce this ban. The governors sitting in the Palace of the Captains General usually made a practice of taking bribes to look the other way. As Pancho Marty said of his career as a slave trader, "I made my fortune buying whites and selling blacks." Britain and Spain then agreed on new enforcement measures, but these only drove the contraband trade slightly further underground. *Cecilia Valdés* features a conversation between Cándido Gamboa and the captain-general about three hundred "bundles" or "sacks of carbon" whom Gamboa is trying to sneak past the Spanish-British commission that inspects incoming ships.

In the short run, the continued importation of slaves to work the ever-expanding sugar plantations generated huge profits for the Cuban oligarchy, of which the Palace of Aldama was proof. In the longer run, however, three dangers threatened the future of this class: First, the contraband nature of the traffic raised the price of slaves more and more, while the price of sugar on the world market fell. Second, with the advent of steam-driven grinding mills (rather than those powered by oxen or by crews of slaves themselves) and other technological improvements, a more skilled and independent workforce could be more efficient than unskilled slaves worked to death over twenty-hour days. Third, the influx of Africans had made whites a minority in Cuba. Census figures are not completely reliable, since their implications were so politically charged, but in the island as a whole whites appear to have become a minority of the population by 1817 and remained so in 1846. In Havana itself, they were a minority of the permanent population; only the Spanish garrisons in the forts and the crews of warships tipped the balance the other way. Thus white independence-minded Cuban intellectuals feared not only a Haitian-style revolt, but also the corruption of their nation-to-be by what the "modern" scientific theories of the time construed as a biologically inferior race.

In this context, with censorship making direct challenges to prevailing policy illegal, and with a nascent sense of nationhood demanding a Cuban literature distinct from that inherited from Spain, Del Monte encouraged his friends and protégés to write novels depicting details of Cuban life and exposing the evils of slavery. The models for these novels included the romances of Sir Walter Scott and Alessandro Manzoni and the social realism of Honoré de Balzac. Del Monte's circle included Cirilo Villaverde, of course. The author of *Cecilia Valdés* was a doctor's son who had seen slavery up close when his father worked on a plantation in Pinar de Río, and then been sent to Havana for education in private schools. He became a schoolteacher himself, and a journalist, but his ambition lay in literature. He published stories and short novels in magazines and with Del Monte's support succeeded in publishing an early version of *Cecilia Valdés* in 1839.

Another member of the circle was Félix Tanco, whose lament about the Africanization of illustrious Cuban youth, quoted in chapter 4, comes from a letter he wrote to his patron in 1837. Tanco's 1838 novel *Petronia y Rosalia* contains harsh scenes of plantation slavery and also anticipates the incest theme of Villaverde's work. During La Escalera he was fired from his job as an administrator of the postal service, and jailed. Del Monte and his group also purchased the freedom of Francisco Manzano, a runaway slave and poet, and paid him to write his memoirs. The book could not be published in Cuba, but a part of it, heavily edited and rendered more acquiescent by the novelist Francisco Suarez y Romero, was smuggled to England and translated and published there. In its earliest pages, Manzano recalls the gentle treatment and education he received as a boy from his first owner, before he was shipped off to a life of misery under successive ones. That first owner was the aged Beatriz de Jústiz y Zayas, removed to her Matanzas plantation many years after she had written her *décima* and memorial at the time of the English attack. Suarez y Romero wrote a novel, *Francisco*, based on Manzano's memoirs as well.

So we can see why Del Monte's circle roused the ire of Spanish authorities and of slave traders, and also why the patrician liberal was in frequent contact with the antislavery British consul in Havana—he hoped to use British pressure to bring about a change in the policies dictated from Madrid. At the same time, we can see why, despite the testimony coerced from Plácido, he would not have been part of any insurrectionary plot. He did not favor abolition, because his wealth and that of his class was tied up in slaves. Nor did he advocate full Cuban independence, much as he criticized Spain's attempts to keep the country subservient and backward. This was the contradiction of the planter class: They wanted liberalization of trade and civil society, freed from Spanish taxation and regulation, but they needed the Spanish army to keep their human property from rising against them. They wanted a rapid end to the introduction of new slaves onto the island, and they vaguely sought some gradual withering away of the slave system itself. But they did not want to make common cause with organized groups of slaves or free blacks, or to place any weapons (physical or political) in their hands.

The Count of Santovenia, whose sugar wealth had made him owner of the mansion that faced the Palace of the Captains-General across the Plaza de Armas and of one of the first estates in Cerro as well, wrote in 1841, just before La Escalera, that slavery was an "odious system," and he called for strict punishment for slave traders and for a campaign to promote the immigration of a free white labor force. Yet he argued that "a state of freedom would be attended with greater evils than slavery itself, because all the foundations of our civil existence would be speedily overturned [and] our beautiful Cuba would return to its previous condition, uncultivated and filled with barbarians, lost at once to us and the rest of the world." The Countess of Merlín, whose visit to Havana came a year before Santovenia's report, challenged potential abolitionists and independence advocates in a similar vein. If slaves were freed and educated, she argued, "under a constitutional regime, in a country governed by egalitarian laws, couldn't they demand to share in those same institutions? Would you give them all of your rights, all of your privileges, make them your judges, generals, and ministers, give them your daughters in marriage? They would feel themselves men like yourselves, and demand a settling of accounts."

At times, white Cubans frustrated with Spanish rule saw their salvation in alliance or possible union with the United States. Del Monte, though not a supporter of annexation, invited the friendship and correspondence of U.S. diplomat Alexander Everett, a Massachusetts Democrat, former ambassador to Spain, special envoy to Cuba, and an unabashed proponent of buying or otherwise acquiring the island and annexing it to the United States. In 1842, Del Monte wrote Everett of his fear that British agents might provoke an uprising of blacks in Cuba in order to increase Britain's influence in the Caribbean. "England has decreed our ruin, and Spain does not *know* or does not *want* to know this, and the Spanish authorities on the Island do not want or do not know how to weather the tempest." He told Everett that the United States should protect its interest and that of its "lesser sister of the great Western Confederation of the Caucasian Peoples of America" by sending American warships if need be.

In the meantime, Del Monte left with his family for a visit to Philadelphia, and then to Paris, where news of his implication in La Escalera reached him. In a letter to the Paris newspaper *Le Globe*, he claimed to have met his accuser Plácido only once, when the poet sought a loan to support his literary work. Del Monte said he was opposed to the slave trade and wanted to promote free white labor, but not by "revolutionary measures." He added, "I do not want my country to have slaves and even less that these slaves be blacks, that is from such a savage branch of the human family." A year later he requested permission to return to Cuba, which was denied. In 1846, he was finally acquitted of charges of conspiracy, but he remained in Madrid, where he died in 1853.

Where Del Monte stopped short of U.S. annexation as a solution to Cuba's problems, Cirilo Villaverde apparently did not. In 1846, he joined an anti-Spanish conspiracy of a new sort. This plot was headed by Narciso López, like Del Monte a Venezuelan by birth and married into a prominent Cuban planter family, but a career Spanish military officer rather than a literary man. López planned on staging an uprising and requesting U.S. aid. In 1848, shortly before the uprising was to occur, the plan was discovered. López escaped to the United States, but his chief aides, Villaverde among them, did not. On the night of October 20, Villaverde was surprised in his home by a group of Spanish soldiers and police, arrested, and taken to the New Jail. Tried and convicted by the Military Commission of Havana he was sentenced to the chain gang, but he plotted an escape along with another prisoner and the gatekeeper of the jail. In April of 1849, they succeeded, spent several days hiding in a thatched-roof cottage in the outer barrios, and fled to Florida in a small sailboat rented by Villaverde's friends.

Though he was able to return to Havana for brief periods, Villaverde lived most of the rest of his life in New York, Philadelphia, and New Jersey, making his living by teaching Spanish and writing journalism, while throwing himself into the politics of the growing Cuban exile community in the United States. He served first as secretary to Narciso López, who from his headquarters in New York and then New Orleans raised a series of invasion forces made up mostly of Americans. Two of these expeditions succeeded in reaching Cuban soil; on the second, after a few victories, López was captured to the west of Havana, brought to the capital, tried for high treason, and sentenced to death. In the sandy open space between La Punta fortress and the New Jail, he was executed on the garrote, a chair fitted with an iron collar and a screw tightened to crush the spinal cord and produce instant death. Many of his American recruits perished by firing squad, shot on the slopes of the Castillo de Atarés.

After López's defeat, Villaverde soldiered on the North, writing in favor of Cuban separation from Spain in a variety of Cuban-exile and other Spanish-language publications. He married the exile activist Emilia Casanova with whom he founded a private high school in Weehawken, New Jersey. Throughout the 1850s he continued to argue for Cuban annexation to the United States, though in later years he shifted to a proindependence view. He finally wrote the definitive version of *Cecilia Valdés* in 1878. Spanish censorship forbade publishing the book in Cuba, so the classic novel of nineteenth-century Havana first saw print in 1882 in New York. Meanwhile, the human profile of Havana was being altered by the one policy on which Spaniards and Cuban-born whites could agree: immigration to promote the growth of a free, non-African labor force.

As early as 1845, Domingo Del Monte's brother-in-law Miguel de Aldama made arrangements to import a group of Basques whom he hoped to put to work in his fields in place of slaves. Thanks to a variety of colonization schemes involving labor contracting, indentures, and subsidized transportation, by 1862 whites had again become a majority in the island's population, roughly 800,000 out of the 1.5 million total. Over the next three decades, some 500,000 more arrived, not counting several hundred thousand soldiers and officials, many of whom also stayed. The bulk of the immigrants came from Spain, especially from poorer areas (Asturias, Galicia, the Canary Islands) or areas subject to political repression themselves (Catalunya). Also included in the "white" category in the census were Chinese contract laborers—little better than slaves themselves for the term of their indentures—who entered Cuba in the third quarter of the century. The Chinese *"culies,"* whose total immigration during third quarter of the nineteenth century totaled about 150,000, were put to work on plantations and in railroad construction.

In Havana, the new wave of Spanish immigrants, especially younger men, competed with white middle-class Cubans in the professions and the lower ranks of commerce and civil service, and they also formed, for the first time, a significant white working class. Between the census of 1846 and that of 1862, the city's white male population grew from 62,000 to 92,000. By 1862, whites— mostly born in Spain—had become a majority of the bakers, butchers, carpenters, carters, shoemakers, day laborers, and even coachmen, all trades previously dominated by Cubans of color.

Cigar rolling, the first factory-based work of any importance in Havana, surged during these years, as Cuban *puros* took the smoking rooms of the United States and Europe by storm. The Havana city directory of 1859 contains ten two-column pages devoted entirely to listings of cigar stores and brands, including not only such names as (translated) Cuban Delight, Havana Rose, and Lovely Cuban Woman's Whim, but also Británica, Crimea, Lord Wellington, Daniel Webster, Washington, Pensilvanio, and even Flor de Henry Clay. The illustrations affixed to boxes of cigars and cigarettes offered the world some of its first comic strips (with relations between white men and mulattas as a frequent theme). By the 1860s, nearly five hundred tobacco factories and workshops employed a free wage-labor workforce of 13,000, about 70 percent of them white. In 1865, cigar workers organized the country's first labor newspaper, *La Aurora*, and the next year the country's first real trade union, the Asociación de Tabaqueros de La Habana, struck against Cabanas and Carvajal cigar factory. The Asturian anarchist organizer and writer Saturnino Martínez introduced the position of Reader into the factories, a tradition maintained ever since, allowing the workers to hear news, articles, editorials, and literary works, without stopping their manipulation of the tobacco leaves. The cigar rollers took up a collection to pay the Reader (often a literate member of their own ranks), and so could democratically choose what he should read. Invented in Havana, this practice spread to factories in Key West, Tampa, New York, and other cities with emigrant Cuban workers.

After serving out their terms in the countryside, meanwhile, many Chinese gravitated to the capital to work in tobacco factories, as well as in construction and on the docks. They settled especially in the outlying zone to the north of La Salud, on the north bank of the old Royal Ditch, where they began to go into business as vegetable growers and street vendors. With the arrival of another wave of Chinese immigrants, the *californios* who had made some money in gold-rush era California but then fled growing discrimination and persecution there, Havana's Chinatown took shape in the area bounded by the modern streets of Galiano, Belascoaín, Reina, and Zanja (Ditch). Alongside laundries, restaurants, and small stores selling imported Chinese goods, whorehouses, gambling parlors, and opium dens grew up in this neighborhood populated largely by men. So too did traditional fraternities (similar to the African cabildos), political organizations with roots in the old country, and eventually newspapers and theaters. By the end of the nineteenth century, Havana's *barrio chino* could be compared only to those in San Francisco and Lima in the New World. The Chinese *charada*, an underground lottery in which bets were placed on numbers represented by different symbols, took its place alongside cards, dice, the Spanish state lottery, cockfights, and other forms of gambling on luck and skill. Ever since then, "horse" has meant "one" in Cuban slang, "butterfly" has meant "two," "corpse" has meant "nine," and the like.

Catalán merchants, meanwhile, played an ever-greater role in the city's merchant middle and upper class. "Five years of privation, and then a fortune," was said to be the motto of the Catalán immigrant. Thanks often to their links with fellow-countrymen of the previous generation, many did succeed in rising from small shopkeepers to wholesale merchants and informal bankers within one generation or two. The thirteen-year-old José Gener y Batet, for instance, stepped off a ship in Havana in 1844 and went to work for his uncle, a storekeeper in Pinar del Río. Twenty years later he was back in the capital, having acquired a position in the state apparatus. He was soon the founder and owner of an important tobacco factory and owner of a sugar mill. Cuban planters, borrowing against the next harvest, often fell into debt to such Catalanes and other Spanish merchants, who thus began to acquire more and more plantations themselves.

In this complex tapestry of classes and nationalities old and new, Havana in the second half of the nineteenth century was not so much "the most loyal," as it was divided and blowing in the wind. The new generation of Cuban-born intellectuals, hundreds of whom had studied in the United States or Europe, felt frustrated with the cautious reformism of their parents or employers. To them, being modern meant independence, democracy, and free labor, yet many were still fearful of the cataclysm that a revolt against Spain could unleash. As they were caricatured by a contemporary, "They have read Proudhon, ride in berlins [four-wheeled closed carriages], love liberty, and own slaves." They conspired in cafes, and when a revolution finally broke out in 1868, they enlisted in it. But the revolution began far from Havana, in and around the old smugglers' port of Bayamo and the cattle lands of Camagüey, in the East. It was led by planters and cattle ranchers removed from the centers of the slave-based economy. Carlos Manuel de Céspedes, Oriente sugar planter and alumnus of Havana's Seminary of San Carlos, freed his small contingent of slaves on condition that they join his rebel contingent, which they did. The rebel army's ranks were quickly swelled by masses of free mulattos and blacks, followed by rural and urban whites of many classes, and by runaway slaves. Though the civilian leadership's position on slavery was equivocal and shifting, that of the rebel army was increasingly clear.

The war was long and bloody, lasting ten hard years. It was fought largely in the eastern part of the island but left an indelible mark on Havana. In the person of General Antonio Maceo, mulatto general from a farm-owning family outside Santiago de Cuba, and in the composition of its officers corps and troops, it unified white and colored Cubans behind an independence ideal without the bloodbath many whites had feared. The Spaniards, eager to portray the war as a racial struggle, called the rebels derogatorily by a pseudo-African term, "mambí." The rebels embraced it, as U.S. independence fighters had embraced the British taunt of "Yankee Doodle" a century before. Many divisions remained, however, between the rebel army, its civilian leaders, and its wealthy sympathizers and diplomatic representatives in Havana and New York. In the end, the war changed Cuba in many ways: increasing the indebtedness of Cuban planters, provoking the gradual emancipation of the slaves, adopting what would later become a new nation's anthem and flag (the flag first hoisted by Narciso López), and driving many of the rural population into cities and towns. But it did not bring independence. It would be followed by a second independence war whose results would change the capital even more.

6

Revolutions and Retributions: From the Teatro Villanueva to the *Maine*

Throughout the Ten Year's War, Havana was a city divided. With some outstanding exceptions, it was divided between *criollos* and *peninsulares*, between those born in Cuba and those born in Spain. Proindependence families sent their sons to the war zone, performed underground support of various kinds, or went into exile. Veterans of the black and mulatto militias (revived in the 1850s, after the fear of La Escalera had subsided) also made their way eastward to join the mambís. Urban Spanish vigilante groups, meanwhile, formed out of the *batallones de voluntarios del comercio*, battalions of immigrant clerks, cigar workers, and other employees recruited in the 1850s to guard against insurrections or invasions of the Narciso López sort. In 1869, the Voluntarios began recruiting Spanish deserters and veterans as well. Their task was to suppress active support for the rebellion in the cities, Havana above all.

On the night of January 21, 1869, three months after the outbreak of the war, a company of Cuban actors put on a musical comedy called *Perro huevero* in the Teatro Villanueva, a theater and dance hall located two blocks south of the New Jail. The title was taken from an old saying to the effect that a dog will go after eggs no matter how often it burns its nose in the pot. Though the play contained no political references, it did have some lines praising the physical beauty of the isle that was now in full revolt. Among the cast was a mulatto singer and actor named Jacinto Valdés, who performed under the stage name Benjamín de las Flores. According to his Spanish police file, he was an unemployed cigar roller who had turned to the theater as a means of support. He lived with Juana Relly, described as a prostitute and fortune-teller. One way or another they were members of the capital's *farandula*, its world where night life, criminality, and bohemia met. At an opportune moment in the drama, Valdés shouted out *Viva Carlos Manuel de Céspedes* in praise of the Oriente planter turned general who headed the rebellion, and he added other *vivas* for other leaders of the revolutionaries in the east. He was fined 200 pesos and warned not to repeat the subversive action, but the news of what had happened at the performance of *Perro huevero* spread.

The next night, both sides of Havana came to the Teatro Villanueva prepared. Many women in the audience came dressed in revolutionary colors, some with the single red star of the rebel flag stitched into their clothes. A group of Spanish Voluntarios, meanwhile, gathered outside. At the point in the drama where one actor's lines proclaimed, "Say it with me, or suffer your shame/Long live the land that yields sugar cane," numerous women and men in the audience chimed in. They stood and chanted the lines, and they launched blue and white ribbons, matching the stripes of the insurrectionary banner, over the crowd. The Voluntarios then burst into the theater, shooting into the audience and making arrests irrespective of age and sex. Over the next two days, the Voluntarios continued their reprisals, firing on patrons in the outdoor sidewalk of the Café del Louvre, a gathering point for the wealthy separatist youth, and then attacking the Palacio de Aldama. This mob was allegedly searching for an arms cache, but in reality they were punishing Miguel de Aldama, the late Del Monte's brother-in-law, for having declared sympathy with the rebel cause. In the course of the three days of violence, fourteen residents of Havana were killed, sixteen wounded, and forty-five arrested. Thereafter the Voluntarios patrolled the streets intent on repressing any signs of disrespect toward Spain. The Aldamas went into exile, and so did Jacinto Valdés.

Since the University of Havana was a hotbed of separatist sympathy, in November the Voluntarios turned their attention that way. On orders of the governor, thirty-five medical students were arrested on suspicion of having vandalized the tomb of a Spanish journalist. Eight were put on trial by a military court, and acquitted. In response, a mob of Voluntarios besieged the jail, intent on retrying the students themselves. The judge of their proceedings was the Catalán immigrant José Gener y Batet, now head of a world famous tobacco firm bearing his name. The Voluntarios lined the eight students up against the wall of the jail and executed them while Spanish regular troops stood by. The rest were returned to the confines of the jail.

Havana tradition says that the eight medical students (all white, of course) did not die alone. Five members of the Abakuá secret society, all construction workers employed nearby, are said to have organized a rescue attempt and been killed in the attempt. One of them, as oral tradition tells it, had been a "milk brother" of the condemned student Alonso Álvarez de la Campa—his mother was wetnurse to the condemned white student. The preeminent historian of the colonial period, Manuel Moreno Fraginals, wrote recently that he had heard the story of the Abakuá rescue attempt in 1940 from a ninety-year-old Abakuá and former slave, and later from a 100-year-old who did not know the first informant. Moreno says he then found same name mentioned by both in the burial records of the city cemetery for that year. Historian Jorge Lozano cites a letter written back to Spain by Ramón López de Ayala, Voluntario captain who commanded the firing squad, which says that "some blacks opened fire on a group of Artillery Voluntarios, killing their lieutenant. Those assaulted then charged the blacks and hacked the five authors of this aggression to bits."

In Havana during the Ten Year's War, lines of nationality cut across those of class, and vice versa. Some militant workers, like Saturnino Martínez who had introduced the Reader to the cigar factories, were also Voluntarios. On the other hand, the Spanish authorities used their wartime powers to suppress union organization and deport the organizers. They shut down *La Aurora* and temporarily banned the Readers, and they finally clamped a lid on the Voluntarios during a carriage-drivers' strike which enjoyed some Voluntario support. More important, however, was the fact that nationality itself was always in flux. As a popular saying put it, "A Spaniard can get anything he wants in Cuba—except

90

Spanish forces preparing to execute a Cuban prisoner by garrote in fornt of the New Jail, 1869.
Picture Collection, The Branch Libraries, The New York Public Library, Astor, Lenox and Tilden Foundations.

Spanish children." The descendants of Catalanes and Asturians and Galicians learned to speak like Cubans. Politically, the sons and daughters of many a *peninsular* declared themselves *cubanos* during the Ten Years War, or in the uneasy interval that followed, or in the new War of Independence launched in 1895.

The most famous example, by far, was the son of immigrants from Valencia and the Canary Islands. Leonor Pérez came to Havana from the Canaries with her parents, who had the good luck to win a sizeable prize in the state lottery shortly after they set foot on Cuban soil. She married Mariano Martí, who had come to the Cuban capital from Valencia as sergeant in an artillery unit, fought against Narciso López, and then retired from the army and taken a job in the police. The couple settled in a small house on Calle Paula in the old city and had a son who was baptized in the Church of the Angel in 1853 with the name of José Julián. The growing family soon moved to a succession of other houses, mostly in the poorer barrios outside the walls, where Mariano served as a neighborhood watchman, though he was sometimes out of work. One of the briefer stays was on Calle Jesús Peregrino itself. Though his parents were loyal to the Peninsula, the boy developed nationalist senti-ments and formed a close tie with his teacher Rafael María Mendive, a poet and fervent nationalist who ran one of the very few secular schools in the city, a private school on the Prado that served the lower middle class.

During the days of the Villanueva events, José Martí, now six-teen, published the first and only issue of a short-lived literary magazine, *La Patria Libre*, printed in a small shop on the Calle Obispo near its crossing with Cuba, aptly enough. Four days later, his patron Mendive was arrested, and shortly thereafter the teenager wrote a patriotic poem in a manuscript paper secretly cir-culated by students. He continued to visit Mendive in the El Príncipe fortress until the teacher's deportation to Spain. Then, in October, a group of Voluntarios raided the house of his schoolmate Fermín Valdés Domínguez, behind the Tacón Theater. The Voluntarios claimed that Valdés Domínguez and friends had been mocking them from a window as they passed by in the street, returning from a military parade. In the house they found separatist propaganda and a poem by the two friends in which they challenged a third schoolmate who had enlisted in the Spanish army, calling him an apostate who had broken ranks. Valdés was arrested on the spot, and Martí two weeks later.

Valdés suffered a year's imprisonment, after which he enrolled in medical school and became one of the thirty-five arrested for profanation of the tomb (though he escaped being one of the eight who were shot). Martí was confined in the New Jail, tried and convicted of "disloyalty," and finally sentenced at the age of seventeen to six years on the chain gang. Prisoner number 113 in the "First Brigade of Whites," every day from April to August of 1870 he trudged from the New Jail to the quarries at the edge of Vedado, manacled just as R. H. Dana had described eleven years before, laboring twelve hours a day under the summer sun near what is now the Hotel Nacional.

Finally his parents prevailed upon the authorities to put him to work in a cigarette factory within the jail, then to exile him to the Isle of Pines off Cuba's southern coast, and finally to deport him to Spain where he could complete his education. He gained a law degree and in the late 1870s made his way to Central America, briefly back to Havana, and then into exile in the United States. Like Cirilo Villaverde, Martí spent more of his adult life in exile than in Havana. He lived most of his last thirteen years in New York.

Propagandist, political organizer, groundbreaking essayist, and modernist poet, José Martí would be the architect and organizer of the Cuban Revolutionary Party and the second Independence War. Around him coalesced a new notion of *Cuba Libre* "with all and for the good of all," one that promised that "the colony would not live on the republic"—that separation from Spain would also include thoroughgoing social reform. The last of the independence struggles of the Spanish colonies, the Cuban struggle was also the most radical. In the years of independence agitation, if open nationalism could not be expressed in the capital without fear of expulsion or arrest, there were other, more subtle ways in which Cuban-born Havana expressed its growing sense of nationhood. One of the most striking of these was sports.

Spaniards went to the bullfight at the *plaza de toros* on Belascoaín or the one in Regla across the bay, both of which featured exclusive boxes from which Spanish authorities would preside. Bullfights were often sponsored by the army or the Voluntarios, and nationalist-minded Havanans shunned the *plazas de toros* like the plague. Martí called bullfighting a "futile bloody spectacle . . . and against Cuban sentiment for being intimately linked with our colonial past." The Cuban alternatives were twofold, one borrowed from the Spanish heritage, and one from the United States. Cuban men had long been fanatics of the *vallas de gallos*, the cockfight pits. Beginning in the 1860s, Cubans of both sexes went to the baseball park.

"Cockfighting," the novelist Abel Prieto would observe with late twentieth-century hindsight, "took root in Cuba even before we knew we were Cuban, before we knew we were different from our fathers. Bullfighting never had a chance, because the cockfight offered a fair contest, and Cubans always prefer what's equal or even, something anyone can win. A bullfight is essentially a trap with no exit for the bull." American businessman Joseph Dimock, in Havana en route to visit his family's sugar mills in Matanzas and Cienfuegos, took the train from Regla to Guanabacoa to visit the famed cockpit there. "Those of all shades were present: white, black, lemon, and mahogany color," he noted disapprovingly. "The cockpit was a perfect pandemonium, and all were equal there—white and black, slave and free—all betting, drinking, and smoking together. It would have rejoiced the heart of the most ardent abolitionist to see the perfect familiarity between the two races." Cockfights generally took place on Sunday mornings, an indication of lack of popular participation in the weekly masses officiated by mostly Spanish priests.

In less bloody fashion, Cubans beginning in the 1860s borrowed from the United States what they saw as a New World and democratic sport. The called it *el beisbol*, or more colloquially *la pelota*. One version of its implantation places the first game in a clearing in the still largely forested El Vedado, organized by a trio of middle-class Cuban youth returned from studying in Mobile, Alabama. The new sport took root in both Havana and Matanzas, finding equally fertile ground among dockworkers who learned it from American crews. It soon spread throughout the island and eventually, via the travels of Cuban ballplayers, to the rest of the Caribbean and Central America as well. The Havana Base Ball Club (so named, in English) was founded about 1870, while the Ten Years' War raged in the East. In 1874, Havana defeated Matanzas, 51–9, in the first recorded professional game. Ex-Fordham University and (U.S.) National Association pro Esteban Bellán held down third base for Havana. Emilio Sabourín scored eight runs. Four years later Sabourín's Liga General de Base Ball de la Isla de Cuba set up headquarters in Havana. Baseball newspapers and magazines proliferated, many of them making the opposition of baseball to bullfight explicit. "We categorically reject the bullfight," the editors of *El Pitcher* wrote in 1888; "we will organize a crusade against the ignoble spectacle," a reporter for *El Baseball* declared. Cuban doctor Benjamín de Céspedes wrote to a baseball promoter that fans of different classes rooting for the same ballclub was "a rehearsal for democracy," nothing less.

The Almendares team's brand new stadium opened in the early 1880s across the street from the Quinta de los Molinos, the summer residence of the Captains General. The Spanish countered with a new bullring nearby. So when six thousand spectators packed the stadium to see the championship ballgame between Almendares and Habana in 1886, their statement was not only about sports. "Everyone was at baseball," a visiting Spanish poet was shocked to observe ten years later. "Men and women, old and young, masters and servants . . . I had a presentiment that Spain had died for Cuba."

Episodic Spanish attempts to outlaw baseball or particular teams proved fruitless, but when war broke out anew in 1895, they immediately instituted a new ban. This time, ballplayers were among those who flocked from Havana to join the rebellion. Three members of the Almendares club's pitching staff became rebel officers. Emilio Sabourín, now player manager of Havana, was arrested for his separatist activity and exiled to the Spanish enclave of Ceuta in Morocco. Among his fellow-prisoners was Juan Gualberto Gómez—Havana journalist, independence organizer, close ally of Martí, and former president of the Central Directorate of Societies of the Colored Race. Sabourín, wrote Gómez, loved three things equally: his family, the nation, and baseball. Sabourín died in Ceuta at the age of forty-three, two years into a twenty-year sentence. Gómez lived to return to Havana, and we will meet him again.

Another site of symbolic confrontation, far from the roar of the baseball crowd, was the city's vast new resting place for the dead in the heights about El Vedado. In the 1880s, Fermín Valdés Domínguez, returned from exile and practicing medicine, took up a public collection to build a mausoleum-monument at the Cemetery of Colón celebrating the innocence of his eight fellow students who had been executed. In November of 1889, their remains were exhumed and brought to the new memorial, in a plot purchased for 920 pesos in gold. In response, José Gener y Batet dug into his personal fortune to add fourteen Italian marble statues to his own mausoleum-chapel and future resting place, so that these could look down upon the column crowning the students' memorial a hundred yards away.

The 1880s also saw the first signs of organization among the city's prostitutes, who published several issues of a magazine called *La Cebolla* (the onion). *La Cebolla* did not touch the question of independence. Its pseudonymous contributors appear to have been both *peninsulares* (La Madrileña, Lola la Sevillana) and *criollas* (La Conga, Teresa Machete). One of their goals was to present a better image of the oldest profession than the image presented in the recent exposé *La prostitución en la ciudad de La Habana* by Benjamin de Céspedes (the same who wrote about the democratic qualities of baseball), who emphasized the sordidness of the red-light underworld and particularly the victimization of children. The magazine's organizers, nonetheless, directed most of their fire at the bribes and sexual favors demanded by the Spanish officials and police. They selected as their editor a progressive Spaniard named Victorino Reinera, who later edited *El Machete,* an embattled proindependence newspaper in Santiago de Cuba, and was deported from that city for publicizing the activities of rebel general Antonio Maceo. The tone of *La Cebolla* was decidedly confrontational: "The ominous times of sitting still and shutting up are gone, never to return," the editorial opening the second issue declared. "Today no one sits still or shuts up, so why should we? Why should we tolerate with our silence the criminal conduct of a pack of thieves who, without cause or justification, are robbing us of what has cost us so many bumps and grinds?" Other articles complained of "the unjust fines they impose on us, because we don't want to accede to the lustful whims of some cop, or because we won't slip them the bribes they expect."

La Cebolla also echoed the universal *criollo* distaste for high Spanish taxes and restrictions on commerce: "The 'horizontals' of this capital pay more taxes to the State than are required to become [in the case of white men] voters or elected representatives. Though we contribute more than other classes to feed the treasury with the sweat of our brows, we are treated as if we were slaves, without protection of the law." The writers complained of new laws requiring them to close their windows or install lattices to block the view from the street, although in practice, one of their poems observed:

> Go ahead and peek out the window
> and stretch your arms out too.
> The soldier won't say a word
> if he gets a coin out of you.

"In what country is the industrialist banned from putting his merchandise on public view?" demanded an open letter to city's Civil Governor. "We sell our flesh—mine, as you may discover, is fresh, velvet, firm, and perfumed, a true *bocatto di cardinali*. Why should we be barred from tempting the passersby with our charms?" A profile of a leading madam praised her as a good and generous soul, a former unionist in the cigarette factories of Madrid, a "revolutionary of other days . . . who stands up before the authorities demanding justice, firm in defense of her rights." To the Municipal President of Havana, on the other hand, they pointed out, "If we are 'public women,' you are also a public man. Your life is nothing to boast about, either."

One reason for the increase in prostitution was an economic depression that hit the country and its capital in the 1880s, followed by the devastating effects in the 1890s of a new war against Spain. Conditions were especially difficult for women who had to support either children or destitute parents. According to estimates by the historian María del Carmen Barcia, in the late 1880s a room cost six to eight pesos a month, and food a minimum of a peso a day, while the daily pay of washerwomen, ironers, seamstresses, maids, and female cigar factory workers was only a peso or slightly more. In the last years of the century, according to the results of official surveys, at least third of the prostitutes in Havana held or had lost jobs in other trades, and half were under twenty years of age.

The depression stemmed from the lingering effects of the disruption caused by the Ten Years War, the rapid spread of beet sugar production in Europe and cane production in Hawaii and South America, and the vagaries of U.S. tariff policies (negotiated not between Washington and Havana, but between Washington and Madrid). Cuba's share of the world sugar market dropped from 29 percent in 1868 to 11 percent twenty years later. To get under tariff barriers, cigar factory owners moved production back and forth from Havana to Key West or Tampa as needed, since the cured tobacco leaves could make the crossing of a half day or less just as easily as the finished cigars. When the factories moved, unemployed Cuban workers followed. Cuban professionals, too, sought in Mexico or the United States the jobs for which they were qualified that were absent or dominated by Spaniards at home. About 250,000 Spaniards entered Cuba in the last third of the nineteenth century, while about 100,000 Cubans left. All these developments culminated in the second Independence War, 1895–98.

This second war began with an uprising in Oriente and with landings on remote eastern beaches, organized in the United States and
led by Martí, Maceo, and the commander-in-chief of the rebel armies
in both wars, Dominican-born Máximo Gómez. Martí died in battle
within six weeks of stepping on Cuban soil, but native recruits
flocked to the insurgent armies and these joint forces soon extended
the war to the countryside all over the island, including the outskirts
of Havana. The insurgents' weapons were machetes, rifles, and "the
torch"—they burned the cane fields of planters who did not
come over to the separatist side. In response to the rebel advance,
Spanish Captain-General Valeriano Weyler, pioneering a tactic later
adopted by American commanders in the Philippines and Vietnam,
tried to dry up sources of support for the independence armies by
forcing hundreds of thousands of peasants and farmworkers off the
land. This policy of "reconcentration," driving now-jobless rural
Cubans into the towns and cities, brought tens of thousands of
deaths from starvation and disease. Between censes taken in 1887
and 1899 the country's population dropped by 60,000 (to just over
one-and-a half million), the first decline in centuries. That of greater
Havana, however, grew by about 40,000 to a total of 250,000.

In Havana, the sick and hungry *reconcentrados* were crowded into
wooden barracks constructed in the *fosos* or pits, steep empty holes
of collapsed limestone that dotted the outer barrios. Families wandered the streets searching for aid. In Nuestra Señora de la Caridad,
one of the three shelters set up for children orphaned or separated
from the families, 4800 boys and girls subsisted on scarce rations
funded by appeals to private charity. To avoid open criticism of the
policy of reconcentration, appeals from pro-Spanish organizations
referred to the needs of "poor children" without specifying who
they were. Agricultural production plummeted, and food prices in
the city doubled. "Not only the *concentrados* lack meat," reported *La
Lucha*, a paper speaking for popular Cuban opinion. "We don't
have it in Havana, because of the scandalous prices charged by the
slaughterhouse. In these days we've seen people who used to
weigh three hundred pounds, and now they're down to skin and
bones." Prices of root vegetables and bread, the traditional foods of
the poor, surged as well. *The Matter of Bread*, a comedy that debuted
at the Teatro Alhambra in June of 1897, featured satirical ditties
about prices: two silver *reales* for a small *ñame* (Cuban sweet
potato), one for a beet or a *malanga*, and twelve *centavos* for a rotten
yucca, "bitter and black."

At the same time, contradictorily, the capital continued its march to modernity. The New York-based Spanish-American Light and Power Company brought electric lighting to Central Park, across from the Hotel Inglaterra, in 1889. Soon its cables and lamps began to snake through the streets. A new aqueduct to replace the old Royal Ditch, begun in mid-century, opened at last in 1893. Designed by the engineer Francisco de Albear, himself born in the Morro Castle where his father had been fort commander, the underground duct depended entirely on gravity to produce pressure. It was an engineering triumph parts of which are still in use today. The first cinema opened in 1897, and the next year the modern La Tropical brewery and ice factory opened on the far side of the Almendares, in the municipality of Marianao.

Modernity was also marching along in the cultural sphere. Danza had become *danzón*, whose sensual rhythms and motions scandalized moralists anew. In the realm of high culture appeared *La Habana Elegante*, a fin de siecle tropical *New Yorker*, a review of poetry, high society, gossip, shopping, travel, and the arts that debuted in the 1880s. Its leading contributor, at least in retrospect, was the poet and critic Julián del Casal. Casal was particularly influenced by the French symbolists, as in his well-known verse, "someone sows evil in my errant path, so that I may harvest it, in flowers that crumble at my touch." He suffered at the hands of Cuban critics not so much for those influences as for more exotic ones, reflected in his habit of dressing in a Japanese kimono and surrounding himself with Oriental objects of all sorts, not to mention his poetic longings for the cold perfection of snow. Attacked as a bearer of unhealthy foreign contamination, and most likely homosexual, he was a forerunner of others who would suffer under those prejudices in periods to come. Yet he was part of the search for a Cuban identity distinct from its Spanish sources. Fired from a job in the state bureaucracy for an article that mocked the captain-general, Casal soon published a sonnet identifying (if pessimistically) with Antonio Maceo when the ex- and future general visited the capital in 1890 to try to rally and reorganize independence supporters there.

Maceo stayed in the Hotel Inglaterra, probably the first Cuban of color to do so. Casal visited him there, and this encounter between the farmer-soldier and the urban aesthete, the man of action and the man of letters, the revolutionary and the decadent, has become a touchstone for modern Cuban intellectuals seeking to reconcile the two. Maceo and Casal posed for a joint photograph, which has been lost, and the soldier also gave the poet a signed portrait dedicated to the "the appealing Cuban bard and intelligent young man Don Julián del Casal." For his part Casal confessed in a letter written soon afterward that he had met only one person lately whom he had found appealing. "Whom do you think? Maceo, a beautiful man of strong constitution, sharp intelligence, and iron will. I don't know whether this affection I feel for our General is the effect of the neurosis that makes me admire those with qualities opposite to my own, but few men have made such a welcome impression on me." In another letter, which has vanished like the joint photo, Casal is alleged to have repeated an impression along the same lines and added, "Although I am a bitter opponent of war, on hearing him talk I felt convinced that it's necessary and inevitable. Within a year, I think, we'll be in rebellion again."

It was five years, in fact, and Casal died before the new Independence War began—suddenly, of an aneurysm suffered during an outburst of laughter in 1892. Juana Borrero, the most promising young contributor to *La Habana Elegante*, died in exile in 1896, of typhoid fever in Key West, where her proindependence family took refuge during the war. Borrero's death at nineteen interrupted her poetic career just as it was taking shape—romantic, melancholy, modernist, erotic, and ethereal all at once. She is known, too, for her love letters to the poet and *Habana Elegante* contributor Carlos Pío Urbach, from whom she was separated first by family vigilance and then by the Florida Straits. "Listen," she reminds him in one of these, "I may be 'the ideal' but I'm not 'the innocent,' you know?"

Pío died in the war, in 1897. So did Maceo himself, in December of 1896, in a small skirmish near Punta Brava, about ten miles outside the capital which many had hoped to see him enter at the head of an army. The conservative, pro-Spanish newspaper *Diario de la Marina* went so far as to throw a banquet to celebrate his death. Even some who favored autonomy or independence relaxed at the disappearance of the dreaded "mulatto republic" that Maceo represented to them. On the other hand, Maceo had been kept informed of Spanish preparedness by an extensive Havana underground, one of whose members had succeeded in smuggling plans out of the captain-general's palace. The clandestine clubs of the Cuban Revolutionary Party kept up this activity, with men and women carrying messages, maintaining contacts between civilian organizers in exile and the rebel armies, raising money, sewing uniforms, and smuggling arms, ammunition, and volunteers to the battlefields. Two female leaders of the insurgency were prisoners in the Casa de Recogidas in Old Havana. These were Evangelina Cossio de Cisneros and Magdalena Peñarredonda y Doley.

Peñarredonda, born in 1846 of a Spanish father and French mother, was a movement veteran from Pinar del Río, the tobacco-growing province to the west of Havana. In the first war she had been a member of the local revolutionary club. When she and her sisters shaved their heads as a sign of solidarity with the *mambís*, they were locked in the house by their father until it grew back. In the 1880s Peñarredonda lived for a period in the United States, contributing pseudonymously to *La Habana Elegante*. She was the "Elga Adman" (an anagram for "Magdalena") whom we quoted about the "sad and monotonous life of the girls of Cuba" in chapter 3, and once back in Cuba she was the alleged recipient of Casal's second letter about Maceo as well. In the 1890s, she was elected an officer of the underground Cuban Revolutionary Party and traveled back and forth to New York to serve as liaison with Martí and other leaders. When Maceo's armies reached Pinar del Río in 1895, she became legendary as a combatant, underground organizer, and spy; exposed and arrested in 1896, she was brought to the capital and imprisoned in the Casa de Recogidas, where she became a leader in demanding more humane conditions for political and common prisoners alike. She remained in prison until the Spanish defeat in 1898.

Evangelina Cossio, by contrast, was a teenage activist who made a dramatic escape to the North, like Cirilo Villaverde fifty years before. The beautiful daughter of a veteran revolutionary organizer from Cienfuegos, she had accompanied her father and sister to internal exile on the Isle of Pines off Havana Province's southern coast. There she organized an attempt by exiles and islanders to take the Spanish governor captive, seize arms and a boat, and join the rebel army. Cossio's plan included luring the governor, who had been pursuing her since she arrived, with a message that said, "I'll wait for you tonight in my room, but come alone." The governor was kidnapped but then rescued, and Evangelina ended up in the Casa de Recogidas, threatened with deportation to the penal colony in Morocco.

The American newspaper magnate William Randolph Hearst then entered the picture, making Cossio a cause celebre in his flagship paper, the *New York World*. A year after her arrest, she was

U.S.S. Maine entering Havana Bay, 1898.

Photography Collection, Miriam and Ira D. Wallach Division of Art, Prints and Photographs, The New York Public Library, Astor, Lenox and Tilden Foundations.

rescued, hidden overnight somewhere in the city and smuggled on board a New York-bound steamship the next day. According to the *World*, the escape involved a ladder, a file to cut through a barred window, and leaps from rooftop to rooftop, all under the firm hand of the paper's special correspondent sent to Havana for the purpose. Other accounts suggest guards were bribed, or even that the Spanish found her a liability and wanted to get rid of her. In any case, Hearst used her escape to build his paper's circulation and public interest in the Cuban rebellion. In October, 1897, Hearst presented Cossio to the American public at an extravaganza in Madison Square Garden. This was the same year in which the newspaper owner reportedly cabled his artist who had complained that there was no fighting to depict in Havana, "You furnish the pictures, and I'll furnish the war."[1]

Three months later, mob attacks by pro-Spanish vigilantes on several Havana newspapers led U.S. Consul Fitzhugh Lee to point to a breakdown of order in the capital and call for the sending of a U.S. battleship to protect American interests there. After negotiations between Washington and Madrid, the *U.S.S. Maine* steamed between the Morro and the Punta on January 25, 1898, her "courtesy visit" balanced by the dispatch of the Spanish cruiser *Vizcaya* to New York. On Tuesday, February 15, at 9:40 p.m., a great explosion shook Havana. Residents rushed out of homes, theaters and cafes, speculating that a bomb had gone off, that a powder magazine had exploded, that the city's natural gas tank had blown up. Then the news began to circulate, by word of mouth, that what had exploded was the *Maine*, taking 191 victims to the bottom of the bay. The sinking of the *Maine* brought the United States into the war.

7

Many Happy Returns?
U.S. Occupation and Its Aftermath

On January 1, 1899, the red and yellow flags that had proclaimed Spanish dominion over Havana for nearly four centuries came down. They came down from the Morro, from the Palace of the Captains General and soon—on orders of Havana's mayor—from private flagpoles and balconies too. Within a month, a commentator in Havana's *El Figaro* weekly reported, the only Spanish flags were the ones flying from the masts of ships repatriating the defeated colonial army, or those hidden under the counters of Spanish merchants' shops.

By contrast, Cuban flags came out of hiding, and the capital filled with them at last. The *bandera cubana* flew from private homes, patriotic and social clubs, union halls, and the new associations of Army of Liberation veterans. Its red triangle with a single white star appeared on brooches and belt buckles, its five blue and white stripes sewn or embroidered onto the clothes of shoe shine boys and socialites alike. An exile recently returned from the North marveled at how, walking through the city, he heard the piano notes of the revolutionary movement's songs wafting out of houses on every street. *Cuba Libre* was triumphant everywhere in Havana—except where it mattered most. The red, white, and blue colors that fluttered in the sea breeze atop the flagpoles of the Morro, the Palace, and other seats of power were the stars and stripes of the United States. Another returning exile, the poet Bonifacio Byrne who had been supporting himself by reading aloud in the cigar factories of Tampa, described his response in a verse that every Cuban child would learn in school:

> In sober mourning I returned
> From a distant shore and clime,
> For a glimpse of my flag I yearned
> But found another in place of mine.

The Cuban war of independence did not end like the American one, with an imperial army surrendering to a rabble in arms while a band played *The World Turned Upside Down*. The war that President William McKinley asked for, in the wake of the *Maine*, was one for "the enforced pacification of Cuba," using "hostile constraint upon both the parties to the contest" to insure on the island "the security of its citizens as well as our own." U.S. ships blockaded Havana, trading cannon fire with Spanish shore batteries, but most of the fighting took place around Santiago de Cuba in the East. There the Cuban army cooperated with the American one, warily, in return for a promise from Congress that "the people of the Island of Cuba are, of right ought to be, free and independent" and that after pacification was accomplished, the United States would withdraw. In the end, beneath a towering ceiba tree at the foot of San Juan Hill, Spanish generals surrendered to American ones, but the Cuban commanders were not invited. U.S. forces in the meantime attacked the other remaining outposts of Spain's empire in America and the Pacific. Then diplomats sat down in Paris to hammer out a treaty which ceded control of Cuba, Puerto Rico, the Philippines, and Guam to the United States as "new dependencies" of various sorts.

In the Philippines, independence forces began a guerrilla struggle against the new occupiers. In Cuba, the tug-of-war over the country's future was political. The spotlight in this struggle centered on Havana, where the occupying government installed itself. A U.S. military governor replaced the captain-general. More troops came to carry out the occupation than had been sent to fight the war. American soldiers pitched their tents in the Plaza de Armas and barracked in the Castillo de La Real Fuerza, while they set

U.S. troops camped in the Plaza de Armas, 1898. The Palace of the Captains-General is in the background (now the Museum of the History of the City) and the Palacio del Segundo Cabo (now the Book Institute) is to its right. El Templete (commemorating the city's founding and housing the murals described in chapter 3) is not shown, but would be to the viewer's right. *Photo*: Library of Congress.

about building a permanent base, Camp Columbia, on a tract of farmland in the commanding heights of Marianao. The new Cuba would be bound to the United States by "ties of singular intimacy," McKinley declared ominously in his State of the Union address at the end of 1899, but "how and how far is for the future to determine in the ripeness of events." No one on the island could say how long the military presence would last, or under what terms it would end.

In the Parque Central, across the Prado from the Hotel Inglaterra, the statue of Queen Isabel II of Spain was unceremoniously toppled from its pedestal one day in March of 1899. The weekly *El Figaro* ran a graphic of the empty pedestal topped by a question mark and polled its mostly upscale readers for suggestions. José Martí beat out a statue of liberty by four votes. Liberation army commander

Máximo Gómez, Christopher Columbus, and an allegorical figure linking the United States, Cuba, and Spain also figured among the top nine. Antonio Maceo came in tenth. Though a committee formed to raise funds for a Martí monument, the pedestal remained empty for three years.

In the "ripeness of events," the occupation lasted three-and-a-half years and left behind an anomalous republic—an independent nation in whose affairs the United States had a constitutional right to intervene. This was, however, only one of many outcomes. The occupation changed the city's patriotism and its plumbing, its language and its layout, its commerce and its entertainment. As in the case of the British occupation, the people of Havana defended their aspirations and their culture, and they simultaneously welcomed, synthesized, or forcibly adapted to what was new.

A political split between the Cubans who had fought for independence and the army of occupation underlay everything else. From the Cuban side, the independence war had been fought for a loosely defined ideal of *Cuba Libre*, a republic, as José Martí said, "for all and for the good of all." If the first war had been initiated by planters, this one had been declared and fought by an army and an underground created, as Máximo Gómez said, from bottom up rather than the top down. The officer corps included planters (many of them ruined), but also professionals, small farmers, and workers. The officers were about 40 percent nonwhite, and the troops about 60 percent so. The series of wars that they had fought over a period of three decades represented a revolution in Cuban popular notions of race and class. "To the American at home," reported occupation veteran Lt. Col. R. F. Bullard in an article called "How Cubans Differ From Us," "the negro as a social, political or even industrial equal is an affront, an offence, nothing less; to the Cuban, he is not."

The expectations of most of those who had struggled for independence included not only racial equality but land reform, an end to great extremes of wealth and poverty, and recompense for those who had sacrificed through exile, military service, displacement, or Spanish confiscation. These expectations also included a foreign and commercial policy friendly to the United States but not monopolized by it. That vision explains why, in his war message, McKinley declared it "not wise or prudent for this government to recognize at the present time the independence of the so-called Cuban Republic . . . To commit this country now to the recognition of any particular government in Cuba might subject us to embarrassing conditions of international obligation toward the organization so recognized." In what it saw as a "Spanish-American War," the United States was not fighting to turn Cuba over to the political heirs of Martí.

In fact, an American notion that the Pearl of the Antilles ought to decorate the necklace of manifest density can be traced back at least three quarters of a century before 1898. As a rich producer, proven market, and military outpost commanding Caribbean sea lanes, Cuba had long tempted U.S. political leaders. "I candidly confess," wrote ex-President Thomas Jefferson in 1823, "that I have ever looked on Cuba as the most interesting addition which could be made to our system of States." That same year, President-to-be John Quincy Adams echoed him in a tone of greater inevitability: "There are laws of political as well as of physical gravitation, and if an apple, severed by a tempest from its native tree, cannot choose but fall to the ground, Cuba, forcibly disjoined from its own unnatural connection with Spain, and incapable of self-support, can gravitate only towards the North American Union, which, by the same law of nature, cannot cast her off." Throughout the nineteenth century, U.S. administrations attempted to purchase Cuba from Spain, as they had bought the Louisiana Territory from the French Empire and then bought Alaska from the Russians. For Cuba they offered considerably higher sums, of 100 million dollars and up. As Adams' quote suggests, U.S. policymakers held not only that the United States was destined to control Cuba and her fruits, but that Cubans—because of their Latin and particularly their African blood—could not govern themselves.

Though Spain refused to sell, U.S.-Cuban commercial ties steadily increased, as we have described. Americans' ownership of Cuban plantations and mills also grew steadily, by purchase or by foreclosure of defaulted loans. When the Ten Years' War broke out, the Grant administration tried again to get Spain to sell the island. "All the civilized nations," Secretary of State Hamilton Fish told the Cabinet in 1869, "would be glad that we should interpose and regulate control of the island."

In the face of the new rebellion that broke out in 1895, both Grover Cleveland's Democratic administration and William McKinley's Republican one followed these same goals. At the time the *Maine* steamed into the harbor, negotiations were still under way for an armistice that would give the island semiautonomous status under Spain, or for a sale of the island to the United States.

These negotiations continued after the battleship exploded and
sank. When Spain would not sell, and the rebels would not agree to
give up the idea of *Cuba Libre*, McKinley decided on war. There
was, however, considerable sympathy for Cuban independence
among the American public, and significant resistance in Congress
to the creation of an American empire out of the vestiges of Spain's.

So Congress amended the war resolution. The Teller Amendment,
named after Sen. Henry Teller of Colorado, stated: "The United
States hereby disclaims any disposition or intention to exercise
sovereignty, jurisdiction, or control over said island except for
pacification thereof, and asserts its determination, when that is
accomplished, to leave the government and control of the island to
its people." These words may still be read on the monument to the
soldiers and sailors of the *Maine* on Havana's seafront Malecón,
though the American eagle that used to crown the monument was
removed in 1961. Cuban representatives in the United States also
demanded and received private reassurances that the U.S. withdrawal would be accompanied by the provision of funds to pay
pensions to the demobilized army of independence.

In Cuba, as in the United States, support for the island's
independence was not complete. Much of the country's commerce
remained in the hands of Spaniards, who did not depart for home
with the evacuated troops. Conservative property owners and professionals, both Spanish-born and Cuban-born, had petitioned for
U.S. intervention in the last years of the war, because they too had
much to fear from Martí's ideal. The McKinley and Roosevelt
administrations interpreted "pacification" in the Teller Amendment
to mean the creation of a government led by the propertied classes.
Such a government might request continued U.S. rule, or would in
any case be a hedge against radical change. The Army of Liberation
was pensioned off as previously agreed, with the troops insisting
on turning in their guns to local Cuban authorities, not the occupation forces—though some units refused to accept their pensions or
turn in their guns until the occupation actually came to an end.

As municipal elections and then elections for a Constitutional
Convention unfolded, military governor Gen. Leonard Wood kept
assuring Washington that "the Cuban people realize they are not
ready for self government" and (paradoxically) that they would
elect "the better class of men." He lent "the better class" his support
by limiting suffrage to the best of his ability through property and
literacy requirements, though he was forced to make an exception

for veterans of the rebel army.[1] He openly campaigned for his chosen candidates as well. But, as he finally reported home, most of them lost. Many of "the worst agitators and political radicals" were elected instead.

Wood cast particular private scorn on long-time journalist, organizer, and civil-rights advocate Juan Gualberto Gómez, former head of the Cuban Revolutionary Party in Havana, whose comment about baseball enthusiast Emilio Sabourín was quoted earlier. Gómez was one of the two nonwhites among the thirty-one elected members of the Constitutional Convention. On his official stationery bearing the letterhead "Military Governor, Island of Cuba, Havana," Wood wrote ominously to Theodore Roosevelt about certain "degenerates of the Convention, led by a little negro of the name Juan Gualberto Gómez; a man with an unsavory reputation, both morally and politically," whose purpose was "to bring forward his own race and see what he can accomplish politically to his own advantage." Before sending the letter off to Washington, Wood changed "degenerates" to "agitators." He did not change his complaint that "it is next to impossible to make them [the Cubans] believe that we have only their own interests at heart."

In November of 1900, after nearly two years of occupation, the delegates began to meet in an imposing former dance hall turned theater, often called the "coliseum of a hundred doors." Just off the Prado opposite the old Spanish military parade ground, it was originally named Teatro Irioja after its Basque developer, then Eden Concert under subsequent owners, and was finally rebaptized as Teatro Martí. The convention's members wrote a constitution very much like that of the United States, although a centralist rather than a federal one. Uniquely for Latin America, it included separation of church and state. Despite the urging of women's revolutionary clubs, the convention rejected a proposal for female suffrage, leaving this question to later legislation. But they adopted universal male suffrage, a clear change in direction from Wood's restrictive and racist rules that had governed their own election.

At the urging of Gómez and others, they twice rejected a proposed limitation on Cuban sovereignty which had been attached to a military appropriations bill in the U.S. Congress by Senator Orville H. Platt of Maine. The Platt Amendment—passed by Congress in a different mood than that of 1898—required Cuba's constitution to ratify all decisions made by the occupation government as binding obligations, to give the United States an exclusive right to build naval bases on Cuban soil, and to include a perpetual right of U.S. intervention in Cuba as needed. Article III of this Amendment stated: "That the government of Cuba consents that the United States may exercise the right to intervene for the preservation of Cuban independence, the maintenance of a government adequate for the protection of life, property, and individual liberty, and for discharging the obligations with respect to Cuba imposed by the treaty of Paris on the United States."

On March 2, 1901, 15,000 residents paraded through the streets of Havana to announce their refusal to accept the Platt Amendment. The protesters thronged through the Prado, Neptuno, Galiano, and Reina, cheered on by many more from sidewalks, balconies, and arcades. They paused outside the Teatro Martí to approve the stand taken by the delegates. After that they crowded their way through the narrow streets of Old Havana to the palace of the Captains General to present a petition to Governor Wood, condemning both the Amendment and the imperial pressure for it to be passed. The Convention soon sought modifications of the Amendment, but were told there could be none. If the Platt Amendment was not adopted verbatim, the occupation would not end. Finally they accepted it, first by a margin of one vote, and then (with four abstentions) by a margin of five.

On May 20, 1902, with the Platt Amendment embedded in the new constitution, Cuban flags at last replaced Americans ones and the occupation troops withdrew. Camp Columbia was turned over to a new Cuban army, while the incipient naval base at Guantánamo Bay remained in American hands, soon to be leased "for the time required." In preparation for the official transfer-of-powers ceremony in Havana, a zinc-and-tin statue of liberty was hurriedly shipped from the United States to fill the vacant pedestal in the Parque Central. The statue held an American shield in one arm and a torch in the other, but a hurricane that tore through Havana eighteen months later destroyed this particular vestige of the occupation. Curiously, the hurricane chose for its visit the date of October 10, anniversary of the original Cuban declaration of independence in 1868.

Finally, in 1905, a Cuban sculptor's marble effigy of José Martí crowned the pedestal, but the first intervention under the terms of the Platt Amendment came during a disputed Cuban election only a year after that. Until the year 1959, the American political and economic presence in Havana would be a weighty and often decisive one, a source of both shame and revolt. And yet, in this cosmopolitan and always curious city, the presence of things American, and the ability to master them, would also be at times a source of pride and hope.

To begin with, at the same moment as they resisted annexation and military occupation, many residents welcomed what they initially saw as American aid in a step toward independence. Spain had been expelled "by the Cuban machete and the American cannon," as one petitioner to the military government wrote. Handbills of popular ballads from the last days of the war include one that said:

> Long live the Americans
> Who come on our part
> We ought to embrace them
> From deep in our hearts.
>
> Long live our flag
> Joined with that other
> Which lives in the heart
> Of each Cuban brother.

In the early months of the occupation it was common to see Havanans wearing both Cuban and U.S. flag pins on their lapels, or other displays of the two flags intertwined.

More profoundly, particularly for those who had lived in the North as political exiles, economic refugees, students, or some combination, the United States had long served as their anti-Spain and anti-colony. Their preference for baseball over bullfights is one example, but much of what they saw during their U.S. exile gave substance to their vision of an alternative Cuban future: independent, democratic, modern, and technically advanced. Furthermore, the occupation government, even when the honeymoon was over, was the government of reconstruction after years of war and neglect, and as such it was the only game in town. If many of the Cubans appointed to staff it had been lukewarm in their support of independence, many others had devoted their lives to that ideal. The Americanization of the capital was not only the work of Americans or annexationists by any means.

English words, one sign of this affinity, had made their way into the city's lexicon far in advance of American troops. Tobacco workers returning from Key West had christened one of the new barrios

of Centro Habana, to the north of Pueblo Nuevo, Cayo Hueso—
literally "bone key," but phonetically and socially an adaptation of
the American name. Cubanizations of baseball terms such as *es-
traik*, *ao*, and *jonrón* were legion. In fact, the Americanism *sport* had
largely replaced *deporte* to describe activities of many kinds. If the
horse track in Marianao was called the *hipódromo*—in Spanish—its
daily program featured a race called the *handicap*. So when *new
women* got opportunities to work for the occupation authority as
nurses, *typewriters*, and occasionally *supervisors*, this only expanded
an existing linguistic trend. Similarly, their male counterparts who
found ways to take advantage of new opportunities in small business became *self-made men*. With the importation of new gadgets for
domestic chores and entertainment—from gas ranges to light bulbs
and Fuller brushes, from electric fans to gramophones to
Champion bikes—the word *comfort*, usually Cubanized as *confort*,
entered daily speech and written language too.

Many stores rapidly adopted English to appeal to the influx of
Americans, not just soldiers and sailors but those who followed, an
army of merchants, investors, tourists, craftsmen, carpetbaggers,
and engineers. The long-established Crusellas family cosmetic and
soap emporium on Calle Obispo in Old Havana hoisted a new sign
upon its doorway declaring itself "Crusellas Store." The cachet of
English also enlivened communications among Cubans themselves. In *El Reconcentrado*, a nationalist Havana paper created originally as the voice of those expelled from countryside by the
Spaniards, Crusellas announced to their Cuban customers the
opening of a new lounge in which *ladies* could buy *ice cream de todos
los sabores* (of all flavors), dished out by *bellas señoritas*. English
brand names for new imported goods became part of the household language just as indigenous words for foods and implements
had done centuries before: whether arriving home to grate *yuca* on
a *guayo* or to cook up some *Quaker* (rhymed with cracker), Havana
cooks first had to unlock the *yale* (pronounced "yah-lay," the lock).
For breakfast, the traditional *café con leche* and buttered toast now
had to compete with something called *jamanég*. The word *blueplate*
entered the city's gastronomic vocabulary, and even a cheap restaurant offered, bilingually, "*A comer barato. 50 cents square meal*," while
a family advertisement in a provincial paper, celebrating the birthday of a lieutenant colonel in the liberation army, concluded,
"*I wish you many happy returns of the day*."

Drinking as well as eating habits mirrored this state of affairs. No one knows who invented the *Cuba libre* by mixing Cuban rum with Coca-Cola, but the daiquiri came to Havana from Santiago de Cuba, where it celebrated the coordinated landing of Cuban and U.S. troops on the beach of that name. It was soon available in long-established bars like the Florida (later Floridita) and new ones like the New England Bar, Manhattan Bar, and Gay Broadway.

The occupation also transformed Havana physically, and many of these changes met long-delayed aspirations. Contrary to the hopes of *Cuba Libre*, U.S. authorities refused to redistribute Spanish or idle private property, rural or urban, or to even to distribute desperately needed supplies or loans which could help Cuban farms and businesses revive. But they did initiate public works on a large scale and turn Spanish military sites over to Cuban institutions for civil use. Thus, many now-classic landmarks of Havana were built or begun at this time.

A plan to convert the city's rough coral oceanfront to a seawall and promenade had been kicking around colonial offices since it was first proposed in mid-century by Francisco de Albear, designer of the aqueduct. Now it became reality. Construction of the city's trademark Malecón began in 1901 and the first stretch opened a year later. Symbolically, the city began to turn its back on the Spanish fortresses, the crowded and polluted harbor, and face the Florida Straits instead.

The new Malecón included one important American modification not foreseen by Albear: a wide boulevard, inside the promenade, for cars. The occupation years brought the automobile to Havana. The very first cars were French models, but soon came a Locomobile and its brethren from Detroit. When Henry Ford's mass production techniques brought him dominance of the auto market in the United States, Model-T's flooded Havana as well. In the rest of the Spanish-speaking world, a car that's not working has *descompuesta* (literary, "decomposed"); in Cuba, borrowing from English, it has "broken down."

Paved streets and plazas suited the bicycle, as well. The environs of the Castillo de la Punta, starting place of the Malecón, had become a garbage dump in the last years of Spanish rule. This was replaced with a paved plaza, lit by electric lights and frequented by residents of every social class. The plaza became so popular with bicyclists—especially children and young women—that

Mayor Perfecto Lacoste banned horse and mule-drawn carriages from nearby streets from four to eleven p.m. to avoid accidents. The French architect Charles Brun, resident in the United States, was contracted to design a bandstand for the center of this area. After its construction, the municipal band played nightly concerts, as Spanish military bands had done in the Plaza de Armas—only now, even under occupation, the concerts began with the Bayamo Hymn, call to arms of the liberation movement and national anthem-to-be. The first film to be made in Cuba, a sixty-second short subject shot in 1899 called *"El parque de Palatino,"* depicts the comings and going of citizens in another brand-new park.

The modern campus of the University of Havana also got its start at this time. The university (under Spanish rule officially the Royal and Pontifical University of St. Geronimo) dropped its old name and moved from its downtown quarters in a former convent to a hilltop site above Cayo Hueso, toward Vedado, an acropolis commanding a view of the city and the sea. There it occupied the buildings of the Spanish Pirotécnica, a munitions factory and depot. "This building devoted for so many years to making elements of destruction and death," said the university's report for 1900–01, "has by the strange winds of destiny . . . become dedicated to shaping our progress, culture, and civilization."

When the Castillo de la Real Fuerza was vacated by U.S. troops moving to their new base at Camp Columbia, the city's oldest fortress became the first site of the National Archives. Among other renovations at this facility were new and modern bathrooms, with flush toilets and sinks "made in the U.S.A.," to replace the ancient Spanish pit latrines. Indeed, plumbing was a fixation of the occupation authorities. Flush toilets were almost nonexistent in colonial Havana, despite Domingo del Monte's innovation in the Palacio de Aldama, and a U.S. army survey showed that only 10 percent of houses had indoor plumbing of any sort. The occupation army's chief sanitation officer personally led a team of 120 doctors to visit the houses of the capital and impart instructions on the use of drains, garbage collection, and other measures. Sinks and toilets were imported from the United States on a grand scale and sold at modest prices. Inspectors issued orders to install and connect these new devices, often when there were as yet no supply pipes or drains for blocks around—but the pipes and sewers were usually on their way.

Sanitation measures, however, failed to stop the outbreaks of yellow fever that had been decimating the occupation troops since their first landings in Oriente and continued to do so in the capital after the fighting had stopped. Since yellow fever was thought to spread through contamination, particularly from the vomit and feces of victims, medical officers intent on plumbing and scrubbing were at a loss. The Havana doctor and epidemiologist Carlos J. Finlay, then sixty-five years old, had been proposing since the early 1880s that the fever was spread, instead, by mosquito bites. Finlay, educated in Europe, Philadelphia, and Havana, went to Washington when the United States entered the war. He used his American medical contacts to enlist in the medical corps. He continued to make his yellow fever hypothesis known, and when all other measures failed, Major Walter Reed, head of the army's Yellow Fever Commission, agreed to carry out a controlled experiment to test it.

The experiments were carried out at Camp Columbia and adjoining rented farmland, where one group of uninfected volunteers lived in a filthy cottage well-supplied with used blankets and bedclothes brought daily from a yellow fever ward, and the other lived in a scrubbed and disinfected cottage supplied with the Aedes aegypti mosquitoes that Finlay had bred, which had been allowed to bite infected men. Finlay's theory proved correct, and the ensuing mosquito eradication campaign effectively solved the yellow fever problem in Havana. Finlay went on to become Chief Sanitation Officer of the new Cuban government, though most of the international credit for "discovering" the cause and cure for yellow fever went to Reed.

Joining the goal of improved transport to that of sanitation, the electric streetcar replaced the old animal-traction lines. "Accustomed to seeing in Havana and Puerto Príncipe the urban streetcars drawn by horses," the exiled journalist and former Almendares baseball star Wenceslaus Gálvez had written of his arrival in Tampa during the war, "one is surprised to see here the same cars operating under their own power." Two days after the Treaty of Paris was signed, a syndicate of U.S., Canadian, and French investors bought up the horse-drawn street railway system from its mostly Spanish stockholders. The following month they incorporated the Havana Electric Railway Company, in New Jersey, and their representatives set off for Havana to begin building an electric plant. In March 1901, the first line opened, from Old Havana to Vedado. Many more followed, reaching as far as Marianao by 1903. Ridership sextupled within the first year, from 10,000 to 60,000 passengers a day. Horse droppings vanished from the rails.

All in all, says historian Louis Pérez, "Havana teemed with activity. Gangs of survey teams, construction crews, builders, and wreckers seemed to be everywhere, and at times they were." Thus the occupation and its aftermath brought to Havana the modernization many had sought, but at a steep price—very little of it was under Cuban control. The streetcars went "under their own power" but subject to U.S. ownership, as was the case with all new and expanded utilities. The majority of contractors were Americans, and so were a great many of their employees. Even the plumbers were American imports, and members of a union—Plumbers' Local 200—to which no Cubans belonged.

Some entrepreneurs came from the United States as civilians to pursue the attractions of this new frontier, while others parleyed their positions in the occupation into sizeable economic stakes. Sgt. Frank Steinhart, chief clerk of the army of occupation, rose by 1907 to the presidency of the Havana Electric Railway, Light, and Power Co., a monopoly which merged several utilities under one roof. He built himself a roof too, a mansion on the Prado to rival that of any departed Spanish count. Capt. Tillinghast L. Huston arrived with the *yanqui* Corps of Engineers and became even more of a Yankee as a result. He formed contracting companies which secured commissions to dredge the city's harbor, install its new sewer lines, and build its new wharves. With his profits from these ventures and others in Cuba's interior, he joined New York brewer Jake Ruppert in buying the New York Yankees in 1915—and Babe Ruth from the Red Sox five years after that. When Ruth in turn visited Havana, at the height of his fame, he stayed in the Hotel Plaza, which by then rivaled the Inglaterra on the other side of the Parque Central. The Plaza was founded by another officer of the occupation, Capt. Walter Fletcher Smith.

A New York construction firm, Purdy & Henderson, remodeled the old colonial building housing the Plaza, and they also built the Lonja de Comercio for importers' and exporters' offices on the Plaza de San Francisco, and the headquarters buildings of the National Bank of Cuba and the Cuban Telephone Company (both U.S. owned firms). By the 1920s, enough of these neoclassical concrete-and-steel structures dotted the colonial landscape of the old city that a travel writer remarked that the office buildings "seem to have been bodily transported from New York."

Havana's upper and middle classes thus found themselves as junior partners to foreign capital rather than the captains of a new nation, as many had hoped. The old landowning class lost of much of its land, a casualty of war, reconcentration, Spanish expropriation, and debt. Without reparations, supplies, or affordable credit to get farmers back on their feet, many (whether larger or small) had to sell out for what they could get. *Trabajar pa'l inglés*, "to work for the English," was an old expression, origin unknown, that meant to work without much hope of compensation, to invest one's effort in vain. Going to work for the Americans now offered the best chance of holding on to some of one's previous status or becoming a *new woman* or a *self-made man*. Among the plantation owners, the luckier and richer could barter their land for shares in new foreign sugar companies. Professionals with university degrees in fields such as law or engineering or architecture could go to work as employees, consultants, or representatives of American firms. Examples of the distance between the ideal of *Cuba Libre* and the role of junior partner are provided by two veterans of the independence war, Perfecto Lacoste and José Lacret.

Lacoste, from a planter family and educated in the United States, had been head of the revolutionary underground in Havana after the arrest of Juan Gualberto Gómez. It was he who smuggled the Spanish military plans stolen from the Captains General's Palace to Antonio Maceo, who also stayed for a few days at the Lacoste family mill. Under the occupation, he became mayor of Havana (and issued the regulation banning horse-drawn carriages from the area popular with bicyclists) and then Secretary of Agriculture. "Nothing has been done toward the improval of our agricultural situation . . . ," he complained in 1901. He called on the military government to provide credit and other aid to farmers, but his plea fell on deaf ears. A year later, he was appealing instead for more U.S. capital and entrepreneurs. "In no foreign country will American capital and enterprise be welcomed so warmly as in Cuba," Lacoste wrote in *Opportunities in the Colonies and Cuba*, published in New York with an introduction by Leonard Wood. "The policy of the new government is to strongly encourage the influx of American capital and brains."

General José Lacret Morlot was born on a coffee plantation in Oriente, the son of Haitian-French planters. Educated in France and having lived in both Florida and New York, Lacret was a veteran of both independence wars. He had been wounded, jailed, escaped, and fought again. Elected to the Constitutional Convention, he sided with Gómez in arguing successfully for universal male suffrage and in refusing to accept the Platt Amendment even on the final vote. "This for me is a day of mourning," he said when the Amendment was approved, "because we have enslaved ourselves forever in grievously heavy chains." But he advertised in the English-language *Havana Post* that he had established a real estate consulting office in the capital. "Having a practical knowledge of the entire island," he offered corporations and individuals his services for "buying and selling farms and plantations, mining properties, native timber, and all kinds of leases."

As Lacret's ad indicates, rural Cuba became a land sale bonanza, another new frontier. Large companies like United Fruit and American Sugar bought ruined plantations and virgin territory. Thousands of settlers arrived too, including hundreds of North American families who set up farming communities across the main island and on the Isle of Pines, bringing their customs and Protestant religions along.

All told, by 1905 foreigners of various nations owned an estimated 60 percent of Cuba's countryside, resident Spaniards another 15 percent, and Cubans only the remaining quarter of the land. In the all-important sugar industry, U.S. individuals and corporations controlled 21 percent of production in 1905. As they expanded production on newly acquired lands, their share rose to 53 percent in 1916 and 63 percent in 1926. In the major industry carried out inside the capital itself, cigar production, American companies bought up many of the Spanish brands. The Havana Commercial Company, a holding company organized by New York bankers, acquired more than a dozen factories accounting for 161 different brands. The once-grand Palacio de Aldama, which had been converted to a cigar factory by a Spanish firm in the 1880s, now passed into the hands of "The Habana Cigar and Tobacco Factories Limited," an English concern.

For white collar jobs, potential Anglo employers were most comfortable with those most like themselves: those who spoke English and had lived in the States. The Lonja de Comercio advertised for "a young gentleman of presentable appearance and absolutely fluent in verbal translation." The telephone company sought out bilingual operators for its rapidly expanding grid. "The more progressive merchants have hired clerks who can speak English," the *New York Times* reported.

Most of all, American firms brought with them traditional American ideas about race. Occupation authorities and their successors in the private sector did not find blacks or mulattos to be of "presentable appearance," and racial integration did not fit American concepts of what was modern or progressive, since this was the heyday of scientific thinking about a hierarchy of racial types. So blacks or mulattos were not welcome as conductors on the electric streetcars. The new department stores would not hire them as saleswomen or cashiers. Even black generals, usually from peasant or working class or slave background, did not find the private sector opportunities their white counterparts did. Quintín Banderas, who had been a sailor and construction worker before rising in the ranks of the *mambís*, ended up distributing advertising circulars for the Cuban-owned Crusellas soap company.

Another general, whose name has been lost, became the centerpiece of a landmark legal case when he was refused service by the American-owned Café Washington in 1899. Though discrimination in private hiring met little effective resistance, attempts to impose U.S.-style Jim Crow in the capital's cafés and restaurants proved too much of an affront to *Cuba Libre* to succeed. In the last years of the colony, once slavery was abolished, a combination of Spanish law and steady pressure from the Societies of Color had more or less established the principle of equal accommodation in Havana at least. So the Café Washington incident became a cause celebre.

City authorities shut down the Café Washington until its owners promised to "obey the laws of the country and serve the public without distinctions or differences." But when the restaurant was allowed to reopen, they placed an increasingly common sign on the mirror behind the counter: "We cater to white people only." This time the owners were tried and sentenced to two months in jail, plus fines. They appealed, claiming the sign did not specifically say they wouldn't serve people of color, only that they would not "cater" to them. A long legal battle ensued, hinging on the exact translation and intent of the English phrase. In the end, the sentence was confirmed. From then on, those who wanted formal segregation turned increasingly to private clubs, though luxury hotels catering to Americans often turned colored clients away with the claim that they had no rooms.

Anything that suggested African culture was even more controversial than the question of access to a restaurant or cafe. To the Cubans in charge of city government, African-derived drums and dances smacked of backwardness and barbarism. They seemed the antithesis of the modern way of life that would prove Cubans worthy of self-government, both to the Americans and to them-selves. The Día de Reyes celebration and similar processions had been banned under Spanish authority when slavery ended on the ground that they conflicted with the Catholic religion and no longer served any purpose. When the Spanish flag was finally low-ered, a group of Abakuá took their rituals openly into the street to celebrate. Local police promptly took them into custody and they were sentenced to a year in prison for illegal association.

A later petition by a Lucumí mutual aid society to allow their *toque de tambor* was denied by North American authorities. Finally a city council ordinance of 1900 attempted to settle the matter. It forbade "the use of African drums in any sort of assembly, whether on the public streets or inside," as well as the processions "known as *comparsas, tangos, cabildos,* and *claves,* or any other that make use of symbols, allegories, and objects which conflict with the seriousness and culture of this country's inhabitants."

However, attempts by Cuban authorities to control popular behavior in Havana were no more successful than those of Spanish or U.S. colonial authorities. In the first year of the occupation, the city government had thumbed its nose at the military government by choosing February 24 (date of the declaration of independence of 1895) for rebel army commander Máximo Gómez's triumphal en-trance into the city, where he was feted in barrios rich and poor, white and black. That night there was a society ball in the Teatro Tacón and an outdoor concert across the street in the park. But a *mambí* veteran's memoir describes another celebration, still less official, by a great crowd dancing through the nearby streets to the beat of conga drums, whirling, singing satirical songs, and making barbed and earthy jokes. Such *comparsas* (street dances, usually by organized groups with practiced choreography) also made their way into the annual celebration of Carnival, which had previously been a decorous white-dominated parade of carriages and floats that occurred parallel to the Día de Reyes. Comparsas of blacks joined the carnivals of 1899 and 1900, dressed in mock uniforms of the Voluntarios and other repres-sive Spanish forces, celebrating their departure. After independence, groups from mostly black barrios like Jesús María demanded the offi-cial right to participate in Carnival. Their repertoire included songs that linked patriotism and race, celebrating the role of black and mulatto soldiers and officers in the independence wars.

Though much farther removed from its African roots, the danzón also came in for—and triumphed over—criticism as being too tropical, sensuous, and uncivilized. "The danzón, very pretty, very typical of our climate and what you will, but not an appropriate dance for a modern soiree. The intervention will bring us a government that's free and stable, and will give us new dances and habits too." So said an article on the society pages of the elite magazine *Cuba and America*. An edict from the civilizers in the city government was more explicit: danzón was permissible, but only if the couple held each other at arm's length, and restricted the motions of their hips. As a result, the danzón took on a new nationalist air and was enthusiastically performed by Havanans of all colors at celebrations of the semiofficial patriotic holidays, weddings and baptisms, in dance halls, and more. A satirical cartoon in *El Figaro* shows a caricatured black couple in which the woman insists she's obeying the new regulation, but the man pulls her close and says, to her satisfaction, that he supposes he'll have to opt for the old regime. In spite of his prejudices, the cartoonist shares his characters' bafflement at what's so modern and democratic about such puritanical rules.

A ditty from a satirical musical by Ignacio Sarachaga, author of *The Matter of Bread* described in chapter 6, contrasted the danzón with the two-step, the North American dance enjoying its moment of chic. The two-step was "fit for a wake," the song declared, and then it played on a rhyme setting *danzón* against *anexión*. As best it can be rendered into English, the number went:

> As long as danzón lives
> And we feel its concatenation
> No one can make us bear
> The weight of annexation

A similar contest ensued over attempts by both the occupation authorities and "modernizing" Cubans with revolutionary credentials to ban the cockfight and the lottery. Both institutions went underground, to reemerge into legality in the 1910s.

An example of how carefully the elite tried to walk a line between multiracial nationalism and "modern" scientific racism was the official commission that examined Antonio Maceo's skull. In a patriotic ceremony, the remains of Maceo and his white aide de camp Francisco Gómez (son of Máximo) were exhumed from their battlefield grave to be placed in a memorial near Santiago de Las Vegas, to the south of the capital. A team of three white scientists, using the "latest anthropometric techniques," examined the skeleton of the "Bronze Titan." The team's most prominent member, Luis Montané, had studied with the leading anthropologists of Paris and headed the University of Havana's Department of Anthropology and Anthropometric Exercises, founded in 1900 by the military government. The meticulously detailed report pointed out first of all that Maceo was a mulatto, and that "the crossing of white and black can create an improved group when the influence of the former predominates, but an inferior group when the two influences are equal, and especially when the black predominates." Fortunately, they concluded that while the size and shape of the general's bones matched his African heritage, his skull capacity "could be mistaken for that of the best-endowed European." Thus the mulatto hero could be celebrated for his prowess as a thinker and strategist as well as his strength and skill at arms, without challenging the notions of progress that emanated from Europe and the United States.

All in all, the period of the occupation established precedents whose echoes continued throughout the twentieth century and continue today. These trends extended beyond Havana, but in the capital—always the point of contact between the "interior" and the "foreign"—they reached their height. North American dominance was felt as a wound on Cuban pride and patriotism, but the standard of living in North American cities became the yardstick against which to measure Havana's life. Cuban culture, language, and idiosyncrasies were treasured as bulwarks of national identity, but American ones were seen as the keys to comfort and success.

8

Symbol of an Era: Alberto Yarini y Ponce de León

At dusk on November 21, 1910, a well-dressed man stepped out of his home on Calle Paula, a block from the birthplace of José Martí. His silver Nautilus wristwatch gave the time as 7:38 p.m. He was twenty-eight years old, and he lived in this house with three women in their late teens or early twenties named Elena Morales, Celia Marín, and Berthe Fontaine or Santerre, a valet called José Claro, and probably other servants whose names have not survived. It was a wintry night in Havana terms, so he was wearing a dark cashmere suit over a starched white dress shirt with six gold buttons, and underwear monogrammed top and bottom with the initials A.Y. In his pocket jingled an assortment of the more valuable coins then in circulation: a Spanish centén, a French louis, and an American double eagle. Around his waist he buckled something he didn't commonly wear, a gunbelt and a holster carrying a nickel-plated revolver with a mother-of-pearl grip, recently purchased in the United States.

A short walk brought him to the Calle San Isidro, the street that gave its name to this barrio of Old Havana near the docks. Untouched by the fever of construction in the nearby financial and commercial district, San Isidro was made up mostly of small single-story houses and quite a few hastily constructed single rooms. It was home to many stevedores, construction workers, laundresses, and other sorts of laborers, its corners replete with bars and cheap cafés. Alberto Yarini stepped into the single room at number 59 to speak to Rosa Martínez, who worked there. Then he crossed to number 60 and spoke with Elena Morales and Celia Marín. When he returned to the street, he saw Berthe Fontaine's countryman and former employer Louis Lotot waiting for him, pistol in hand. Before Yarini could draw his own gun, he was cut down by a hail of bullets from Lotot and his confederates stationed across the street on the sidewalk and on the cracked red clay shingled roofs.

Once the shooting stopped and police arrived, they found Lotot dead, shot by Yarini's friend and de facto bodyguard Pepe Bastarrechea, who carried a revolver that matched the one Yarini had not had time to fire. Yarini lay on the sidewalk, in the arms of Elena Morales, bleeding from multiple wounds. He was taken to the nearest first aid station and then to the Emergency Hospital, where he died at 10:30 p.m. The next morning, a large crowd followed his casket to the home of his parents, brother, and sister on fashionable Calle Galiano a few blocks from the seacoast and the nascent Malecón. There his body was waked for another day and night, with a constant stream of visitors, before the funeral procession set off on the 24th.

Alerted by notices in the newspapers, masses of Havanans had already filled Galiano and the nearby cross streets. A marching band set a somber cadence for the crowd, which swelled to an estimated 10,000 mourners of all races, classes, and sexes, as four pairs of horses pulled the richly adorned funeral coach for four miles to the Cemetery of Colón. There, senator and ex-general Miguel Coyula—by most accounts one of the few officeholders of the era to live off his salary rather than graft—spoke in the name of the Conservative Party and for himself. Memorial wreaths came from relatives, political figures, the San Isidro branches of both Conservative and Liberal parties, sugar workers, well-to-do café companions, and more. Nearby, a group of ñañigos sent the dead man off with the farewell drumming and chants almost never performed for outsiders.

Alberto Yarini y Ponce de León was the third child of a family with an old Cuban pedigree, owners of Matanzas sugar plantations in times past, now well-to-do professionals in the capital. His father

was a dentist and professor of dental surgery, his uncle a medical
surgeon, his older brother a dentist and professor in the father's
footsteps, and his sister an amateur pianist of note. Until his
untimely death, Alberto Yarini was one of the city's leading *bon
vivants*—a man about town, a habitué of its dance halls, theaters,
and opera, at home in both the bars of San Isidro and the posh cafés
of the Acera del Louvre. Educated in the United States, he spoke
fluent English and perfect Spanish and dressed almost always in a
three-piece suit of pure white or somber black, topped by an elegant panama hat. He was the reputed lover of various married
women of standing, the holder of a no-show job in the city government, and the president of the Conservative Party committee for
San Isidro and the neighboring barrios of San Francisco and Belen.
He was what in U.S. political terms of the period would have been
called a ward boss, in charge of handing out favors and delivering
votes. He was said to have ambitions to run for a seat in the House
of Representatives, though his political friends urged him to give
up his main business first. But what made all of the rest possible
was just that entrepreneurial activity. Yarini was the King of San
Isidro, and San Isidro was the city's red-light district. Alberto Yarini
y Ponce de León was famous and infamous throughout the island—
then and now—as its capital's most stylish and successful pimp.

After his education in an American private school, where he had
been sent to avoid the hardships of the capital in the years of the independence war, Yarini had returned to Cuba during or shortly
after the U.S. occupation and taken advantage of one of the less
savory artifacts the occupiers left behind. In their pursuit of
hygiene, the authorities had decided to relocate the city's scattered
sex industry, as much as possible, to one specified "tolerance zone."
San Isidro was recommended because of its working-class character and proximity to the docks. The rows of single rooms were
rented mostly to pimps, who made their nightly rounds collecting
the lion's share of the take from the women working within them.
Pornographic nickelodeon parlors, live sex shows, gambling
houses, and low-end music bars migrated to the new red-light district, which attracted married and single Cuban men, new single
immigrants, and sailors, tourists, and businessmen from abroad,
especially the United States. San Isidro became famous as far away
as Paris and New York. Along with the sex establishments came the
requisite shooting galleries, pool halls, drug sellers, and ubiquitous
stands of Chinese vendors selling the Cuban foods they had

mastered—fried pork skins, sweet rolls, corn tamales, and plantain chips.

Diverse sectors profited from the industry. Landlords charged the pimps double rents, police and inspectors demanded bribes to let operations run smoothly, and unemployed men became the pimps' assistants and enforcers. Yarini roamed his kingdom, greeting everyone by name, handing out coins to children, slapping his admirers on the back. He was quiet and charming as a rule, violent when he needed to assert his authority over either women or men. In myth, journalism, and literary works, he and his legend have come to symbolize Havana in the earliest years of the Republic, and in certain ways this makes sense. Havana was the capital and showcase of a sovereign state, but the state could not be said to direct the affairs of the country, because the real levers of power lay elsewhere. Cubans denied center stage in the nation's economic development succeeded in the corners that were available. The nexus of political office, graft, and patronage was one of these, and prostitution was another. Yarini lived at the intersection of the two.

Bribery was an old tradition left over from the colony. Graft in the awarding of contracts and embezzlement in public office had taken root during the public works boom of the occupation, since the American occupiers came well-versed in the operations of late-nineteenth century big-city political machines like that of Boss Tweed in New York and the handing out of government jobs to cronies through the "spoils system." The Cuban administrations that followed developed all of this into a fine art. Because the state apparatus offered one of the relatively few lucrative avenues of advancement for ambitious Cubans of all colors and classes, government became increasingly corrupt. The Conservative and Liberal parties drew to some extent on different constituencies; the Liberals, for instance, had a greater following among people of color and nominated Juan Gualberto Gómez for a congressional seat. The parties occasionally came into armed conflict over contested elections, twice settled by U.S. intervention. But the basis for their competition was not so much opposing programs as competing groups of loyalists who expected to be rewarded with public posts, from the cabinet member on high to the lowest lottery ticket seller on the street.

Local bosses like Yarini, called *sargentos políticos*, handed out jobs, got a troublesome relative off without a jail sentence, or found a sick one a scarce hospital bed. In return they borrowed their constituents' voting cards, to make sure the votes were cast the right way. Liberal Party leader José Miguel Gómez, president during Yarini's ascendancy and death, earned the nickname "The Shark" due to the bite he put on those seeking government contracts or jobs. But there was wisdom in the popular saying that derived from his nickname: "When the shark swims, he splashes." His successor, Conservative Mario G. Menocal, was called "The Overseer" because he had managed a sugar mill for the Cuban-American Sugar Company of New York. On his watch, Yarini's lieutenant and avenger Pepe Bastarrechea (already kept out of jail in a deal brokered by Conservative politicians) was able to leave San Isidro behind and rise through the bureaucracy as, successively, lottery official, customs official, and port inspector. Gómez and Menocal, like their successors Alfredo Zayas and Gerardo Machado, were all white ex-officers of the Liberation Army who walked a political tightrope between enriching themselves, rewarding Cuban supporters, and cooperating with American businesses, an act often richly compensated by a seat on the company board. *El que tiene un amigo tiene un central* ("a friend is as good as a sugar mill") goes a popular Cuban saying that dates from this period. It doesn't refer to the spiritual value of friends.

Available corners of the economy also included the flesh trade, whether as entrepreneurs like Yarini or as sex workers like his prostitutes who—their position fundamentally unchanged since the days of the colony—sold their bodies to feed their families and themselves. Despite the opportunities that opened up for a minority of women in salesrooms, offices, and schools, census data from 1907 show that only about 75,000 women out of a total Cuban population over 1.5 million had legitimate paid work. Maids and washerwomen (self-employed or working in Chinese laundries) accounted for 65 percent of these female workers, followed by cigar or cigarette makers, teachers, and seamstresses. Prostitution filled the cavernous gap.

"I had long wavy hair, a good body, cinnamon skin, I was friendly, and I had a family dying of hunger," testifies Lulú, a San Isidro veteran of Yarini's time, in an oral history recorded much later by cultural historian and poet Dulcila Cañizares.

I didn't have any brothers and my father had died of tuberculosis. All my sisters were younger and my mother was a poor woman without the strength to iron or wash. So I had to find a pimp to buy

me clothes and shoes and put me to work in a room. He abused me
and took almost everything I gained, but I didn't have any other way
to get into the business. It wasn't easy, to go to bed and satisfy men
of every size and shape—white, black, mulatto, Chinese, Spaniards,
or wherever they were from, clean ones and dirty ones, ones who
stank to high heaven and not just of bad tobacco and worse rum. But
I had to put up with anything, or Pepe would beat me and then I had
to throw my arms around his neck and tell him I loved him so much.
When I could, I dropped him for another, and so on, because
everyone exploited us.

Neither political corruption nor economic necessity, however, fully
explains the mystique that surrounded Alberto Yarini. He is the
only sex trade entrepreneur and the only *sargento político* in the
city's history to be so widely remembered, so honored at his death,
so surrounded by a halo of romantic myth. It's impossible to know
how much of what was said about him is exaggeration increased
over the years, but the fictions as much as the facts testify to the collective aspirations that gave rise to his myth. He was a Prince
Valiant to a population—especially its male segment, which continued to be a majority—insulted by all sorts unfulfilled promises,
and a Prince Charming even to women who knew there were no
such Princes to be found. He had a populist touch without pretense
of superior morality, in contrast to those of his background who
displayed the opposite tendencies on both counts.

Lulú, quoted above about her exploitative pimps and the squalor
in which they kept her, went on to say, "Yes, I saw Yarini a lot. He was
handsome and clean, going by the door of my room, where I stood
waiting for customers. I would have given anything to be his
woman, not just to sleep with him but so I'd be respected a little,
because everyone respected him." Another, Consuelo la Charmé,
recalled how she escaped from her first situation in San Isidro and
found protection among women working for Yarini, whom her ex-
pimp would not dare to attack. "He wasn't the type that shakes your
hand and greets you because of who you are. He couldn't stand
people who first wanted to know were you this or were you that.
He'd just as soon talk with a black as a Chinaman, and a Chinaman as
anyone else. What [his murderers] did to him is worse than I can say."

"Yarini had more women than he knew what to do with, and he
dressed like a millionaire," recalled Alberto Cárdenas, who
watched the funeral procession at age fourteen and went to work as

a gravedigger in the cemetery the following year. "Kids my age, my friends, we envied him a lot, would have given anything to be like him. When they killed him, it was like they had killed the hero of our lives."

"He was famous for the harem he had in his house," said Federico Morales Valcárcel, the young Conservative Party organizer who gave Yarini the matched set of revolvers that didn't manage to save him from death at twenty-eight. "People in the street, in high society, in small towns and in Havana all said to themselves, 'What is it about him?' We took advantage of that popularity to gain adherents in the neighborhoods by the docks." Yarini avoided making speeches, according to Morales, but was always the perfect representative to resolve internal disputes over who should get what job. "Nobody knew how he did it, but he did. He settled these problems with *cosas de cubaneo*, with his Cuban touch."

On the afternoon before his death, according to stories collected by journalist Leonardo Padura, Yarini stopped by a broken-down house on the Calle Compostela to consult about a troublesome dream with María la Gambá, an old black woman who had been a prostitute in her youth, one of fifteen such women whom he maintained in their old age in return for their supplying him with desserts. María la Gambá gave him *arroz con leche*, Cuban rice pudding, and consulted with her spirits. She warned him that there was something like a runaway train bearing down on him.

There is one other key element in Yarini's myth, besides his alleged generosity, his way with women, and his accessibility to people of all stations. Certain key moments of his legend stood for Cuban nationalism in opposition to both North American arrogance and European immigration which threatened Cuban jobs and pride.

The confrontation with competitors that led to his death was, of course, one of these. Lotot and his confederates were French and Italians from France, Canada, and the United States, all in the business of luring young French, Belgian, and other women to Havana and putting them to work on the street. *Las francesas* (Frenchwomen, as all the European prostitutes were called) were exotic and popular with the customers of San Isidro, and were said to have introduced oral sex into the trade. Yarini had just taken the most beautiful new arrival, La Petite Berthe, away from Lotot, and he had allegedly vowed to take the rest. In the days of tension leading up to the shooting, the ballad singers in the bars of

San Isidro invented a new verse that went:

> Frenchmen so lacking in honor
> You'd better leave Cuba tonight
> If you don't want Yarini
> To snuff out your miserable life.

When Yarini was ambushed instead, nationalist pride took over. New verses predicted revenge. The news of his shooting spread "as if he'd been the President of the Republic," dockworker Esteban Cárdenas later recalled. "A whole crowd of us met up in the Alameda de Paula—the pimps, and more of us who had nothing to do with that business, but we came because we were young and those were our friends and we were furious that Yarini had been shot in an ambush, not a man-to-man fight." The crowd, a typically Cuban mix of white, black, and Chinese extraction, decided to wait in ambush on the slopes below the Castillo del Principe and kill the foreign pimps as they descended the hill from Lotot's funeral. Cárdenas's family responsibilities gave him second thoughts, and he didn't go. Others did, and murdered two of Lotot's confederates. They were convicted and sent to jail, but pardoned when the Menocal administration later came in.

The other famous confrontation—and the one in which Yarini came out on top—had taken place two years earlier in El Cosmopolita, one of the series of fancy restaurants and cafés on the Prado that made up the Acera del Louvre. Yarini, sitting and drinking and conversing with some of his political friends, overheard a man at a nearby table complaining in English to his companion about the disgraceful customs of a country where blacks mixed with whites at such a respectable place. The black man in question was General Jesús Rabí, who had, among other accomplishments, commanded Cuban troops in an attack on Spanish forces to cover the American landing at Daiquirí. Rabí was now a government inspector of mines and forests, a member of a Masonic lodge and, it was said, also an Abakuá. Altogether, a man admired by Yarini, so the pimp and politician excused himself from his companions, walked over to the Americans, and demanded in perfect English that they show a hero some respect. When they didn't, he knocked the first man to the ground. The offender turned out to be one J. Cornell Tarler, temporary charge d'affaires of the American embassy, and the other his commercial attaché. Yarini was arrested and charged with assault, but acquitted with the help of his friends. The affair made the papers in Cuba and eventually those in Tampa as well. In Havana it passed from mouth to mouth in many versions (some had the Americans as naval officers) but the moral was always the same: Alberto Yarini had stood up both for Cuba and for a raceless ideal.[1]

The story was rendered all the more compelling by increasing evidence that the raceless ideal was far removed from fact. In 1908, a group of black and mulatto veterans disappointed by both the Liberal and Conservative parties had formed the autonomous Independent Party of Color to fight for an end to discrimination in general and, especially, equal treatment of the colored population in access to elected office and government jobs. Two years later, the established parties outlawed the new one on the legal basis that it was racially exclusive. This prohibition led in 1912 to a brief rebellion in Oriente province and then a bloody pogrom by army troops and white vigilantes that took the lives of thousands of mulattos and blacks.

Lurid tales of that rebellion in the capital's press added fuel to a fire already lit by fantastic reports of Afro-Cuban societies kidnapping and killing white children for their blood, supposedly required for "witchcraft" of *santería* or the rites of the Abakuá. "Until the triumph of the revolution," the conservative Havana daily *El Día* fulminated in 1918 after a decade of such scares, "blacks raised white children without eating or abusing them . . . Cuba has been liberated from Spanish tutelage, legal equality and the rights of all citizens have been established, and those people have begun to drink the blood of white girls, and even to martyrize their own daughters . . . Where is progress, then, where is civilization?" The next year the same paper came out in support of lynching "in certain cases," and indeed, in a rare case in the history of Havana, a mob in Regla the next day killed José Williams, a black Jamaican immigrant accused of attempting to rape a white girl. This was the same type of mass-media hysteria that fueled lynching and the growth of the Ku Klux Klan in the United Sates in these same years.

Colored social organizations fought back against lynching and the association of blacks with savages. The Club Atenas, which represented the elite of colored Havana, issued a statement signed by representatives of black organizations of all strata, in which they argued that "the history of this class [slaves, former slaves, and their descendants] is coterminous with that of this nation," and that "we have the right to be considered civilized men, not barbarians." Such social clubs continued to denounce discrimination, but after the suppression of the Independent Party of Color, blacks and mulattos did not organize politically along racial lines again.

As a result of the scandal around the shooting of Yarini, the government closed the San Isidro tolerance zone. The sex trade moved, barely underground, to other areas, especially the Centro Habana barrio of Colón. Periods of official crackdowns and unofficial bribery and toleration would continue throughout the next half century, including a crackdown in Colón in the 1940s that drove some of the business back to San Isidro again. The role of pimps declined, according to some studies, to be replaced by madams, independent prostitutes, and protection rackets mediated by organized crime figures from both Cuba and the United States. There were no more gentlemen pimps, in any case, and indeed opportunities for men of Alberto Yarini's class broadened as a new sugar boom fueled by World War I brought explosive growth to Havana's economy again. Before we leave San Isidro behind to look at the capital's rapid growth far beyond the precincts of the old city, however, it's worth noting that in Havana as in its sister port of New Orleans, the red-light district was linked not only to national politics but to national culture. It was a place where musicians and musical genres got their start.

When residents of war-devastated eastern Cuba migrated to Havana in the first decade of independence, they brought with them both sounds the city knew and sounds it did not. San Isidro was often the first place that the musicians among them found work. Balladeer Manuel Corona—later famous as composer of "Mercedes," "Longina," and others of the most beautiful love songs in the repertoire of Cuban *trova*—frequented the barrio in his transition from cigar-roller to musician, during what he later called a "bohemian period that was not the most honorable of my career." He played at the bar on the corner of Egido and Merced, enjoying the generosity of the profiteers and protectors of the sex trade. Gonzalo Roig, who became the most famous composer of boleros and light operas (including a musical version of *Cecilia Valdés*) and was a founder of the Havana Symphony, played piano to accompany the sex shows at the Zaza theater, notorious among male tourists and sailors far and wide. The legendary troubadour and composer Sindo Garay was already playing better venues, but he wrote a bolero dedicated to Yarini, who was often in his audience at the trendsetting Café Vista Alegre on Belascoaín:

> Don't worry, for life smiles upon you
> In your pursuit of orgies and pleasures,
> Because the poor ladies of the night
> At your feet lay all their treasures.
>
> But in the midst of your enjoyment
> Which you may think comes for free,
> More sincere than women's kisses
> Are these words of advice from me.

In the shadows of San Isidro grew up, also, the first Havana gay community about which any written record has survived. There were homosexual men among the prostitutes at Alberto Yarini's funeral, and openly gay and effeminate Cuban men had found employment and a measure of acceptance as domestic servants doing the washing and cooking in houses of prostitution since the days of *La Cebolla*. Yarini's valet José Claro was one of them. Rogelio Martínez, a taxi driver who frequently drove for Yarini, remembered San Isidro as "like a carnival in the morning, when the *efeminados* in their pastel-colored undershirts swept out the street-front rooms. Passersby would yell things, and they'd answer with scandalous comments, with giggles and gestures and not getting upset. But there was one they called the Queen of Italy, as queer as they come, who could fight like a lion. Later he became a *santero* and moved to the barrio Jesús María, I happen to know."

With the clampdown on San Isidro and the spread of cinema in the 1910s, meanwhile, many of the musicians moved on to earn their bread and butter accompanying silent films in the movie palaces that sprang up all over, like the two-screen rooftop Polyteama opposite the Parque Central and others in outlying barrios throughout the city. Here the musicians provided yet another odd counterpoint in the city's eclectic mix: off-the-cuff improvisations in every Cuban musical genre to try and match the antics of Buster Keaton, Theda Bara, Clara Bow, Rudolf Valentino, or Tom Mix. At the Cine Oriente on Belascoaín, the pianist and violinist played inside a cage to protect themselves from audiences who didn't like what they made up. "You developed dexterity, speed," recalled trumpet player Lázaro Herrera of his stint at the Cine

Valentino in El Cerro. "If you screwed up and didn't pay attention, you'd get run over by a train."

While the output of U.S. studios dominated Cuban movie houses, newsreel photographer Enrique Díaz Quesada, the author of *El Parque de Palatino* mentioned in the previous chapter, succeeded in 1913 in producing the first Cuban feature film. Entitled *Manuel García or The King of the Cuban Countryside*, it played to sold out crowds on both screens of the Polyteama. The film itself has been lost, but its scenes of large crowds in action were said to have matched those of Eisenstein in Russia and D. W. Griffith in the United States. In content, *Manuel García* presented a myth parallel to that of Alberto Yarini. García, a legendary bandit of the late nineteenth century, appeared as a tropical Robin Hood who collaborated with the revolutionary army while he robbed from the rich and gave to the poor. In the meantime, the capital entered a new era in which the gap between rich and poor became more evident day by day.

9

Catch a Ford on the Malecón: Republican Havana's Growth and Decay

In the two decades after 1910, Cuban sugar boomed as it had a hundred years before. This time, the industry got new life from a commercial treaty which gave Cuban sugar and tobacco favorable tariff terms in the North, while increasing the island's dependency by giving U.S. food and manufactured goods equally or more favored terms in Cuba. In addition, U.S. investment fueled the opening of bigger mills and plantations further from the capital, in newly felled forests of Oriente and in the plains of Camagüey. Though many mill owners (American, Cuban, or a combination) maintained headquarters in Boston or New York as well as Havana, Havana remained a magnet for sugar wealth and the funnel for everything Cuba imported in return. The sugar industry got its most emphatic boost from the effects of World War I, which drove wholesale prices to unprecedented levels, from 1.9 cents a pound in 1914 to 9.2 cents in 1918 and an incredible 22.5 cents in 1920 at the peak of the boom. The capital lived a moment of delirium called "the Dance of the Millions" that gave rise to a new upper class and accelerated the rush to plan, pave, design, and build. By the end of the first three decades of the Republic, Havana's skyline had begun to take on its modern form.

The Malecón, completed most of the way to the Almendares in 1930, curved for nearly four miles from the docks of Old Havana past the Castillo de la Punta and along the Florida Straits to El Vedado's tree-lined boulevard, Calle G. In hurricane season or when winter cold fronts swept down from the North, waves battered the wall and splashed over onto the pedestrian promenade and the street, making the ramparts feel like the prow of a ship cruising through wind and mist and spray. When, more often, the sea was calm and the weather clear, the Malecón became a picture-postcard place: sun drenched in the daytime with immense blues beyond, romantic and Technicolor at sunset, the sea "a prodigy of light and color," as Federico García Lorca wrote during his 1930 stay "The city's window," the Malecón has been called—a window to which residents could escape on hot summer nights, sitting on its concrete sill. Havana's eye on the sea, its smile welcoming guests, the gently curved arm of the sea holding the city in its embrace.

As it marched westward in the 1910s and 1920s, this seaside drive covered what had once been the tiny bay of San Lázaro at the beginning of Cayo Hueso, which was filled in to make a park dominated by Antonio Maceo on his horse. Balconied hotels and clubs and apartment houses lined its landward side, some built around grand entrance halls and open staircases in imitation of the old aristocratic palaces, others with elevator lobbies or narrower, tile-lined flights of marble stairs. Further out, near the quarry where Martí and hundreds more had toiled on the chain gangs, car dealerships clustered around the intersection with Calle Infanta, inviting potential purchasers to take their wares for a spin along the sea. "Foot it and go!" advertised the Ford Motor Company, a slogan which gave rise to the Cubanism *fotingo*, still in use today for the venerable cars of bygone eras that dot Havana's curbs and streets. The first taxies in the city were Fords too. For many years, the way to say "let's take a taxi" was "let's catch a Ford."

On the bluff beyond Infanta, where the Spanish shore battery of Santa Clara had traded cannon shots with American battleships and English men-o'-war, the old guns decorated the new gardens of the elegant, fourteen-story, twin-towered Hotel Nacional, designed in Mediterranean revival style by the New York firm of McKim, Mead, and Wright and completed in 1930. From there on, the Malecón embraced El Vedado, no longer an isolated suburb of rustic estates, but a riot of turrets, towers, gables, and widow's walks, steep Swiss roofs and flat Italian ones, covered with old-fashioned red clay tiles or modern poured concrete. El Vedado filled, month by month and year by year, with private mansions surrounded by fences and gardens, as well as more modest middle-class homes and apartment buildings. It also featured a scattering of tourist hotels: first the Trotcha (which expanded into two new buildings in the first decade of the Republic), then the ten-story Presidente near the seaside end of Calle G, the ten-story Palace at its upper end, and the Nacional. Further out, where the seawall and drive did not yet reach, the Vedado Tennis Club built an imposing gingerbread clubhouse for its members who were drawn from the Cuban and resident North American elite. It looked (and, turned to new uses, still does look) as if the Great Gatsby might emerge from its doors. We will turn to some of the flamboyant residents of this district, both old rich and new, soon.

The construction of Vedado provided a playground for Cuban-born and immigrant architects and craftsmen who offered their clients all manner of architectural display. To Havana's already eclectic architecture, they added a competition of styles from all over Europe and North America, a riot of conspicuous consumption that some architectural historians have dubbed "cockadoodle-meow." In contrast to the narrow, crowded, haphazard streets of Old Havana, with barely a sidewalk separating walls from vehicles, Vedado was and is a garden city, with broad, tree-lined streets and wide sidewalks in front of yards large and small. In contrast to the old city's picturesque street names that meant avocado, light, sun, bitterness, souls, or friendship, the new district followed a mapmaker's grid with odd-numbered streets running parallel to the seacoast, and even numbers and letters running uphill from the Malecón.

At the far end of Vedado, the year 1921 saw construction of a drawbridge across the Almendares that led to the still more exclusive suburb of Miramar. This bridge, where the Fifth Avenue tunnel is today, was popularly known as El Puente de Pote after the nickname of its developer, the immigrant José López Rodríguez ("Pote" is a bean stew from his native region of Spain). Through hard work, advantageous marriage, and political friendships, the legendary Pote rose from bookstore clerk to lottery ticket printer, store owner, and publisher, and then to land speculator, sugar mill magnate, and banker in the feverish years of the boom. He bought a controlling interest in the National Bank of Cuba from J.P. Morgan, then hanged himself from the shower of his Vedado home when plummeting prices broke his bank and stripped several of his millions away. His Matanzas sugar mill, like many others in the early 1920s, soon passed into North American hands.

At the mouth of the Almendares, below the bridge, glowed a copper-roofed gazebo on the seaside estate of one of Pote's real estate rivals, engineer Carlos Miguel de Céspedes, minister of public works in the administration of President Gerardo Machado (1924–33). Céspedes was in charge of many of the great works of those years, from another modernization of the Prado to the construction of the new Capitol building on its upper reaches, from the paving of the Central Highway (the first to link all the country's provinces) to the extension of the Malecón. These projects spread copious sums of public and private money among landowners, contractors, politicians, and real estate entrepreneurs, not least of them the Secretary himself. Carlos Miguel had interests in Miramar, but the bulk of the land on that side of the river belonged to the González de Mendoza clan—sugar magnates, plantation owners, bankers, politicians, corporate lawyers representing U.S. firms, and the owners of the Almendares Scorpions baseball team. For his own headquarters, Céspedes decided to buy up and demolish an old honeymoon hotel on the Vedado side of the river, on the bank where fishermen built shacks to house their nets and catches, and where the first settlers had erected their short-lived village of thatched huts. On this spit of land the Minister built his pleasure dome of house and gardens. To make amends for shunning the neighborhood which he had helped to develop, he did not call it Xanadu—or Monticello or Versailles—but simply Villa Miramar.

Behind the Villa, and linked to it by an arched bridge spanning a narrow channel, was an island in the river to which the new owner gave the name Kotsima, Japanese for the Isle of Love. There he assembled a private zoo of monkeys, flamingos, iguanas, macaws, two lions, and a bear. In a greenhouse alongside the menagerie his gardeners raised great quantities of exotic flowers. Kotsima also boasted orchids, porcelains, decorated screens, and a great lion of the bronze variety, acquired in London as the model for those cast to adorn the Prado's park-like median strip. Out in the river were anchored the Secretary's yacht *Miramar*, for fishing and cruising, and his speedboat *Cuba*, famous for the number of regattas it had won.

A bit inland from the coast, just behind the Tennis Club, was the home of a family typical of Vedado in a very different way, the Loynaz. The poet María de las Mercedes Loynaz, known all her life as Dulce María, became the only Cuban and the only woman from all the Americas to win the Premio Cervantes, the Nobel Prize of Spanish-language literature. Born in December of 1902, the year of Cuban independence, she sprang from two prominent families of the criollo aristocracy. Her father, General Enrique Loynaz del Castillo, fought the independence war's battles and also, in celebration of the landings of Martí and Maceo, wrote the lyrics to one of its main anthems, *El himno del invasor*. Her mother and namesake, Maria de las Mercedes Muñoz Sañudo, descended from a landowning fortune on her maternal grandparents' side. The Loynaz fortune was swallowed up by in the war; the Sañudo money, though nearly lost to Spanish authorities in an earlier period, survived. When the young General Loynaz passed a photographer's studio shortly after his arrival in Havana at the end of the war, he saw María de las Mercedes' portrait in a display of Havana's most beautiful young women. He took the photo and sought her out.

Soon after Dulce's birth, the family followed high society westward from a house on the Prado to one in Centro Habana, a few blocks from Galiano at the corner of San Rafael and Amistad. General Loynaz went out on the front balcony to make speeches to cheering crowds of the Liberal Party, but the children's life was protected, as if to keep them purer than their times. They did not go to school, even to a private one, but received their education from tutors and their visits from carefully selected offspring of their father's comrades-in-arms. They grew up indoors, surrounded by antique vases, marble statues, paintings and portraits, and a library full of books. At her mother's urging, however, Dulce María enrolled in the university to study law, and on her own account she fought for and won the right to go unaccompanied to her classes and exams.

When Dulce María was in her teens, her mother divorced the General because of his frequent and public extramarital affairs. Hers was one of the earliest divorces to be granted in Cuba under a new republican law. This first Cuban divorce law had to overcome objections from both the Catholic hierarchy and William Jennings Bryan, then U.S. Secretary of State, but Cuban legislators (regardless of their varying attitudes toward other rights for women) saw it as an emblem of the separation of church and state. Soon after the divorce, grandparents and mother and children moved to Vedado, where Dulce María would live for the next seventy years.

They bought one of the oldest houses in the district, a *casa-finca* on Calle Línea with tiled walls, tinted glass, exuberant plantings, an inner courtyard, and extensive grounds. The property bordered that of the Tennis Club, extending nearly to the coral seacoast where the Malecón had not yet arrived. "The house stood in middle of a leafy garden," the poet recalled later, "filled with begonias, jasmines, rare lilac-hued dahlias, honeysuckles, vines of blue and white and red, and sturdy trees; everywhere were comfortable benches, antique marbles, fountains with brightly colored fish, and white peacocks—never before seen in Cuba—who admired their reflections in the pools." In the late 1920s and 1930s Dulce María and her three siblings—all poets too—turned this retreat into a salon. Every Thursday at five o'clock amateur and professional literati of many schools and tendencies assembled to read from the classics and their own latest works. The salon took place in a large blue-grey room with the signs of the zodiac and silver stars painted onto the ceiling in addition to a quote in Italian, borrowed from a princess, "Maybe yes, maybe no." After a disastrous hurricane blew down the nearest telephone pole in 1926, the house on Línea had no phone because none of the brothers or sisters bothered to get the pole replaced. For a time they even banished electricity from their salon, lighting the room with antique candelabras instead. Regardless—or attracted by the eccentricity—literary guests found their way.

When Federico García Lorca visited Havana in 1930, he came not just on Thursdays but every afternoon to play the piano, drink whiskey and soda, and read from his work. His favorite Loynaz was not Dulce María but Flor, the youngest sister, whose rebellion mirrored her namesake, the black revolutionary general Flor Crombet. In Flor's new Fiat, Lorca accompanied her and her brother Carlos Manuel to El Templete, not the memorial temple but a sailors' bar, a customary haunt. Once when the General protested Flor's unconventional habits (she shaved her head, for instance, to proclaim that men should find her attractive for more than her looks and locks) she replied, "In these times it's very hard to live a moral life. It's even harder to seem to."

What her sister did in public, Dulce María Loynaz did in her verse. "In my poems I'm free," she wrote. "I walk on water . . . on waves unfolded out of waves and other waves." In these poems, which range from unrhymed classical Spanish meters to long declamatory prose poems and short ones like Zen parables, she often put herself in the position of women seen or seeing from unique angles. Her verse speaks for Lazarus's betrothed when, returning from the dead, Lazarus demands that she pick up right where things left off—and for the pregnant Virgin Mary when another expectant villager wants to gossip about ambitions for their sons. It speaks for a woman visiting Egypt (as Loynaz did, traveling with her mother and sister, without male accompaniment) who falls in love with the famous mummified king.

At the same time, much of Loynaz's poetry invokes Cuba, and especially her corner of it, El Vedado, because her central metaphors evoke the river and the sea. One of her poems to the Almendares describes how it "drinks in the sun at daybreak, wraps its lover's arm around the city's waist, rises in the spiral winds of the Cuban hurricane." Her long, untitled prose poem beginning "Island of mine" likens Cuba's shape to "the antenna of America," "a fine gold iguana," and "the drawn bow an invisible archer wields from the shadows, aimed at our heart."

Thanks to her father's position, Loynaz's poems began appearing in Cuban newspapers and magazines when she was still a teenager, but she did not pursue publication herself. "Out of a mixture of shyness and pride," she explained later, "a bad combination for the game of life." When her first collection was published in 1938 at the urging of literary friends, it attracted little notice, failing even to be included in the new books display at El Encanto, the department store catering to Havana's elite. Stung by this indifference, she vowed to never publish again and to destroy the rest of her writing before her death.

That this did not happen was due in part to the recognition she soon gained from prominent female contemporaries in South America, such as the Uruguayan poet Juana de Ibarbarou who, after Loynaz's visit there, called her "the greatest woman in America." But it was due mostly to one of those juxtapositions of opposites always close at hand in Havana: in her mid-forties, the reclusive and aristocratic daughter of the *mambí* general married a social butterfly, a Spaniard, and a model of the self-made man.

Pablo Álvarez de Cañas had arrived in the port of Havana as a struggling immigrant from the Canary Islands at the tail end of 1918. To the impoverished regions of Spain, Cuba was still a powerful magnet, and Havana exercised the strongest pull. Between

1902 and 1934, more than a million immigrants entered the country, three quarters of them from Spain. As in the colonial period, they were predominantly young men seeking to *"hacer América"* (to "do America," to make it there and make it theirs). That America was now independent did not dampen their ardor, so a new wave of Spaniards became Cuban, adding to the capital's genetic mix and somewhat bleaching its skin. This white immigration was promoted by the Chamber of Commerce (still largely dominated by Spanish-born merchants) and by the government of the Republic through generous laws. The Centro Gallego, the social club and mutual aid association of the most successful Galician immigrants, hired Purdy & Henderson to build a sumptuous headquarters that literally surrounded the Teatro Tacón. Inside this new structure, they rebaptized the historic auditorium the "Teatro Nacional."

Álvarez de Cañas was part of this flood. He worked over the years as bookkeeper and salesman for a variety of firms in the capital and their branches or mills in the interior, while cultivating his social ties to high society at every turn. He first proposed marriage to Dulce María Loynaz when she was only eighteen, two years after his arrival, but the romance and proposal were quashed by her mother out of hand. In the early 1930s, Álvarez de Cañas landed a job with Senator Alfredo Hornedo, yet another of the dubiously self-made millionaire politicians and real estate moguls of the era. Thanks to his friendship with President Machado, Hornedo had won a monopoly status for his Mercado Único meat and produce market (today Mercado Cuatro Caminos), and to defend this and other interests he had founded the newspaper *El País* and was looking for ways to boost its circulation. Álvarez de Cañas, depending on ghost writers to pen the actual copy, used his connections and his incisive eye to make *El País*'s society page the most popular in Havana, read by both the elite and those who wished they were.

Showered with gifts and services by merchants, professionals, and plutocrats anxious to see their names in the paper, the columnist soon had his own fortune—and he finally married Dulce María Loynaz (now divorced from her first husband, a Loynaz cousin) in 1946. The fabled recluse of Línea and 14th became the hostess of a new colonnaded mansion at the corner of 19th and E, her husband's companion at social events, and the author of "The Event of the Week," one of the columns that appeared under his name. Her new husband was a born promoter who—among many coups—was to become chief publicist for Cuban tobacco in the United States

Dulce María Loynaz in her house at 19th & E in El Vedado. Portrait on wall is Loynaz in the 1920s or 1930s. Photo was taken many years later, when the poet lived in seclusion well after the revolution of 1959 (see chapter 13).

Photo: Biblioteca Nacional José Martí.

though he neither spoke English nor smoked. His picture soon filled U.S. dailies as he presented boxes of cigars and cigarettes to Gary Cooper, Clark Gable, Bette Davis, and other stars. In similar fashion, he began to get Loynaz's work published in Spain. A triumphant reading at the Ateneo of Madrid in 1947 established her international reputation, though she remained better known in Havana for her role as hostess and her eccentricity than for her literary work. For her part, she continued to credit the former family salon: "[Nothing] would have been possible without the house," she wrote later. "The repose of its gardens that shut out the loud hum of the city, the atmosphere where every object showed off not its price but the art and skill of the hand that had created it. [That was] my attempt to revive in Cuba a salon in the style of 19th century—a refuge for the aristocracy of the spirit."

If the Loynaz salon in Vedado represented one extreme of Havana culture and society, the other extreme was an equally emblematic living space, the *solar*. *Solar* in conventional Spanish means land or building lot, and by extension it means both noble lineage and mansion house. Thus the mansions of Old Havana were originally called *solares*. When their owners left, the poor and the new arrivals moved in, but the old name stuck.

On Calle Tacón across from the ancient Castillo de la Real Fuerza, for instance, the eighteenth-century house of the ex-slave Juana de Carvajal, enlarged and upgraded by the Calvos de la Puerta as we have seen, had passed in the later nineteenth century into the hands of the Catalán businessman Salvador Samá, recently named Marqués of Marianao. Samá, who partnered with a British company in the development of the first railroad to Marianao, lived on his suburban estate and rented out the Old Havana building piecemeal. His descendants, absentee landlords in Barcelona, continued the practice, and by the twentieth century it had become a tenement made up of single rooms rented out to the poor.

In similar fashion, the descendants of the Counts of Bayona, whose ancestral mansion faced the Cathedral, sold a fifty-year lease to a real estate entrepreneur with rights to transform it as he saw fit. So the old palace began to resemble Swiss cheese, its nooks rented out to poor families, generally black, who crowded into the interior and hung their laundry from the balconies where the countesses had once sat to watch the *volantas* pass by. The same occurred to many of the grand colonnaded villas of Cerro, when their residents either lost their fortunes to American or Spanish creditors, or prospered and moved on to the chic neighborhoods of the moment, Vedado and Miramar.

Thus *solar*, in Havana, came to have a new meaning entirely opposite to what it had meant before. A *solar* was now a tenement, called elsewhere a *ciudadela* or *cuartería*, a place where many families crowded into a single room each. All the residents did their washing and cooking and bathing in common facilities in the courtyard, sharing a single cookstove and tap. At the coming of independence there were already more than two thousand *solares* of one sort or another, housing over a third of the city's population. During the Republic the process continued apace, as the city's population swelled not only with immigrants from abroad, but with immigrants from the Cuban countryside. To poor Cubans in the interior, Havana was the place to go in search of work.

When times were good, with large purchases and high prices for sugar in the United States, the capital offered the possibility of advancement. When they were bad, when U.S. imports or prices plummeted, the capital offered the possibility of survival. Small farming families who had lost their homes and scant fields to landlords or bankers sought jobs in Havana to stave off the threat of death from malnutrition or disease. So did the landless canefield and mill workers who fled the "dead season" of unemployment between harvests. As domestics or delivery men or dockworkers, they had a better chance of feeding their families and themselves—and likewise as secretaries or shoeshine boys or sellers of lottery tickets, as entertainers, electricians, or elevator repairmen, as employees of cigar factories or whorehouses too.

Poor families who rented from the new managers or owners of old mansions often added makeshift rooms themselves, narrowing the courtyards down into passageways. It's common today to walk into a decayed colonial palace or *casa-finca* and find a wall running smack into the middle of a colored-glass *mediopunto*, or a spider web of do-it-yourself electrical wiring in the entranceway where the coachmen used to wait for the master's or mistress's commands.

To a higher stratum in the interior, the hilltop campus of the university—symbolized by the marble statue of Alma Mater at the top of the majestic entrance stairway of a eighty-eight steps—was a magnet drawing young men and a few women from provincial towns and cities in search of both professional careers and cosmopolitan sophistication: "At the end of the journey he will see the university, the stadium, the theaters . . . ," imagines a provincial tailor's son in novelist Alejo Carpentier's *The Chase*. "Then he will stroll into a café and order a martini. At last he will know how it tastes, that mixture they serve with an olive at the bottom of the glass." Many such students lived in new or converted rooming houses, but the tailor's son in the novel goes to live in a turret in a sort of solar, subletting his room from an old black woman who had been his wetnurse long ago and had in the meantime come to the city and worked for the family that then abandoned the house. The statue of Alma Mater was herself a similar symbol of the city's mixed heritage (and of the city fathers' ambivalence). The sculptor crafted her body after that of a mulatta model, and her face after a statue from ancient Greece.

As pressures and opportunities grew, landlords and speculators built new *cuarterías* or *solares*—even in Vedado, where they were hidden behind neoclassical facades, but especially in Cayo Hueso, Pueblo Nuevo, and other old barrios of Centro Habana, the former neighborhoods "outside the walls." Such *solares* took on names like El África, El California, or even El Ataúd (coffin). Makeshift squatter settlements also sprang up on empty lots, growing into shanty towns with equally eloquent names: Las Yaguas (palm thatch), Llega y Pon (squat and build), La Timba (guava paste, a traditional food of the poor), and Cocosólo (coconut, that's all). If the poet Dulce María Loynaz has served to exemplify the Cuban culture that took root in the salon, the musician Luciano "Chano" Pozo González may do the same for that of the solar—all the more so because, like most paths in Havana, the paths of their twin stories will nearly cross.

Chano Pozo was born in a solar called Pan con Timba on the outskirts of Vedado. After his mother died, the family moved to El África, at the border of Pueblo Nuevo and Cayo Hueso, close to where his father shined shoes on the corner of Zanja and Belascoaín.

"El África was a hell of a place," recalled Herminio Sánchez, a longtime resident of this barrio, trying to describe Chano Pozo's roots. "At night the courtyard was lit with one single bulb, and the clotheslines full of wash made it even darker than that. Something like two hundred people lived there, all of them black. The police didn't go in there. And if they did, or anybody came after you, the place had five exits. That was the beauty of it. You could go in on one side, and come out anyplace else." Short but strong, and with a temper, Chano got in his share of fights, petty thievery, and trouble with the police. He was sent to reform school in the countryside, where he learned to read and write. He got back to Havana in the early 1930s, in the depth of the Great Depression which caused both sugar prices and U.S. purchases to plummet, and went to live in El Ataúd, in the barrio of Colón. Pozo shined shoes like his father, sold newspapers, did whatever else he could to survive. Then he too went to work for senator Alfredo Hornedo, just as Dulce Maria Loynaz's future husband did around the same time.

Exactly what Chano Pozo did for Alfredo Hornedo is not clear. He may have started out selling *El País* on the street, but oral history says he was a bodyguard or enforcer as well. In any case, Hornedo supported him, and he became a habitué of the magnate's home on Carlos III, a modern castle (now the Casa de Cultura of Centro Habana) with a massive first story, two recessed levels above, and a terrace with two-story watchtower. Whatever the reform school graduate might have done for the politician-businessman-publisher with his fists, what made Chano Pozo's career was what he could do with his open hands and a goatskin stretched across a wooden tube. For all its privations and cruelties, the culture of the *solar* was also the culture of the *rumba*. At the center of *rumba* was the drum.

From various parts of Africa, the slaves had brought knowledge of sacred hollow-log drums, played with the hands rather than with sticks, and tuned by tempering the skins over a fire. They made and played these drums in the cabildos, and their descendants continued the tradition in all of the Afro-Cuban religions and secret societies—despite near-constant prohibitions by Spanish, U.S., and Cuban authorities on the public use of anything resembling African drums. Over time, among the black working class of both Matanzas and Havana, these sacred drums gave rise to the modern conga drum or *tumbadora*. And they gave rise to *rumba*, a Cuban creation, the secular music of the *solar*.

Rumba was a lively, flexible, improvisational music of congas, *clave* sticks, and voices, danced by soloists or by couples, in one of its most popular forms as a pantomime of flirtation and sex. In the courtyard of the solar, rumberos improvised lyrics that displayed their knowledge of African languages or that dealt with gossip, politics, neighborhood characters, romance, sex, and work.[1] When there was no drum—or to avoid trouble with the police—the *tumbadores* played wooden crates instead, creating the famous "box rumba," the *rumba de cajón*. At carnival time, the congas and the rumba came out of the *solares* and into the street as comparsas, performed in conga lines and featuring brief, repeated, catchy lyrics. Even these constantly went in and out of legality—and, when officially illegal, in and out of control.

In the 1920s and the 1930s, however, a new generation of national- ist artists and intellectuals, both white and colored, began taking a new look at Afro-Cuban influences and incorporating them in fields ranging from anthropology to literature to visual and musical arts. Nicolás Guillén, who had newly arrived in the capital from Camagüey, began introducing Afro-Cuban rhythms and colloquial urban working-class language into his poetry, in a similar fashion to what Langston Hughes (soon to be Guillén's friend) was doing with the blues in New York. Havana poet and journalist José Z. Tallet had already published a poem called "La Rumba" that tried to capture the rumba's music, its lyrics, and the presence of the Afro-Cuban deities. Composers of avant-garde orchestral music such as Alejandro García Caturla, Amadeo Roldán, and Gilberto Valdés added elements of rumba and other grassroots Cuban genres to their works. García Caturla wrote an orchestral piece called *La rumba* (1933) attempting to capture its essence, and in the late 1930s Valdés finally brought the African drums themselves into a symphonic orchestra.

In pop and dance music, meanwhile, the *son* invaded Havana from Oriente, and like contradanza and danzón before it, made the gradual transition from being considered black to being considered Cuban. In the process it picked up the influence of rumba. Miguel Matamoros brought his trio from Santiago to sweep the capital off its feet with "*Son de la loma*," while Ignacio Piñeiro and the Sexteto Habanero converted the choruses of the wooden-box rumbas into classics like "*Échale salsita*" and immortalized picaresque Havana characters such as Papá Montero in their songs. In the musical melting pot of Havana, where instrumentation was always on the move, not only the sextets and septets of *son* suddenly wanted to add the forbidden *tumbadora*, but also Cuban jazzbands and inter- preters of other genres as well. Changing tourist tastes, too, began to demand more openly Afro-Cuban music as part of the package of sun, rum, and sensuality that brought Americans to Cuba during Prohibition and after. By the same token, rumba rhythms and sani- tized lyrics were adapted for groups featuring brass, piano, and strings. Chano Pozo, self-taught conga drummer, composer, dancer, singer, choreographer, itinerant newspaper vendor, shoe shiner, and bodyguard found himself in demand.

In the late 1930s, Pozo performed and composed with the neighborhood groups that prepared *comparsas* for Carnival: El Barracón (slave barracks) of Pueblo Nuevo, El Alacrán (the crab) of Cerro, La Jardinera of Jesús María, and La Sultana of Colón. The diva Rita Montaner brought him into the standout group Los Dandies de Belén, in Old Havana, for which he coauthored the prize-winning carnival song of the same name. He was also in demand by musical groups performing in private parties, beachfront bandstands, and musical theaters. His compositions—though not yet his too black

Chano Pozo, autographed publicity photo from radio network Cadena Azul.
Photo: Biblioteca Nacional José Martí.

skin—were featured in revues at tourist hotels and recordings by
the groups that played there. In 1938 he debuted on the grand stage
as conga player in works by Obdulio Morales and Gilberto Valdés
at the Teatro Martí and the open-air Amphitheater of Havana by
the neck of the bay.

Finally, in the 1940s, Pozo played and danced in the Afro-Cuban
ballet extravaganza Congo Pantera at the new open-air Tropicana
night club, which also featured his own evocation of life in the
solar, "*Parampampín*." His songs were recorded by top Cuban
artists including Arsenio Rodríguez, the blind *tres* guitarist, bandleader, and composer, and by Cuban musicians working in the
United States. Both mainstream Cuban audiences and North
American devotees of "Latin" music found themselves singing and
dancing to his numbers with onomatopoetic titles and lyrics
like "Blen, Blen, Blen," and *lengua* (African-derived) ones like
"Ariñañara" and "Guagüina yerabo." He found a new patron,
tobacco heir and radio mogul Amado Trinidad, for whom he
guarded the door of the Radio Cadena Azul's studios on the Prado
and led the house band Conjunto Azul. When he was shot in the
stomach by a music publisher's bodyguard in a dispute over royal-
ties, Trinidad and Senator Hornedo got him the best of medical care.

Once in the money, Chano Pozo became one of the best dressed
men in Havana. One hot, sweaty day in the 1940s in the solar
El Ataúd, according to musicologist Jesús Blanco, Pozo covered his
bed with five and ten peso bills and declared that the amount
which stuck to him was his budget for the day. Stores and tailors
vied for him to wear their latest suits and jewelry. In carnival comparsas he appeared in immaculate white dress clothes, from top hat
to tails. "He drove a Cadillac and wore Chanel #5," recalled Litico
Rodríguez, ex-dancer and comic actor. "He and [pianist, composer,
and singer] Bola de Nieve were the only black men who could shop
in El Encanto, the most expensive and chic department store at the
time." But Chano Pozo continued to live in *solares*, drink in neighborhood bars, buy marijuana and cocaine from the dealers in the
notorious Parque Trillo and elsewhere, and join in whatever rumba
was at hand. Some time in the 1930s he joined an Abakuá chapter
in Cayo Hueso, though rumor had it that he was expelled, finally,
for incorporating its sacred songs into recordings for Cadena Azul.
He was about to take on a patron *orisha* in the rites of *santería* when
he got an invitation to work in the United States.

In 1946, Pozo set out for New York, center of the recording industry and therefore a beacon for Cuban musicians. He boarded ship along with a new red Cadillac convertible he bought with the advance money. In New York he recorded a few pure percussion rumbas as well as a variety of popular tunes—including "El Pin Pin," his celebration of the defeat of fascism with the addictive refrain *pin pin, cayó Berlín, pon pon, cayó Japón* ("pin pin, Berlin fell; pon pon, so did Japan")—and performed in nightclubs and theaters specializing in Latin music. Then he was introduced to Dizzy Gillespie, who was looking for a "tom tom player" ("I didn't know it was called a conga") to add a new dimension to music bebop. And that, said Gillespie, "is when the Latin innovation in [U.S.] jazz began." Afro-Cuban bebop was the result, with Pozo playing his rumba rhythms alongside Gillespie's trumpet in Carnegie Hall in 1947, the same year that Dulce María Loynaz read to a packed house at the Ateneo de Madrid. With Gillespie he recorded the classics "Cubana Be," "Cubana Bop," and "Manteca," and toured Europe, the West Coast, and the American South.

Life in the United States, however, was no freer of trouble than in Havana, and it brought its own dangers. Pozo left the southern tour when his drum was stolen in North Carolina, and decided not to return because of the discrimination he ran into there. Then, on the cold northern night of December 3, 1948, he was standing in the Rio Café and Lounge on 112th St. in Manhattan's Spanish Harlem, playing his own hit *Manteca* on the juke box, when an ex-sharpshooter World War II veteran from Puerto Rico (Cuban born in some versions of the story) pulled out a revolver and killed him with a single shot. A bad drug deal, a debt, an insult, an assassination paid for out of envy, a punishment for his failure to *hacerse santo* with the *orisha* Changó—theories abounded, but Chano Pozo returned to Havana a corpse, leaving his compositions and the future of Afro-Cuban jazz behind. All in all, says novelist, journalist, and critic Leonardo Padura, "Chano Pozo was the underside of Havana of his era, and he was also Havana itself: mistreated and joyful, boisterous and suffering . . . able to express with his hands a way of life, a way of understanding the world."

So Dulce María Loynaz and Chano Pozo may represent both the extremes and the unexpected intersections of Havana's society and culture in all the decades between the Dance of the Millions and the World War II. Between those extremes of the tree-shaded mansions of Vedado and the crowded *solares* downtown, of course, lived the majority of Havana—working, looking for work, striving to survive or get ahead. Therefore we need to briefly sketch the city's physical growth during this period, and introduce some ordinary families, not famous but equally representative, whom we can follow during these years and the ones that will follow.

From the coming of independence to the mid-1940s, metropolitan Havana's population quadrupled, from about 250,000 to a million inhabitants, fourfold growth in a little more than forty years. To house the increase, the city grew both outward and upward. As the city of the rich expanded to the west along the seacoast, that of the working and lower middle class expanded everywhere else, especially along the streetcar lines, the old roads to surrounding villages, and the ferry routes across the bay.

Across the Almendares but inland from Miramar, the old outlying settlement of Marianao spread eastward to the banks of the Almendares and westward to La Lisa. Its living links to the city's core strengthened with the opening and expansion of entertainment centers such as the Oriental Park racetrack (owned by the Cuban-American Jockey Club) and the beer gardens opened by the Tropical Brewery to promote its brew. The Jardines de la Tropical, designed by Catalán architects in the spirit of Gaudí, featured riverside pavilions that blended Moorish cupolas and mosaics with tropical jungle motifs, linked by sinuous paths that wandered among royal palms and other trees. In the 1930s and 1940s, the Jardines de la Tropical became one of a limited number of social venues where almost all segments of Havana society met.

To the south of the city spread working-class barrios like Lawton, Diezmero, Arroyo Apollo, and Mantilla, and middle-class ones like Santos Suarez and the euphoniously Spanglish Vibora Park. Along the main roads heading south and southeast, neighborhoods like El Calvario, Párraga, and San Miguel de Padrón likewise became part of what was known as La Gran Habana, while the old villages of Guanabacoa, Regla, and Casablanca across the bay were tightly connected to the economic, social, and cultural life of the city through tiny passenger ferries that crossed at all hours of the day and night.

In the meantime, the old city grew vertically to match the horizontal sprawl. Though Havana remained a low-rise city in comparison to many, apartment houses of three, four, five, and sometimes more stories replaced the one-and two-story structures of many older neighborhoods. In Centro Habana, a new shopping district grew up along such streets as Galiano, Neptuno, and San Rafael. Its signature venue was El Encanto (where Dulce María Loynaz was angry that her book was not put on sale, and Chano Pozo finally became able to shop) at the corner of San Rafael and Galiano. Along these streets and others, an endless procession of columns and arcades provided shade for shoppers and less exclusive storefronts while supporting multiple stories of apartments above. If Centro Habana lacked the space and capital that made Vedado an architect's paradise, a walk through its streets still reveals myriad decorative touches in cement and iron, wood and glass, plaster and tile, mica and marble dust, in styles ranging from beaux art to Italian renaissance to art deco and art nouveaux. All of this brought work to craftsmen and artists, while the stores and shoppers brought business to the milliners and seamstresses of the district, which like Old Havana housed a population mixed in every way.

Early in the century, for instance, the sisters Cecilia and Virginia Larrinaga, dressmakers and hatmakers with roots most likely in Oriente, set up shop on the Calle San Rafael and rented an apartment upstairs. They made women's clothes and hats to order, and they saved their money to offer the best future they could to their nephew Luis, whose father worked nearby as a cook. The Larrinaga sisters were mulattas, and while they wanted to send Luis abroad for high school, they feared the racial prejudice he would meet in the United States, so they managed to send him to France. When he returned, he went to work for the weekly newsmagazine *Bohemia* as a French translator, but since the pay was by piecework and there was less demand for French than for English, he worked mostly as a chauffeur for the publisher of the magazine. After Luis married, he and his family moved frequently from apartment to apartment around Centro Habana, along the borders of Cayo Hueso, in accord with what they could afford in the face of ever-rising rents. His son Carlos remembers the devastating hurricane of 1926 (the same that deprived the Loynaz of their telephone service) blowing down the wall of the *solar* across the street and leaving its many inhabitants exposed to view. Carlos in turn went to work at the Victor Adding Machine Company on Galiano, a Cuban-owned franchise of the American company, where he repaired adding machines and typewriters, Remingtons and Underwoods above all.

In the meantime, Pablo González Palacios had come to Havana from Santa Clara in 1914, and begun to do what the Chinese had pioneered most recently, and the free blacks of the treasure port long before. He sold fried meat patties and corn tamales from a cart, first on the southern edge of Miramar, and then alongside the private clubs and the public beach in the nearby Playa de Marianao, where he became known as "Pablo el Cumbanchero" after a popular dance. With his savings, he bought a lot in one of the most affordable of the new working-class suburbs, called Buenavista, recently laid out on former farmland south and east of Camp Columbia.

Buenavista was first subdivided into lots by a U.S. speculator named Joseph Barlow in 1906 and 1907, the years of the second U.S. occupation when American troops again occupied the Camp. In the early teens, the developers received formal authorization for building and paving, on a plan of small lots and narrow streets with set back sidewalks, a sort of mini-mini-Vedado for the working class. About 1920, Pablo el Cumbanchero bought a lot in Buenavista, hired local carpenters to build him a house, and set up stone ovens in the patio to bake bread and sweets to add to his wares. Buenavista was then mostly empty, and up the hill was still an open grassland called "*el parque de los chivos* (goats)" where locals pastured their animals; in the patio behind the house he grew fruit trees—a mango tree, a banana, an *anón*. But Buenavista soon gained a reputation as a barrio both hardworking and tough.

"I love Buenavista," recalls his granddaughter Raquel Cañizares who still lives in that house on what is today Calle 64 of the municipality of Playa, "and I was a protected child, too, but it has always been a *barrio caliente*, a hot place, and I remember how they used to go to the park to rob people and steal the goats." Buenavista even became famous for a gang of female thieves, Las Villalobas, who would sometimes assault the customers in local stores. Like many popular neighborhoods, it was also memorialized in songs such as "Buena Vista en Guagancó," by Arsenio Rodriguez and "Social Club de Buenavista" by the bassist and mambo innovator Orestes "Cachao" López.

There was indeed a Social Club of Buenavista, one of many societies of "recreation and instruction." Distant descendants of the old cabildos, these private societies were created by and for Havana's working- and middle-class population of color whose access to other venues was limited by discrimination, high prices, or both. Founded by Julio Dueñas on Avenida 31 about six blocks from the house of Pablo el Cumbanchero, the Buenavista club had no house band (the internationally famous Havana oldies band of the 1990s was an amalgam put together by the U.S. guitarist Ry Cooder), but it did welcome prominent black and mulatto musicians who performed for public dances as well as private parties to celebrate weddings and *quinces*, the parties held to celebrate girls' turning fifteen.

Besides hosting the dances which nurtured musicians and musical innovation, these clubs sponsored other forms of recreation (such as athletic teams and domino competitions) as well as offering classes in English, skilled trades, and domestic arts. The societies thus provided Havanans of color with a measure of support in the economic competition to stay afloat in Havana, which was severe in spite of the economic growth. Raquel Cañizares and her family were also members of the Club Ameno, another society based in Marianao, which in December of 1946 rented the clubhouse of the Oriental Park horse track for a New Year's dance. That was where she met Luis Larrinaga's son Carlos for the first time. They married in 1949, uniting the Centro Habana family with the Buenavista one. They lived for two years (and had their first two children) in two rented rooms on San Rafael in Centro Habana. Then Carlos bought a used 1948 Lincoln in which to commute to his job at Victor Adding Machine, and they moved back to Buenavista for good.

Still more strands of ethnicity and culture wove their way into popular neighborhoods of Havana as the century moved on. In the mid-1930s, the Cañizares and their Buenavista neighbors began to be visited by a peddler whom they referred to as *el polaco*, literally The Pole. *Polaco*, in the city's terminology, had come to denote anyone from Eastern Europe and, by extension, any Jew. The peddler in question, Alberto Motola, was the son of Sephardic Jews from Turkey who had emigrated to New York at the outbreak of World War I. His family soon heard of opportunities in Cuba, and after a spell in the cities of the interior, they settled in the capital. Jews made their way to Havana by other routes as well. Composer Moisés Simons, who turned the chants of black peanut vendors into the popular hit "El manisero," came from a family of Basque Jews who reached Havana in the nineteenth century.

By the time the Motolas arrived, Jews had established a foothold in the textile and clothing businesses along Sol and Luz and Muralla streets in Old Havana. The Sephardim, whose ancestors had been expelled from Spain the same year Columbus set sail for the new world, established a synagogue on the ironically named corner of Luz and Inquisidor. Alberto went to work by the age of ten, first running errands for a Greek shoemaker, and then sweeping floors and delivering messages for a clothing wholesaler on Muralla. In 1936, he began taking the streetcar out to Buenavista to peddle clothes and fabrics on time payments, door to door. Eight years later he married Maria Roffe, whose parents had made the same journey from Turkey to New York to Havana, and this couple in turn moved from downtown to an increasingly crowded Buenavista, where they rented an apartment and a tiny store a few blocks from the Cañizares house. Alberto too now commuted to the city center, in his case to buy from contacts in the wholesale houses. For this he depended on the streetcars and delivery trucks, until finally, in the early 1950s, he bought an old Model-T.

The Motolas, the Larrinaga-Cañizares, and their neighborhood of Buenavista provide a glimpse of some often-hidden dimensions of Havana during these decades, which go unmentioned in histories of architecture, entertainment, and the culture of either salon or solar. There is still something else to be considered, however. The residents of the city did not act only as individuals or members of families, but sometimes as masses of citizens in the political sphere. As we did with the nineteenth century, we need to refocus on the period we have just covered with a different eye. The political centerpiece of those years in Havana, which left its mark on the city forever after, was what is known as the Revolution of 1933.

10

The Battle of Havana, 1933–35

Juan Criollo, the protagonist of Carlos Loveira's 1927 novel of the same name, described the Cuba of the early years of the century this way:

> [It's] a soccer ball covered with ants, to which an unknown player has given a tremendous kick, sending it spinning through space without the ants having the slightest idea where they came from or where they're going or why. That doesn't stop the little animals from clinging to the surface or from killing each other so as to keep holding on to the ball and their dreams.

Juan Criollo is a novel foremost about Havana, the story of a boy who lives by his wits, who climbs from a miserable shack on the undeveloped seacoast into the realm of politics as the city grows along with him. Loveira had been a teenage exile in New York, an officer in the army of independence, and then a translator for the U.S. occupation force. "At first, just knowing English was enough to change you overnight into the representative of some official or firm," he said later. "But soon, even the cobblestones started speaking English," so he had to look for other work. He found it on the railroads as a brakeman, baggage handler, engineer of a sugar mill locomotive, and eventually machinist. Finally he became a journalist, government bureaucrat, and prominent novelist. But in his railroad period, he was a founder of the Cuban League of Railroad Employees, and he remained attached to union and socialist sympathies in the years that followed. *Generals and Doctors* (1920), his other best-known novel along with *Juan Criollo*, ends with a worker's general strike against the pervasive corruption and inequality which defined that era.

Loveira knew what he was talking about. In 1933, a general strike that began among the capital's bus drivers toppled a government and unleashed the only Cuban revolution truly made in Havana. Years before that, manual workers and their unions, in and out of the capital, were among the first to emerge from the political passivity that followed the frustration of the hopes of 1898.

Even during the first U.S. occupation, the notion of founding socialist or workers' political parties had emerged within the trade unions of Havana. Proponents included old activists of Martí's Cuban Revolutionary Party, such as Carlos Baliño and Diego Vicente Tejera, both connected to international socialist organizations. Among the strongholds of union organizing were the city's cigar factories, whose workers built on the militancy that had made their unions in exile a base of support for the independence movement in Tampa, New York, and Key West. In the expansive open rooms of the Gener, Partagás, H. Uppmann, and other factories, the old tradition of the *Lector*, or Reader, continued. This designated employee declaimed the news and editorials of the daily press and chapter after chapter of famous literary works. As a result, the cigar workers, like the typographers in the newspapers and publishing houses, were generally well-informed and in possession of a level of culture beyond their formal education. The papers they "read" through the voice of the reader included workers' publications of a socialist bent.

Strikes for higher wages or better conditions emerged along with the founding of the Republic, bringing frequent street clashes between unionists and police. In 1907, during the second U.S. occupation, seven thousand tobacco workers in factories belonging to the Henry Clay/Bock & Company trust walked out and stayed out for more than six months, until the company agreed to pay them in U.S. dollars (rather than the less valuable Spanish and French currency also in circulation in the city). Shortly afterward,

Havana cigar factory, early 20th century.

Photo: Library of Congress.

railroad workers striking United Railways (likewise American-owned) had to confront a group of fifty strikebreakers brought directly from the United States to maintain train service between Havana and surrounding towns. Masons, carpenters, lithographers, and teamsters also walked out in spite of warnings from U.S. provisional governor Charles Magoon, known in popular songs as the Hothead for his impulsive personality. In January of 1908, while houses along the coast from the Castillo de la Punta to the mouth of the Almendares were flooded by a storm surge from the ocean, the cigar rollers of the Romeo & Juliet factory struck in protest against impending layoffs. Havana sewage system workers likewise struck against the Huston Contracting Company (whose profits helped Tillinghast Huston buy the Yankees, as noted earlier), and construction workers walked out on the Cuban Engineering Company.

Soon after this strike wave, the Hothead departed along with his Army of Pacification, leaving the restive city in the hands of its Cuban officials. In 1914, a National Workers Congress assembled in the capital, with 1200 union delegates from all parts of the country. The mid-1920s saw the formation of the National Workers

Confederation of Cuba (Spanish initials CNOC) led by Alfredo López, a typographer by trade. López was an anarchist given to trade union unity and political dialogue, who had gained a strong reputation for incorruptibility in a country where money bought anything. With the founding of the CNOC, general strikes on a national level began to occur.

In the 1910s and especially the 1920s, this nascent labor movement was joined by movements in other sectors, as Cuban politics and intellectual life emerged from the torpor that had set in when the promise of full independence and thoroughgoing reform was blocked. Pent up demands for national sovereignty, cultural independence, social justice, and an end to corrupt government reemerged in overlapping national organizations of labor, war veterans, students, women, professionals, and small business owners. In 1919, while the government prohibited the flying of red flags in demonstrations, the movie "The Harvest in Six Acts, or The Blood of Sugar" debuted in the Payret Cinema on the Prado across from the site where the new Capitol building was going up. Expressions of social unrest had come to form part of the city's life. The many new reform groups won some important victories in the late 1910s and early 1920s, most notably tariff protection for local industry, wage increases for unionized sectors of the workforce, reform of the university, and some small steps toward gender equality.

Women's groups fought for access to education and jobs, changes in family law, and the vote. As early as 1913, Magdalena Peñarredonda, the independence fighter and organizer of fellow prisoners in the Casa de Recogidas in 1896–98, published an article entitled "Feminism in Cuba" in which, among other things, she called on women to boycott stores that did not hire female employees. The following year, the new divorce law was passed. At the first National Women's Congress, held in Havana in the Teatro Nacional (formerly Tacón) in 1923, the more radical delegates challenged the sexual double standard as they called for equal rights for illegitimate children and unwed mothers, and for jobs and respectability for former prostitutes. One legal victory for the women's movement was the repeal of the colonial-era law legitimizing a husband's murder of an adulterous wife. Among the Cuban feminists or proto-feminists of the early 1920s were Dulce María Borrero, sister of the late poet Juana, and Mariblanca Sabás Alomá, journalist and one of two female members of the Grupo Minorista, Havana's new cultural avant garde.

They called themselves *minoristas* (the minority) because they saw themselves as bearers of a national ideal of freedom, independence, renewal, and social progress in the midst of the pervasive atmosphere of decadence and corruption which had categorized the first two decades of the Republic. Meeting in weekly *tertulias* (salons or talk sessions), the Minoristas founded new magazines and lecture series, forming a Cuban point of contact with a wide variety of modernist, antiimperialist, and socialist schools of thought abroad.

Among the Minoristas were the writers José Z. Tallet and Nicolás Guillén (not a founder, but a participant), and the composer Alejandro García Caturla, whose incorporations of Afro-Cuban popular culture into Cuban poetry and classical music we have already described. The group also promoted several soon-to-be famous painters who did the same for the visual arts. Alejo Carpentier, a prominent Minorista, began his literary career exploring African roots, and noted about the *avant garde* composers of his circle that "Those who already knew the score of *The Rite of Spring* began to notice, justifiably, that in Regla, on the other side of the bay, there were rhythms as complex and interesting as those created by Stravinsky."

Guillén's body of work would make him a leading poet in the years stretching into the 1970s, and Carpentier would become the most important Cuban novelist of the century and a leading chronicler of Havana's architecture, history, and music. Other Minoristas became political leaders as well as influential intellectuals. These included the poet Rubén Martínez Villena and the essayist Juan Marinello (both later to join the Communist Party) and the brilliant polemecist Jorge Mañach (liberal and anticommunist, who would later write the best political biography of José Martí).

Denouncing government corruption and U.S. domination, the Minoristas and their fellow travelers allied themselves with the political wing of the Cuban intellectual renewal, which was based at the hilltop campus of the University of Havana. In 1923, while students in Argentina and other Latin American countries were demanding and proclaiming the reform of higher education, the new Cuban University Students' Federation forcibly occupied the campus's buildings and plazas, demanding removal of anachronistic and corrupt professors, modernization of curriculum and textbooks, free higher education, and autonomy from the government.

One of the main leaders of this action was Nicanor MacPharlan—better known by his nomme de guerre Julio Antonio

Mella—who was at one and the same time a rowing champion in the university regattas, disciple of the union leader Alfredo López, and an organizer of the independent José Martí Popular University. Mella and López were among the small group who assembled in 1925 in a building at the Vedado corner of Calzada and B (on the site where the Hubert de Blanck theater now stands) to found the Cuban Communist Party. The party's initial base was a small group of Central European immigrants and other Cuban workers, some veterans of the Cuban Revolutionary Party, and some former anarchists. Mella himself was soon expelled by a Stalinist faction within the party that found him too much of a free spirit. In the late 1920s and the 1930s the communists became increasingly influential in the union movement and among middle-class intellectuals, as both of these sectors fought repression by the state.

In the late 1920s, the winds of change blowing through Havana ran up against the dual barriers of the Great Depression and the dictatorship of Gerardo Machado, president from 1925 to 1933. Machado was, like his predecessor Menocal, a former Liberation Army officer who entered politics and managed a U.S.-owned sugar mill before reaching the presidential chair. He was first elected president as a reformer but then solidified his grip on power and wealth through increasingly brutal methods, including murder and torture of opponents, chief among them radical students and unionists.

As the 1930s dawned, the "years of the fat cows" were followed by "years of lean cows." In Cuba just as in the U.S. unemployment soared and wages dropped. The poor subsisted on a diet of "corn and boniatos" (Cuban sweet potatoes) and "water with brown sugar"—and these popular expressions were not far from the literal truth. Alberto Motola's Jewish immigrant father, for instance, brought home only forty-five cents a day to feed nine children, on soup fortified with bread and a little cheese. It was in that context that Alberto went to work at the age of ten. As the Machado dictatorship met growing protest with intensified repression, many members of Havana's political opposition and its intellectual *avant-garde* were driven underground or into exile.

Julio Antonio Mella, one of the earliest to denounce Machado, was expelled from the university and arrested. He went on a hunger strike in jail, and finally into exile in Mexico after his release. In 1929, he was shot dead by agents of Machado's political police. His image of light-skinned mulatto Adonis was immortalized in a portrait by Tina Modotti, the photographer and professional revolutionary who moved in the Mexico of the 1920s in the same circles as Frida Kahlo and Diego Rivera. Union leaders including CNOC founder Alfredo López, and the Abakuá and communist Aracelio Iglesias, leader of the stevedores on Havana's docks, were tortured and thrown into the sea from Navy ships by Machado's assassins, who sowed terror on the capital's streets.

The Student Federation founded by Mella, now converted into the underground University Student Directorate, gave birth to a labyrinth of clandestine groups who proposed to fight terror with terror by way of armed attacks against politicians and others associated with the government. The most audacious act of this underground resistance was directed against the dictator himself. The plan was to assassinate one of Machado's key lieutenants, Senate President Clemente Vázquez Bello, and then blow up the entire top echelon of the government including the dictator when they assembled at the Colón Cemetery to pay their last respects. For weeks, the revolutionaries toiled literally underground, digging a long tunnel from a house on Calle Zapata to the Vázquez Bello family tomb. A group armed with machine guns ambushed Vázquez Bello on the street as planned, while confederates placed enough explosives under the tomb to convert it into a gigantic land mine. Then the Vázquez Bello family decided at the last minute to bury Clemente in Santa Clara, their home town. The plan failed and brought on a new wave of government repression. It was later immortalized in fictionalized form in John Huston's film, "We Were Strangers" (1949), a surprisingly sympathetic portrayal of revolution just before the McCarthy era came to Hollywood.

Demanding an end to Machado's rule and relief from the desperate economic straits of the Depression, a defiant public grassroots opposition emerged alongside the armed underground. The government found itself besieged by protests, strikes, and assassinations on all sides. During this time Flor Loynaz joined the University Student Directorate and drove her Fiat in one of these violent demonstrations. For years afterward its bullet-scarred chassis, hidden in the family garage, bore testimony to the lengths to which even such patrician rebels were driven by the times. Luis Larrinaga, chauffeur and translator, had joined the Communist Party, influenced both by the gravity of the Cuban crisis and the

political ideas he had picked up in France. He too participated in the
uprising against Machado, as did thousands more. Finally in 1933
a work stoppage by Havana's bus drivers turned into a general
strike that paralyzed the city. Clashes between strikers and
Machado's police had the capital teetering on the brink of civil war.

In a well-known image from the Revolution of 1933, jubilant Havanans on
the Prado celebrate an army corporal who has just changed sides and shot
a notorious member of Machado's secret police.

Photo: Biblioteca Nacional José Martí.

On the morning of August 12, 1933, the orchestra of competing sounds to which Havanans had been accustomed since time immemorial suddenly changed into a chorus chanting in unison one and the same phrase: Machado is gone! Streetcars and trucks overflowing with exultant young people circled through the city in a triumphal march, seeking out those who collaborated with the dictatorship and breaking into mansions in a gesture of anarchic reprisal for everything stolen during the preceding years. The strike that brought down Machado had been called by the CNOC and seconded by the university students, the communists, the paramilitary organization ABC, and other groups fighting against the dictatorship. But none of these revolutionary organizations could control the populace of Havana. In the streets, crowds seized and executed agents of the feared political police of the dictator, popularly known as La Porra (the blackjack). They sacked the luxurious Villa Miramar at the mouth of the Almendares, carrying off many of the treasures Machado's Minister of Public Works had amassed. In Buenavista the looting was more practical. Raquel Cañizares has never forgotten how at the age of six she watched two diminutive women, her neighbors from down the block, staggering under the weight of a great sack of rice.

Machado and his closest collaborators, including the head of La Porra and the owner of the Villa Miramar, had already escaped into exile, in most cases to the United States. From that distance they observed the events that spread throughout the country over the next twenty months. If the struggle against Machado had ended, the Revolution of 1933 had just begun. It had started in the streets of Havana, and there it would be fought to the end.

In the middle of the cacophony on that first day of celebration, the city's radio stations announced the formation of a provisional government led by sixty-two year old Dr. Carlos Manuel de Céspedes Quesada and Gen. Alberto Herrera Franchi. Céspedes was a lawyer, former ambassador to Washington, and most importantly the son and namesake of the man who had proclaimed independence from Spain sixty-five years before; Herrera on the other hand was head of the armed forces under the regime that had just collapsed. But the people of Havana were fed up with "generals and doctors" in any case. Even many rank-and-file police and soldiers refused to follow orders from these figures of the old regimes, and soon the revolutionary organizations (armed and unarmed) named their own government, whose short life would leave a deep imprint on Cuban history. The new president was a physiology professor at the University of Havana, Ramón Grau San Martín, and his minister of justice and armed forces was a young graduate of the college of pharmacy and ex-pharmaceutical salesman, born in Bala Cynwyd, Pennsylvania, of a Cuban father and Irish mother, Antonio Guiteras Holmes. Citing Martí's dictum that the colony should not be allowed to live on in the republic, the government adopted the slogan "Cuba for the Cubans" and sought, as Grau put it, "to liquidate the colonial structure that has survived in Cuba since independence." This was the first government in the history of the Republic to take office without the approval of the United States—which, in fact, withheld recognition for as long as the government survived.

As in no other moment, the people of Havana, according to a phrase popular in Cuba, "threw themselves into the street." Teachers, longshoremen, cigar rollers, students, and feminists flooded the city's public spaces in perpetual demonstrations carrying all sort of banners and demands: eight-hour day, female suffrage, laws to protect Cuban-born workers against low-wage immigrants, subsidized breakfasts in the elementary schools, raises for the public employees, and more. The Government of the Hundred Days (as it would be known in retrospect) would proclaim many laws, including price controls, mandatory collective bargaining, and eventually the first nationalizations in Cuban history, which affected the telephone and electric companies as well as a few sugar mills belonging to American corporations. It also declared the Platt Amendment null and void. In spite of these audacious policies, much of Havana wanted more. The accumulated effects of the Depression, together with seven years of strong arm rule, censorship, and repression, had them feeling that they could not take any more. They erupted into demands for still more sweeping change, which overwhelmed the capacities even of the most radical government they had ever seen.

This wave of demands was so intense that it whipped through the armed forces themselves. A few weeks after the fall of Machado, the soldiers and sergeants of Camp Columbia, under the influence of the leaders of the University Student Directorate, had mutinied against the officer corps and ousted the high command of the army, made up of sons of the upper class. This so-called Revolution of September 4, led by sergeants Pablo Rodríguez and Mario Hernández, took possession of the headquarters of the general staff. Also part of this movement, lurking in the background, was a stenography sergeant who spoke some English, a native of the small town of Banes on the eastern end of the island, the illegitimate son of a laundress of mixed blood. His name was Fulgencio Batista y Zaldívar. Sgt. Batista soon demonstrated his capacity for leadership, negotiating with the civilian revolutionaries behind the backs of his colleagues to make himself head of the army, from which position he gave the formal coup de grace to the deposed high command.

Instead of going into exile, however, the ex-chiefs of the armed forces decided to take refuge in the luxurious Hotel National, barely three years old. Convinced that the U.S. embassy would support them, and armed to the teeth, they held out for several days against a siege mounted by the mutinied troops who—together with civilians from the revolutionary organizations—surrounded the magnificent hotel and fired their artillery at its Mediterranean revival facade. In the first days of the Battle of the Hotel Nacional, members of the army's skilled sharpshooter corps practiced their marksmanship against the soldiers from the advantageous position of the fifth floor balconies. Finally, suffering from hunger and thirst as the supply lines to their luxurious rat trap were cut and their ammunition ran out, the aristocratic officials put up a white flag. Some were shot immediately in the hotel's gardens, while others were tried and sent to the Model Prison on the Isle of Pines. The first potential counterrevolution, mounted by the remnants of the power structure that sustained Machado, had been crushed.

The capacity of now-Col. Batista to find solutions to problems had caught the attention of the U.S. ambassador in Havana, Benjamin Sumner Welles. At Welles' request, the *U.S.S. Wyoming* and other warships had been dispatched to the Cuban capital and were anchored expectantly in the legendary bay with marines on board—a reminder to one and all that as far as the U.S. government was concerned the Platt Amendment was still in effect. Welles invited Batista to sit down and talk in his office, which overlooked the Plaza de Armas in the solid building of North American architecture that now houses the Museum of Natural History and was then the embassy of the United States. The two discovered they had some things in common. Nonetheless the ambassador decided emergency measures were needed. He telegraphed Washington to say that neither the government nor the revolutionary organizations nor the right wing were capable of controlling the crowds that had taken over the streets.

The first great confrontation involving these crowds took place on September 29, when Julio Antonio Mella's ashes, brought back from Mexico, were carried in a funeral procession down Calle Reina toward the new Parque de la Fraternidad (the old Spanish parade grounds) at the head of the Prado between the Palacio de Aldama and the Teatro Martí. Rubén Martínez Villena, one of the moving spirits of the former Grupo Minorista and at that moment secretary of the Communist Party, addressed the assassinated revolutionary in a voice nearly extinguished by tuberculosis: "Here you are, yes, not in this heap of ashes but in the immense demonstration of the people that accompanies you." A few moments later, mounted police under Batista's orders received a command to break up the demonstration. When they attacked with gunshots and clubs as the police of Machado had done, hundreds of demonstrators sought refuge in the doorways and behind the columns of the former mansion of the Aldamas. Along Calle Reina, the dead included old men, women, and children. The communists, the unions, and some of the general population blamed the government for this violence, weakening its popular support.

Events like this were not the only factors which kept Havana in a state of permanent turbulence and expectation. On the other side of the political spectrum, a new right, also armed, acted without rest. The clandestine organization ABC placed bombs on street corners and organized assassinations. Explosions could be heard in the capital day and night. Inspired by the paramilitary structure of Mussolini's blackshirts, and created originally as a group of shock troops to destroy the power of the Machado dictatorship, the green shirts of the ABC had joined the Céspedes-Herrera government and been left out of its replacement. They now made war against the Government of the Hundred Days, the communists, the unions, the student movement, and the new generation of the army.

This new counterrevolution attracted support within the air force and some discontented sections of the army. In early November, a convergence of the fascist-leaning ABC, the surviving old guard of the military leadership, and some in the lower ranks who felt they had missed their chance on September 4 staged an uprising that turned parts of the city into a battlefield. This battle began with the bombing of Camp Columbia by air force mutineers, followed by an unsuccessful attack on this base by police and the ABC. As had been the case with the former officers in the Hotel Nacional, the commanders of this rebellion believed they would receive decisive aid from the United States. The *Wyoming*, still anchored in the harbor, assumed battle alert and unsheathed its cannons, which were pointed at the Presidential Palace. By the time the rebels discovered that the U.S. ambassador was supporting the loyal sector of the army, under Batista, it was too late. Commanded from the Castillo de La Punta by Guiteras (still the minister of justice and armed forces), loyal forces cornered the dissidents in Atarés castle, south of Old Havana. Forced to surrender after a prolonged mortar and cannon barrage, the mutinous officers were sent before a firing squad. The new counterrevolution found itself leaderless, for now.

In the midst of this theater of war within which the daily life of the city unfolded, newspapers and radio transmitted reports and rumors of the most unexpected events. Guiteras visited the navy units, which had all remained loyal to the government, and handed each officer a copy of *Ten Days That Shook the World*, John Reed's chronicle of the Russian Revolution of 1917. The radical American journalist Carleton Beals interviewed Guiteras, calling him the "John Brown of Cuba" in a series of articles published in mid-September in the United States. Meanwhile, the cigar makers' union went out on strike, paralyzing the most important factories of the capital. From the eastern provinces arrived news that councils of workers, peasants, and solders had taken over several sugar mills. While the U.S. government refused to recognize the administration of President Grau San Martin, its ambassador announced that Cuban officers would be welcome to train at West Point.

After a conversation with Guiteras in Camp Columbia on November 15, and frustrated in all attempts to tame or coopt him, Ambassador Welles wrote secretly to President Franklin Roosevelt that Guiteras was the most dangerous enemy of the United States in the Cuban government. A plot to depose him, with the participation of sugar mill owners, Welles, and Colonel Batista, got under way. This time there was a counterrevolutionary conspiracy that brought together the interests of the old regime, the United States and the military wing of the revolution itself. Welles returned to Washington, replaced by the experienced diplomat Jefferson Caffery, who was entrusted with the mission of overseeing a coup.

By the time Caffery arrived, the situation had become more polarized still. The American companies that controlled telephone and electricity service had refused to comply with government price controls that lowered their rates to levels the bulk of the population could afford. At Guiteras's urging, these utilities were nationalized in response. To resolve the uprisings on at the eastern sugar mills, two of those were nationalized as well. As if to symbolize a break with the past, one of them was the Chaparra, which former president Menocal had overseen for the Cuban-American Sugar Company.

With its ability to govern weakened by the disobedience on all sides and the ever-rising popular demands for more radical measures, and shot through internally with political tensions and tendencies, the government of the Hundred Days found itself alone between the left and the right. It proved an easy target for a coup d'etat. Relieved not to have to land the marines, Ambassador Caffery announced to his government that democratic forces had replaced Grau San Martín and Guiteras with the ex-colonel Carlos Mendieta, who represented the interests of the sugar mill owners and was a friend of the United States. Among this new government's first measures was the return of nationalized properties to their American owners. The government's true strongman was not Mendieta, but the head of the army, the ex-sergeant from Banes, Fulgencio Batista. His pending tasks were the elimination of the revolutionary leaders and the restoration of social peace.

For a time, the Havana of the Caffery-Batista-Mendieta government remained a beehive of insurgency, street confrontations, and uncertainty. The jail in the Príncipe Castle, on the heights at the far end of the university campus, filled with students and unionists once again. The repression of the workers' and students' organizations grew worse as the new police commander, Batista's friend and ally José Eleuterio Pedraza, boasted that he would meet any threatened strike with "*palmachristi* and rubber." Every resident of Havana knew the meaning of this cryptic term. *Palmachristi* was a laxative, a home remedy made of castor oil, which in sufficient doses could do away with anyone's intestines. Rubber was the generic term for the blackjack. Both ingredients of Pedraza's formula were applied to the prisoners in police stations under his command.

With the leftists under government attack, and encouraged by the rise of Mussolini and the earliest signs of Hitler's ascension in Europe, Cuba's indigenous fascist forces felt more daring. On the morning of June 17, 1934, more than fifty thousand adherents of the ABC, wearing their bright green shirts, covered the surface of the Paseo del Prado from the Parque Central to the Malecón. But

among the crowds of onlookers milling beneath the columns of the
buildings were squads of two separate opposition groups, the communist party and a secret organization created by Guiteras among
his old and new followers, then known as TNT. In the midst of the
speeches and slogans of the ABC, the communist and Guiteras
squads, each acting on its own, attacked with gunfire and sticks,
catching the green shirts unawares, causing several deaths, and
scattering the crowd. In its first attempt at public rather than clandestine action, Cuban fascism was severely shaken.

In this convulsive context, while the hopes for change that had
been raised by Machado's fall faded into smoke, new armed
groups of self-declared revolutionaries multiplied. Their names
flashed through the headlines—Brigade of the Dawn, ORCA,
Liberation Army—as they carried out attacks on the most notorious police officers and on U.S. businesses, landowners, and
spokesmen for the establishment. The multimillionaire sugar baron
Eutimio Falla Bonet paid 300,000 pesos ransom to free himself from
a revolutionary commando group. Pepín Rivero, publisher of the
daily paper *Diario de la Marina* and dean of the conservative Cuban
press, escaped as if by a miracle from an assassination attempt in
the middle of the street.

With the advantage of a new system of "emergency tribunals"
created to send elements considered subversive directly to the
Castillo del Príncipe, Col. Batista launched an offensive which
militarily occupied the University of Havana and dissolved all the
unions in one stroke. At the same time, to protect himself against
any possible "friendly fire," he ordered the assassination of his old
colleagues, the surviving leaders of the sergeants' revolt. Without
unity or coordination, and above all overtaken by the popular des-
peration in Havana and the rest of Cuba, the organizations in
opposition found themselves caught between the withering fire of
the Batista regime from above and an explosion from below. In a
desperate and largely spontaneous general strike in March of 1935,
workers attempted to create a new crisis like that which had pre-
cipitated Machado's fall in August of 1933. But this time the establishment had consolidated itself and was prepared to confront
opposition at every turn. For several days Pedraza's police forces
distributed the promised *palmachristi* and rubber, while hunting
down revolutionary groups in the streets of Havana and sowing
terror among the population. Luis Larrinaga was one of many who
suffered imprisonment during this time.

On May 8, 1935, in what would be the last act of this tragedy, the former Minister of Justice Antonio Guiteras and his closest collaborators gathered at a small military outpost called El Morillo, on the Matanzas coast between Havana and the Varadero beach resort. Among them was the Nicaraguan Carlos Aponte, a former colonel in the guerrilla army of Augusto César Sandino which had kept the U.S. marines at bay for years. They planned to leave for Mexico by boat, and there undertake military training so as to return to the island's mountains to begin a guerrilla war at home. But they were surrounded by the army and killed. With the death of Guiteras and the triumph of Batista—who would control Cuban politics for the next nine years—the epilogue to the Revolution of '33 came to an end.

Three months later, the American warships finally departed from Havana Bay. Many Cubans who had seen their revolutionary dreams broken also took ship, via New York, for Spain. There they joined with other Latin Americans and not a few North Americans to defend the Spanish Republic against Franco and his allies. In proportion to their country's population, the Cubans in the International Brigades made up the largest share of the foreign fighters defending the Spanish Republic and rose highest in its ranks. Among them were leading writers like Pablo de la Torriente Brau, journalist and veteran of the Havana student movement and underground, who died fighting the fascist advance toward Madrid.

The most conspicuous of the North American writers who covered the Spanish war soon installed himself in Havana to chronicle it. In a room in the Hotel Ambos Mundos in Old Havana, Ernest Hemingway wrote *For Whom the Bell Tolls*. He would then stay in Havana, to write and to fish in the Gulf Stream, and he would still be there, together with the rest of the city, when history returned to its roots twenty-five years after the battles of 1933. This time the crowds would not be shouting about the departure of Machado. "Batista is gone!" they would exult instead.

11

Radio Days

Habaneros of the 1940s and early 1950s lived with their ears glued to the radio. Cuba ranked first among all Latin American countries in per capita radio ownership, and its capital city was largely responsible for this figure. In playwright Virgilio Piñera's classic drama about this period, *Aire Frío*, a working-class household that can't afford an electric fan in the summer heat nonetheless owns a radio. The radio is practically a member of the family, its voice heard all through the play.

Havana boasted thirty-four stations (twice as many as Buenos Aires) whose listeners could choose among a vast array of programs. For news junkies, the all-news, all-the-time Radio Reloj then as now reported bulletins punctuated by the sound of a ticking clock and announcement of the time, minute by minute, day and night. Elsewhere on the dial, the Marine Corps Hymn introduced the evening news show sponsored by General Motors, which reported on events from the halls of Montezuma to the shores of Tripoli and beyond. Listeners devoted to adventure serials hung on the episodes of Tarzán (pronounced tar-SAHN), played by the famous actor Enrique Santiesteban, whose face would become as familiar as his voice in the Cuban cinema of the next fifty years.

Lovers of true-crime shows tuned in to the dramatic, macabre, and daily recreation of bloody events, narrated by the popular singer Joseíto Fernández and introduced by a catchy country-style melody of Fernández's own composition. This tune, *La Guántanamera*, would later be appropriated by Pete Seeger and spread throughout the world attached to the verses of another well-known Cuban, José Martí. Naturally, during baseball season, the feats of the professional teams competing for the championship were delivered as radio play-by-play. Three of these four teams represented metropolitan Havana. Fans could hear detailed descriptions of the hitting prowess and basepath speed of Marianao Tigers star Orestes Miñoso, or the catches of Havana Lions outfielder Edmundo Amorós, both of whom would become familiar to U.S. listeners (if anglicized as Minnie Minoso and Sandy Amoros) when the Major League color bar finally came down. Miñoso became a frequent guest of honor at the societies of color, including both the upper-crust Club Atenas and the more popular Buena Vista Social Club. The Almendares Scorpions games were broadcast from La Tropical stadium, their home park, built by beer magnate Julio Blanco Herrera above his brewery and beer gardens. The Lions' new Gran Stadium de La Habana in Cerro, seating 30,000 fans, opened in 1946.

Housewives at home and cigar-rollers in the great factories of Partagás and H. Uppman cried with equal ardor over the tragic events of the soap opera, *The Right to Be Born*, by Félix B. Caignet. Playing throughout Latin America, it became the model for the later radio and television *novelas* produced and aired in Mexico, Colombia, and Brazil. Musical shows featured the young composers and singers of the new music called *feeling* (Cubanized into *filin*), a form of the traditional bolero influenced by the sounds of cool jazz. *Filin*'s leading promoters included a station known by its broadcast frequency, 1010 or Mil Diez. This was the voice of Cuba's reconstituted and legalized communist party, the Partido Socialista Popular.

One of the most-listened-to programs on Cuban radio at the very beginning of the decade, however, was neither fiction nor music nor sports, but live transmission of the debates over a new Constitution to replace the one adopted in 1902. Fulgencio Batista, once he had established himself as Cuba's ultimate behind-the-scenes authority and put a definitive end to the revolutionary currents of 1933–35, displayed his usual capacity for maneuver. In the late 1930s, he entered into a populist and fence-mending phase. Unions took advantage of the opening to regroup into a new confederation. Likewise, the outbreak of World War II in Europe, followed by *habaneros* with the same intensity they awarded to the championship baseball series, had brought a new pluralism to the political scene. Exiles including the Hundred Days president Grau returned from their refuges in Mexico and the United States. As elsewhere in the world, the left enjoyed a summer of legality that preceded the Cold War, and under the politics of the Popular Front the communist parties themselves were more inclined to cooperate with former enemies than to compete with them. For all these reasons, the delegates elected to the constituent assembly—itself a delayed effect of the sweeping away of the old regime—brought all of Cuba's ideological currents into their deliberations in the Capitol building on the Prado, which only on the outside was a carbon copy of the one in Washington D.C.

Held in a semicircular chamber adorned with precious Cuban hardwoods, the sessions of this constituent assembly went out over the radio, live and unmediated, to the country at large. At one extreme were figures like the Italo-Cuban Orestes Ferrara, ex-general of the independence struggle, able orator, former cabinet minister and ambassador to Washington under the government of Machado, and leading conservative political figure ever since. Enriched through all possible mechanisms of the political apparatus of the Republic, Ferrara had built a Tuscan palace alongside the walls of the University of Havana, commanding a panoramic view of the old city below. At the other end of the spectrum, Salvador García Agüero, black and communist, pressed for a guarantee of workers' rights alongside his party's leader Blas Roca, a shoemaker by trade. In between, an array of old Conservatives and Liberals were surrounded by more youthful figures who had emerged from the revolution of 1933 and now took their inspiration from such varied currents as European social democracy, Latin American populism, Italian fascism, and the New Deal. This radiogenic assembly debated and finally approved one of the most advanced constitutions of its time, including such progressive measures as an agrarian reform, the final guarantee of votes for women and their right to hold office, and a percentage of the Gross National Product to be devoted exclusively to public schools. It was the first Cuban constitution free of the Platt Amendment, which Franklin Roosevelt, as part of his "Good Neighbor Policy" of avoiding direct military interventions in Latin America, had allowed to lapse after the fall of the Hundred Days government in 1934.

Not just radio but also railroads brought Havana and the rest of the country the presidential election campaign of 1940, a campaign of whistlestop tours that pitted Grau against Batista, now retired from his post as army commander and seeking the official presidential chair. By the end of the campaign, their smiling faces had been pasted on every street and wall of Havana and the interior. Grau was backed by a center-left coalition grouped around his new party, the Auténticos; Batista, by the Socialist Democratic Coalition, a strange conglomeration of conservatives and communists. Batista won. Four years later, in a peaceful, electoral transfer of power, he was succeeded by Grau San Martín, who returned to office as the embodiment of the hopes of '33.

In 1944 Havana was also shaken by a hurricane, the worst since 1926, which dumped great quantities of rain onto the city. Residents stocked up on candles and cans of guava paste and chocolate as was their custom, but the storm flooded low-lying neighborhoods, the water overflowing front steps and doorways and pouring into homes. Juan Valdés, an eight-year-old child of a single mother, watched the blocked sewers turn his street into a lake at the corner of Manrique and Salud in a Chinatown that had become as Cuban as it was Chinese. Though Juan didn't know it yet, the winds and rain had already destroyed the *solar* in Old Havana, just off the Plaza de la Catedral, where he, his mother, and his older brother had lived a few years before. Now the boys of his new block observed a group of grown-ups trying to clear a clogged drain, laughing at the fears expressed by older onlookers that the current could sweep one of these neighbors into the sewer.

But hurricanes were not the only threats to the tranquility of the citizens. The political renewal marked by the new constitution did not bring any new security to residents' lives. Many of the provisions of the Constitution of 1940 remained merely words on paper, without legislation or enforcement to put them into effect. In Havana, it could not be said that order and social peace reigned. On the contrary, the 1940s and the early 1950s turned out to be an era dominated by organized robbery, murder, violence, and administrative greed and neglect. The settling of scores among competing factions and gangs was the daily bread of the capital, and so was corruption in the halls of state.

From jobs and sinecures in government ministries to positions of leadership in the University of Havana, access to public employment and influence fell into the hands of mafias, often armed to the teeth. The various gangs were made up of ex-revolutionaries, hit men employed by political chieftains, or bandits pure and simple, all of them manipulated or tolerated by government itself. Student leaders carried revolvers as if they were fountain pens. Their armed factions, in the ever-present borrowing from the language of the northern neighbor, were called *bonches*, a species of Wild Bunch. The gangster films starring Edward G. Robinson and Paul Muni, which showed in Havana's movie houses, found their analogue in the city's public life. Gang battles, in addition to the standard baseball games and constitutional assemblies, came to be broadcast live. A sampling of headlines from the era yields many such as these: "While attempting to rob the cash box of the District Court of Guanabacoa, the mayor of that town was gunned down by an Army detachment." "Professor Ramiro Valdés Daussa shot dead by members of the university Bunch." "Student event gives rise to incident; deaths and injuries result." "Well-known concert composer Alejandro García Caturla murdered in full view on the street." "Leaving the apartment building Metropolitana, Dr. Modesto Maidique, ex-senator from Camagüey, shot dead."

In January of 1948, an army officer assassinated the leader of the sugar workers' union, largest workers' organization in the country, in full daylight in a railroad station, before witnesses—and got off. The coffin of Jesús Menéndez snaked through the streets of Havana, followed by a multitude; his assassination inspired the *Elegy to Jesús Menéndez*, one of the major poems of Nicolás Guillén. Not only worker and student leaders or ex-underground-revolutionaries and political figures fell victim to this fratricidal settling of accounts. Presidential security guards, ex-officials of the secret police, civilians, and military officers alike were assassinated on the street or in public offices, their murders attributed to political vendettas and quarrels over spoils among the factions and gangs.

The most spectacular case of political gang violence was known as "The Events of Orfila," and it was this one that most famously made its way onto the air. In the afternoon of September 15, 1947, members of the National Police led by Major Mario Salabarría surrounded the residence of a rival police captain named Antonio Morín Dopico, head of the force in the municipality of Marianao. The attackers laid siege with machine gun fire for almost three hours straight and received answering fire from within. This battle between opposing factions took place six blocks up Calle 64 from the house of Raquel Cañizares, just outside Buenavista in a more prosperous district commonly called Orfila, after a store on the corner of Avenida 31. Radio Reloj reporter Germán Pinelli (later to become one of the most popular television icons of the 1950s), who was present from the start, positioned himself as close as possible and narrated the firefight as if it were a ball game, giving a minute-by-minute account over the background of his station's signature ticking clock.

The residents of Havana listened, horrified, to the moment in the bloody spectacle when the attackers, after swearing to respect the life of Morín's wife Aurora Solar if she would leave the house, shot her down as she walked out waving a white sheet. Only at the end of the carnage, when the massacre was over, did a detachment of the constitutional army appear from nearby Camp Columbia, ensconced in tanks and tossing tear gas grenades.

Hand in hand with gangsterism, government corruption matched any of the true crime stories on Joseíto Fernández's show. Though run-of-the-mill embezzlement by the "kleptocracy" had ceased to be news in Havana, the case of José Manuel Alemán was an exception, a story out of the Arabian Nights. Alemán was Minister of Education in the Grau government that took office in 1944, and he was the most spectacular practitioner of the *botella*—the bottle, universal Cuban term for no-show jobs in the government apparatus. In the Ministry of Education in the 1940s, an estimated 13,000 jobholders appeared only to collect their pay—if they appeared at all, because many *botelleros* were phantoms whose invented names covered direct embezzlement of funds. José Manuel Alemán's rolls of *botelleros* swelled to such proportions that he was said to keep a soap opera writer on retainer to invent the necessary mass of ghost names. In his moment he was the richest man in Cuba, wealthier than any sugar baron, piling up real estate within the borders of the national territory and colonizing South Florida as well. He bought the Miami sports stadium in the name of his son, and apartment buildings along Biscayne Boulevard in the name of his wife, while for himself he acquired Cape Florida, a palace to the taste of Al Capone who had in fact been its owner in earlier days. Alemán's gifts to friends ranged from Cadillacs to night clubs, and on one occasion, to a very special friend, he gave the Marianao baseball club worth half a million dollars at the time.

On the afternoon of October 10, 1948—the eightieth anniversary of the outbreak of the Cuban independence struggle—Minister Alemán led a fleet of trucks from his offices through the narrow streets of Old Havana, to the Treasury of the Republic at the corner of Obispo and Cuba, where they had a mission to fulfill. Alemán's men, with himself at their head, entered that edifice through the doors of its Wall Street façade and passed through the Art Deco interior to the vaults, where they withdrew funds variously estimated from $50,000,000 to $174,250,000, loaded these stacks of bills into the trucks, and then drove to a chartered aircraft. The Minister, his followers, and the money all took off for Miami, where they passed through customs without any difficulty, and that was that. The only thing that kept Alemán from living happily ever after was his death from natural causes, which came seventeen months after his great feat of embezzlement.

Grau's Auténtico successor Carlos Prío took office with pledges to respect citizens' lives and the public treasury, but matters did not improve. The official two-year investigation into the details and the guilty parties in the Alemán case pointed a finger at President Grau himself. On the eve of the judicial process, however, the five thousand pages of inquiries and evidence disappeared as if by magic from the office where they were held. Neither Alemán nor Grau was ever formally charged. Grau would die of old age in 1969 in a very different Havana, a relic of the old order, still ensconced in the mansion on Fifth Avenue in Miramar which he called "The Shack." After his death, the estate became a home for children with no parents able to care for them.

Amidst theft and violence, Havana went about its business, still its noisy and vibrant—if increasingly cynical—self. With the coming of World War II, sugar crops and export revenues finally regained the levels of pre-Depression years, illustrating the thesis once propounded by Orestes Ferrara that the country lived off a "vulture economy." In Havana, as was always the case, the numbers employed in commerce, transport, and public or private services dwarfed those in manufacturing, since most consumer and industrial goods were imported from the United States. On this precarious foundation, outside the docks and government offices and the financial district, the city hummed to the rhythm of retail trade much as it had in the days of the Spanish fleet.

Every few blocks, a corner store, a butcher shop, a bar, and a pushcart or two of root crops and vegetables spread out along the street, joined by a laundry, a stand that took barely-clandestine bets on the numbers, a small *botica* or pharmacy, and stands selling tiny hamburgers called *fritas* or small cups of oysters in cocktail sauce.

A twenty-centavo *frita* accompanied by a three-cent glass of cold pressed sugar cane juice could quickly kill the hunger of those without time or money to lunch on anything else. The oyster stands were surrounded by standing clients, almost always men, who attributed sexual stimulant properties to this dish. The *botica* owner was happy to save his customers the cost of consulting a doctor, by recommending Cuajaní Jordán elixir with ephedrine to combat a cold, or Scott's Emulsion as a general pick-me-up.

All these establishments created a dense network of immediate goods and services within a radius of one-or two-hundred yards, or less in the poorer and more populous barrios. The web that connected all these elements was an impalpable buzz generally called the *bulla*, the city's commotion and its noise. Vendors took to the street early in the morning with their chants which had been passed down over generations, offering treats that might be tamales or snowcones, peanuts or mangos, sour-sweet mamoncillos or coconut filled caramels. They offered door-to-door services ranging from sharpening knives to tightening bedsprings, fixing irons or sweeping ceilings free of the city's grit and soot. They hawked newspapers by calling out the headlines, or they proclaimed their willingness to shine shoes.

These hawkers' chants had long since made their way into popular music, so that Rita Montaner's piercing voice singing, "Housewife, don't go to bed without eating a peanut cone," was as famous in Paris, London, and New York as in Havana, where it echoed through the city on radios and *victrolas* (as record players were universally called). Every bar had its community victrola, ready to play the tunes of the customers' choice, and from early in the day they filled the air with the boleros, guarachas, and sones that radio disc jockeys and word of mouth had enshrined as hits. The voice of Roberto Faz made whole barrios vibrate as he crooned, with double entendres equal to those of Montaner, "I tighten springs, children's cradles or old folks beds, I tighten springs" or "Some are not and some are not, the tamales that Olga sells."

At the center of this web was always the corner store or *bodega*, humming with the murmurs of news and gossip while news or music played on the radio as well. The bodega was open before the neighborhood residents set off for work, and housewives and other clients showed up early too. This market supplied the basic foods of the working–class Cuban diet—rice, beans, butter, corn meal, sugar, coffee—as well as nonperishables such as canned sweets and conserves. Most buyers depended on a popular system of credit, the *fiado*, which allowed them to acquire the so-called *factura* (literally a bill, but figuratively the weekly or monthly market basket of basic goods) and make good on their debt when payday came at the end of the month.

The bodega-keeper, whether Spanish, Cuban, or Chinese, offered not only credit and supplies but also the use of his telephone, and he served as barman to customers who stopped by to drink "the morning" or "the evening"—the shot of aguardiente or cheap rum taken on the way to or from work. Sometimes the bodega itself was the place to play one's daily number, at the same counter that dispensed Lucky Strikes, Peter's Chocolate Bars, and the Hershey's Kisses which enabled Cuban sugar to make its way from the Hershey mill east of the capital, north to Pennsylvania, and back again. This diversity of functions meant that movement in and out of the bodega door was constant, and the murmur emanating from it spread from the corner down the street. In districts like Vedado, the bodega was also where the housewives and the servants of the block rubbed elbows and chatted across class barriers.

Alberto Motola never acquired a *bodeguero*'s license, but he did prosper in Buenavista. He expanded his store to reach the nearest corner, adding glass display windows, broadening his stock beyond kitchenware and fabrics to clothing, hardware, housewares, school uniforms, and books. By the end of the decade, he managed to buy the building he had previously rented, with an apartment upstairs for his family, by way of a mortgage from the branch of an American bank. He rented another storefront, across the street next to the local café, and set up a bargain shop where he sold out-of-season clothes and leftover goods. Surprisingly or not, he also joined the Popular Socialist Party, enrolling in courses offered by an affiliated social organization about both politics and commerce, from which he graduated with a certificate in bookkeeping.

Small businesses like Motola's were not exempt from the reigning corruption. His Old Havana suppliers on the Calle Muralla arranged to import clothes and fabrics without paying even the reduced tariffs levied on U.S. consumer goods. "A ship would come from the U.S. carrying refrigerators," his son Daniel later recalled, "and inside they'd be stuffed with clothes that weren't declared to customs. The extra profit on the clothes paid for the refrigerators, almost." Local merchants had to pay off the local police in return for protection, because the police in barrios like Buenavista had ties with both merchants and thieves. "My mother had been working late decorating the shop windows," Daniel also recalled, "and had two dolls from a famous factory, that cost forty pesos each, which was the top of the top, there was nothing more expensive. When the store closed for the night, the police chief came by with his wife, and they saw the doll and wanted it, so they took it. There were other kinds of bribes to pay, but my mother was particularly bitter about this one."

The distinctive character that the webs of small stores gave to each neighborhood belied an instability as Havanans both new and old moved and moved again when they failed to keep up with rising rents. Juan Valdés's mother and her two sons—white and poor—moved frequently throughout the 1940s and the early 1950s, from one room to another in solars and cuarterías from Old Havana to Chinatown to Casablanca, La Vibora, and Luyanó. This cycle ran from the day they arrived with their bundles of belongings and paid a month in advance, to the day they couldn't pay any more, had used up their security deposit, and had twenty-four to forty-eight hours to move to another and always transitory home. In Juan's childhood memory, that constant movement was marked by the changing faces of the other boys who spun their tops in the doorways of the various solars. At the home he remembers best, the one at the corner of Manrique and Salud where he witnessed the hurricane, the web of stores included an agency with a moving truck, another staple of the time.

The radio offered something for such families too. To the vast numbers of working- and middle-class Havanans who dreamed of escaping from the spiraling rents of the ever-more-crowded capital, the Crusellas soap company offered prizes inside its popular bars of Jabón Candado laundry soap, which wives, daughters, grandmother, and housemaids all over the city used to launder clothes in washboard sinks. Along with the company's radio jingles about the purity and endurance of its soap, Crusellas advertised that the lucky buyers of certain bars of Jabón Candado would find a small plastic capsule embedded in the middle of the soap. Inside that capsule would be a slip of paper announcing what gift the customer had won. The top prizes were houses or apartments. There were two of these "*casas de Jabón Candado*" on 41st Avenue near Buenavista, halfway between the Tropical Stadium and the block where the Events of Orfila had taken place. They're still standing

"Casa de Jabón Candado," Avenida 41 and Calle 58, a few blocks from Buenavista. These houses were given as prizes to lucky buyers of Jabón Candado brand soap—the padlock design that decorates the house was the soap brand's logo. The second story was added later by the owners, probably post-1959.
Photo: Nancy Falk.

today, identifiable by the padlock logo (*candado* means padlock) pressed into the plaster, as it was into the bars of soap.

When Juan Valdés contracted tuberculosis, a common enough ailment in the crowded neighborhoods where he lived, he began a series of stays in hospitals and boarding schools for poor children in need of medical treatment, arranged through relatives with the necessary low-level political connections to get him in. But at the age of fourteen, much like Alberto Motola a generation before him, he went to work. His first job was in a Centro Habana laundry called El Buen Gusto (good taste), for twenty-five pesos a month. His morning walk of twenty blocks took him through the barrio of

Colón, a dense area six square blocks made up almost entirely of brothels, relatively peaceful at that hour because the employees were not soliciting customers at their doors. He recalls something hypnotic about the whole walk, "because in Havana you went walking and melodies accompanied you, from victrola to victrola, a new one each time you crossed a street, each playing a new song, and varying from neighborhood to neighborhood according to class and taste, though with a certain repetition of the hits."

A few years later, still in his teens, Valdés got a new job nearby the old one, joining his brother Tony in the Indochina department store. The Indochina, property of a Jewish Cuban named Max N. Lichy, was so called to make the store seem exotic, not because of the independence war then underway in that far-off land. It was on San Rafael near Galiano, close to the legendary El Encanto, in the busy retail district. El Encanto was joined in the early 1950s by two modern and sophisticated department stores, Flogar and Fin de Siglo. Some called this intersection "The Sinners' Corner" in honor of both the expensive purchases and the extra-marital flirtations that inevitably took place there. On the fourth corner of Galiano and San Rafael stood one of the capital's several Woolworths— known in the language of the city as the Tencén (ten-cent).

For those who couldn't afford to do their shopping in such bastions of style and taste, window shopping was a cheap and addictive form of entertainment for Havanans of all classes and colors. The culture of decorative shop windows reached its maximum expression there. El Encanto, above all, was famous for dressing mannequins in a dozen gleaming windows in its own designers' versions of the latest styles from the runways of Paris and New York. At the beginning of September, when the sun still fell with full summer force on the polished granite sidewalks of the shopping district and the people of Havana sought refuge in the central air conditioning of these retail palaces, an annual announcement that "It's Autumn in El Encanto" accompanied the mounting of a new seasonal display.

When Juan Valdés got a job as floor cleaner, elevator operator, and window display assistant in the Indochina, that meant a salary of sixty pesos a month as compared to the twenty-five he'd been making in the laundry, or the legal minimum of forty-five. It meant, too, working in an establishment that complied with the legal eight-hour day. Every month he gave half of his salary to his mother, with whom he still lived, and had the rest for his personal

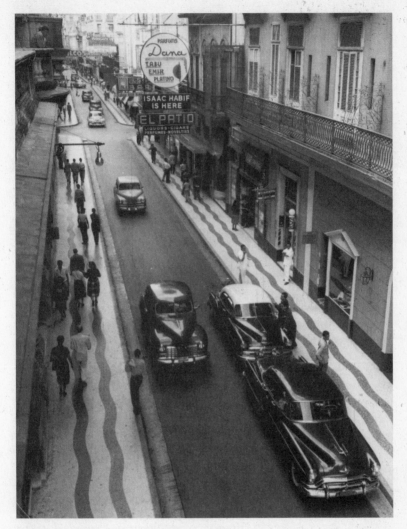

Calle San Rafael, in the Centro Habana shopping district, with polished granite sidewalks, late 1940s or early 1950s.

use. So he dreamed of a MacGregor brand shirt he had seen in window of Fin de Siglo, emblem of distinction, elegance, and current style that he could wear on Sundays, freshly pressed at the Chinese laundry, with pride. A MacGregor cost fifteen pesos, half of his monthly budget, so he availed himself of another institution of the era, a charge account. Some of the big stores issued their own charge cards, like their North American cousins, and others cooperated in an arrangement that offered a credit of fifty pesos, payable over a period of five months and good in several different stores.

Thus the two poles of credit and commercial advertising drove the popular imagination, in a consumer market which was highly stratified yet among the most sophisticated of Latin America and the Caribbean at the time. Cuba had one of the highest per capita incomes in Latin America, and the distribution of this income was skewed toward Havana. But the cost of living in Havana rivaled that in U.S. cities where average incomes were several times greater. In addition, of the total national labor force, 55 percent worked less than thirty weeks a year. Though the dead season in the countryside accounted for much of this high percentage, unemployment threatened wage workers and professionals in the capital too. Economically, residents of Havana lived with uncertainty. This increased public anger at the evident pilfering of the public treasury all the more.

It was no aberration, therefore, when the ageless Caballero de París, who had made himself a popular institution as he walked the streets of the capital for the past thirty years, decided to write in large letters on the wall of a prominent building, "Long Live King Dr. Carlos Prío Socarrás"—a protest against the impossibility of holding the president accountable in any way. Arrested and brought before a judge for this act of disrespect, the Caballero was sentenced to confinement in the mental hospital of Mazorra, on the city's southern outskirts. This action against one of the city's treasured characters brought an outcry from the public and press, and the president himself decided to make amends.

Acting under presidential decree, Havana's chief of police Cornelio Rojas took custody of the Caballero, brought him to a clothing shop where he could be fitted out in a decent suit and tie, and delivered him to the Presidential Palace for a personal interview with Prío Socarrás. The content of their conversation was not reported (though the press in general attributed to the president an affinity for nightlife and bohemia)—only that the Caballero left the palace, recovered his cape *a la* Three Musketeers, his rope belt and pencils, his mysterious bundles, and installed himself again along the city's streets, from whose sidewalks and arcades he declaimed speeches such as this: "I assure thee all that, God be Praised, the worthy Minister of Public Works restoreth to our metropolitan capital its ancient sense of beauty and loveliness. See thee not those potholes that so resemble miniature valleys, that in traversing them we enjoy the exquisite sensation of treading in the footsteps left behind by prehistoric animals of the remotest and most distant times?"

In a way that would have much greater reverberations, anger at corruption also found its outlet on the radio. Attacking the rampant corruption tolerated and promoted by the Auténtico administrations, a new breakaway opposition party called the Ortodoxos adopted the slogan "morals over money," gaining instant popular support. The chief communications medium of its charismatic leader, Havana Senator Eddy Chibás, was his radio hour. From the studios of station CMQ, he denounced cases of public embezzlement and the abuses of the Cuban Electric Company (which was, despite its name, owned and headquartered in the United States). Naming names and exposing more than twenty individual cases of high corruption, Chibás' weekly broadcasts made him a dangerous magnet for popular discontent, a likely candidate for president in the elections scheduled for 1952, and a growing threat to the powers-that-were: political parties, sugar barons, government officials, the established press, and even the radio networks themselves.

Among the many who listened regularly to this program were Carlos Larrinaga and Raquel Cañizares, now married and living in the old Buenavista house that Raquel's grandfather had built. Carlos also knew Chibás personally, because the Café Las Villas, on Galiano near the showroom and repair shop of Victor Adding Machine Company, was a regular haunt of both. While not Ortodoxos, the couple respected Chibás's political agenda and his radio show.

In typical stormy style, Chibás one Sunday afternoon denounced Minister of Education Aureliano Sánchez Arango, the infamous Alemán's successor, for having diverted school breakfast funds to buy real estate in Guatemala. But the minister mounted a spirited defense, questioning the basis of the charges, and enlisted the support of powerful groups including the owners of Chibás's own platform, Radio CMQ. Research by Chibás's associates failed to turn up definitive proof.

Put on the defensive by the acid attacks from Sánchez Arango and his followers, and seeking to keep the morale of his movement alive, Chibás came to the studio on Sunday, August 5, 1951 with something dramatic in mind. He broadcast his most famous speech, the most dramatic appeal to the public conscience heard during the years of the Republic. "People of Cuba," he concluded, "this is my last clarion call!" Then, with the radio microphone still open, he shot himself in the chest. His motives have never been completely established (some say he meant only to wound himself), but he lingered for a week in critical condition, and his funeral ceremonies lasted for another three days—the largest popular funeral to that date in a city that, as we have seen, knew many.

Although Chibás's death was a blow to his new party, some of the younger Ortodoxos who came of age in the shadow of his leadership played important roles during the tragic days surrounding his death. One of them, whose statements over the radio during Chibás's deathbed days first made him known outside the precincts of the university, would later be the subject of a good deal of talk. As a law student he had been involved in one of the campus *bonches* but had lately taken another path. He was running as an Ortodoxo congressional candidate in the elections scheduled for the following year. Fidel Castro was his name.

12

City Lights: The Fabulous Fifties

When public works czar Carlos Miguel de Céspedes's sumptuous Villa Miramar was sacked in the rioting that followed the fall of Machado in 1933, among his treasures that disappeared was, appropriately enough, a painting that depicted the fall of Rome's Iberian city of Numancia to the Visigothic hordes. Some years later, considerably after Céspedes had returned from his brief exile in the United States, he found the missing canvas quite by chance. He spotted it on a wall in the Hotel Sevilla-Biltmore, just off the Prado, property of one Amleto Battisti, an Italian immigrant by way of Uruguay. The ex-official demanded his property back, and the hotel owner complied.

That's a true story, reported in *Bohemia*, the popular magazine for which Luis Larrinaga worked. The Sevilla-Biltmore also figures in a fictional story, perhaps better known. In Graham Greene's *Our Man in Havana*, an unassuming British vacuum cleaner salesman named Wormold is summoned to an appointment in the magnificent though slightly tattered Sevilla of the 1950s, in room number 510. Wormold had lived in Havana for fifteen years, Greene tells us, long enough to watch the boys who had once charged a nickel to guard his car grow up into men offering him taxis and girls. He declines these offers, even though he walks with a limp through a city that seems to "turn out human beauty on a conveyor belt." When he gets to the Sevilla, at eleven in the evening, he takes refuge in the darkened, air-conditioned bar, which he finds to be full of American tourists nursing their drinks. Then he goes upstairs to meet his fate, which is to be inducted into his country's secret service as a spy.

Our Man in Havana is set in the Havana that has lodged in the nostalgic American imagination ever since: a city of bright lights and dark corners, glamour and grit and gambling, open-air shows and secret conspiracy, high rollers and traveling salesmen, strategic position and sensual allure. Or as Greene put it in a note about the impressions that caused him to set his novel there, "this extraordinary city where every vice was permissible and every trade possible." That Havana did exist, alongside others. The Hotel Sevilla may serve as an entry point.

The Sevilla was famous for its courtyard café where mambo king Damaso Pérez Prado held sway, and for its illuminated Roof Garden where Cuban and American elites had long held their luncheons and balls. It was also famous for its casino, just upstairs from the cafeteria, where silver roulette balls danced in spinning wheels and blackjack dealers held sway. Like a growing number of Havana's tourist hotels, it was controlled by the mafia. Amleto Battisti surely felt no chagrin about being caught in possession of a purloined painting, because he was founder of one of the leading crime families of the capital. His silent partners in the Sevilla's gaming room included Santo Trafficante, Jr. and Meyer Lansky, both of them increasingly present in Havana as American mafia interests and investments grew.

Gambling was no U.S. export to Cuba, of course. Cards and dice had been favored pastimes of all classes in the port city since the days of the Spanish garrisons and fleets, with bets on cockfights joining soon after. The state lottery became a major national institution under the colonial administration and then, after a brief hiatus, under the republican one, through which tens of thousands of itinerant ticket vendors represented the lowest rung of political patronage. The *bolita*, the extralegal numbers racket, emerged first in the Barrio Chino and then spread throughout the city under the aegis of various syndicates, of which Battisti's was a major one. The capital's pattern of comings and goings, the contrast of immense inherited riches with immigrants or freedmen starting from nothing, its folklore of chance meetings and striking coincidences, its rituals of divination drawn from *santería* and spiritism—something in its soul fed Havana's addiction to games of chance.

Guiding themselves by the symbols of the Chinese *charada*, residents of Havana who dreamed of a horse ran out to bet on the number one in the weekly national lottery or any of the underground games which took bets and paid out pots every day. Those who passed a nun on the street hurried to bet on five, those who had just caught a fish along the Malecón bet on ten, those who like Miss Muffet were visited by a spider bet on thirty-five, while those on whom a butterfly magically alighted were sure that the winning number would be two. Those who passed by a funeral cortege crossed themselves or didn't, but either way they bet on number eight. To drum up more business, some numbers racket bankers would offer a hint for the players to interpret—such as announcing that the winning number would be linked with "an animal that walks on the roof without breaking the tiles." Customers would hurry to bet on four, which the charada represented as a cat; the swindle became apparent when the winning bet drawn was the elephant, number nine.

Besides these games of chance played in barrios of every class, and the cockfight which was most common on the outskirts of the city, Havana also boasted the Oriental Park horse track in Marianao, where Carlos Larrinaga and Raquel Cañizares had met at the Club Ameno dance. Oriental Park was joined in the 1950s by a dog track on the traffic circle by Marianao's beach district, across from the imposing Havana Yacht Club. At these posh locations where victory depended on the feet of thoroughbreds or the paws of greyhounds, the prevailing bets were not the *centavos*, *medios* (nickels), *reales* (dimes), and or *pesetas* (twenty cents) of the lotteries, but Cuban pesos, pegged to the dollar at the rate of one to one. So the U.S. mafia did not arrive in Havana to implant a new vice. Rather, it promoted a particular new style of gaming—luxury casino gambling dominated by blackjack and roulette. This was an evolution, one more instance of the meeting of "interior" and "exterior" in Havana.

America's organized crime families had founded their fortunes, in part, on the traffic in Cuban rum during Prohibition. After the demise of Prohibition, they returned to Havana in the late 1930s and 1940s as advisers and investors in casino gambling, working with whoever was in power at the time. In 1946, the Hotel Nacional had been the site of a famous mafia conclave convened by Meyer Lansky's boss and boyhood friend Lucky Luciano, at which the major chieftains met in safety, entertained by Frank Sinatra among other headliners, to plan their postwar rackets and division of the spoils in the United States and abroad. This was the conference at which the execution of Buggsy Siegel was decreed. The best of all relations with the U.S. crime families, however, was formed by Fulgencio Batista, who had originally brought Lansky to Cuba in 1938 to reorganize and professionalize gaming rooms in the Oriental Park clubhouse and the nearby Gran Casino Nacional. When Batista returned to power in the 1950s, therefore, the stage for a new act was set.

Batista, like Eddy Chibás, had declared himself a candidate to succeed Carlos Prío in the presidential elections scheduled for November of 1952. But his prospects were not encouraging, even after Chibás's suicide, and in that unsettled climate he decided to seize the moment at hand. On Monday, March 10, Havana woke up to the news that the retired general and ex-president had taken power in a coup d'etat. The coup began in Camp Columbia, seat of the army general staff and site of the coup that Batista had helped lead nineteen years before. Within forty minutes, the general and fifteen other plotters took control of the main military bases in the capital. The remaining major bases, in Santiago de Cuba and Santa Clara, were soon in their hands as well. Without making any effort to resist the coup, President Prío abandoned the Presidential Palace, boarding a plane for Miami with his family. Batista declared himself president in law and in fact.

The surgical efficiency of the coup—which occasioned no deaths—was not so much a testimony to its planning as a symptom of the country's political state. The Spanish language *Reader's Digest*, widely read in Havana, described the coup in its Latin American edition a few months later as a "model revolution" carried out in a "lush, passionate, and fickle country" by a figure endowed with "the softness, swiftness, and daring of a panther." The magazine added that "Cubans are too disillusioned by a long succession of corrupt, inefficient governments—even though duly elected—to care for anything more than a hard hand at the helm." Asked about Communism—the issue of the day—Batista declared, "I'm a friend of the United States and the United Nations. Besides, I won't stand for any foolishness." The governments in power in Washington, London, and other Western capitals immediately

recognized Batista's dubious claim to the presidential chair.
Dwight Eisenhower's reasoning presumably reflected what
Franklin Roosevelt had once remarked about the Nicaraguan dictator Anastasio Somoza, "He may be a son of a bitch; but he's *our* son
of a bitch."

Once restored to power, Batista decided to take the business of
gambling more seriously than ever before. It became the centerpiece of his ambitious program to put Havana firmly in the center
of the American tourist map and to collect a personal share of the
gaming industry's profits in return for assuring its security and
safety. He put his old associate Lansky on the state payroll as an
official adviser, and offered licenses and matching funds to anyone
who would invest. "Havana will become the Monte Carlo of the
Caribbean," he declared.

The center of this Monte Carlo was to be El Vedado, no longer
"barred" as its name meant literally, but rather no-holds-barred,
and increasingly taking shape as the city's new downtown. Meyer
Lansky's personal project, the twenty-one-story seaside Hotel
Riviera, opened in 1957 on the site of a former sports arena at the
foot of Paseo along the Malecón. The world's largest hotel-casino
complex outside Nevada, the first hotel in Havana with central air
conditioning, the Riviera was topped by a giant neon-script logo
visible from both directions along the length of the Malecón. If it
cost an extravagant 18 million dollars to build, its gambling operation alone produced a net profit of 3 million dollars in the first year.

On the other side of Vedado, toward Centro Habana, a glittering
new gambling, entertainment, hotel and retail complex took shape
in the area called La Rampa, where Calle 23 plunged down a steep
slope from the heights near the university to the stretch of the
Malecón between the Ambar Motors showroom and the gardens of
the Hotel Nacional. Meyer Lansky took over management of the
Montmartre Club, just off 23rd, and made it the venue of choice for
the most serious gamblers with the most money to put at risk. He
set up another casino in the Nacional, which he entrusted to the
capable hands of his brother Jake. On Calle 21, his associate Santo
Trafficante, Jr., controlled the casino and the Salón Rojo nightclub in
his own new skyscraper hotel, the Capri. Trafficante, heir to the
numbers racket and other enterprises built by his father among
the Italian- and Cuban-American communities of Tampa, was the
mafioso who knew Havana best. He also ran the Sans-Souci nightclub and casino in Marianao, while he and Lansky shared interests

in the gaming rooms at the Comodoro in Miramar, the Deauville along the Malecón in Centro Habana, and Amleto Battisti's Sevilla-Biltmore downtown. The third of the towering new hotel-casino-nightclub complexes, the Havana Hilton, opened at the top of La Rampa in 1958.

High-end gambling was not the only manifestation of the mafia or of Havana's renewed role as a tourist magnet drawing Americans eager to see and to do what they could not see and do at home. American and Cuban gangsters used Havana as a way station for heroin smuggling to the United States, and facilitated increased domestic sales of heroin and marijuana as well. Drugs went by such street names as *manteca* (lard, as in the Chano Pozo number), *maní* (peanuts), or *taladro* (drill, for a joint). More visibly, prostitution flourished even more than in the past. No longer Paris but not yet quite Monte Carlo, Havana was increasingly called the Brothel of the Caribbean. Unlike during the times of Yarini, the sex industry of the 1950s was not contained within a single red-light district or tolerance zone, but rather distributed throughout the city in zones differentiated by class.

The sons of the Havana bourgeoisie, the moneyed tourists, and the mafia aristocracy rubbed shoulders in the elaborately decked out entrance rooms of the exclusive Casa Marina, located on the street of the same name, near Maceo Park along the Malecón. In this luxury bordello, just blocks from El Vedado, the services of the most exclusive Cuban and foreign prostitutes were sold. Their prices, differentiated by specialty, were equivalent to what many of the city's white collar workers earned in a month. There were also private live spectacles in Vedado palaces. Frank Ragano, Trafficante's lawyer, recalls in his memoir going to one such luxury residence redesigned as a series of stage sets where visitors could preview the actors and choose which they wanted to watch having sex with whom.

The middle-class and white-collar patrons, like the tourists of average means, went to the Calle Pajarito, south of Carlos III. These discreet brothels—known in Havana slang as *bayús*—were administered by madams under strict rules set up to maintain hygienic conditions. Their employees worked in rooms with individual baths and charged prices on the order of three pesos and up. A rung further down was one of the most famous red-light districts, the old barrio of Colón through which Juan Valdés walked to work, densely packed into a few square blocks between the commercial district along Galiano and the Prado. Here the sex business spilled out onto the streets, the bars, and the corners, where the prostitutes hawked themselves to factory workers, American sailors, employees of bodegas and laundries, and other men for a two-peso price. On a smaller scale, the sexual market of the Barrio Chino competed with that of Colón. Some of the prostitutes from each of these districts also performed as showgirls and actresses in the productions at the Shanghai Theater, famous mecca of Havana pornography on Zanja, the street that covered the route of the old Royal Ditch. The Shanghai's live shows competed with those offered by certain bars of the Playa de Marianao, immortalized in the film *Godfather II* and the novel *Three Trapped Tigers* by Guillermo Cabrera Infante. Finally, in the lowest echelon of Havana's sex market, the streetwalkers of the Avenida del Puerto served sailors for one peso or a few pesetas— usually without beds, often in doorways or between trucks or underneath boxcars on the rail line. They were still called *fleteras* (rented boats) as they had been centuries before.

As in the past, the sex industry was a way of life for thousands of women, most of whom stayed in it for many years. Tomás Fernández Robaina quotes a sex worker about her life during this era:

> Not all of us were always *fleteras*, or always worked in bars, or *bayús* or the better houses. Many of us passed through all these classes, or some of them. Everywhere, we had to pay bribes. The madams and landladies had to pay a quota every week to the Secret Police, the Bureau of Investigation, and the local police captain, and besides that each had to pay the cop on the beat a half peso or box of American cigarettes, because they wouldn't accept Cuban ones, and a full peso on Saturdays, or else they'd take us to jail. If we made some money, we'd run out and buy jewelry, bracelets or gold rings, though people never understood why. It was practical. If you got sick, or had a family problem and needed money, you could run to the pawn shop and take care of it that way. It wasn't just to show off. In other circles, people put money in the bank. Buying jewelry to pawn was what we did.

North American tourism, shipping, and naval "courtesy calls" all added to this business. "My fellow countrymen reeled through the streets," Arthur Schlesinger, Jr., later recalled of a visit to Havana in the 1950s, "picking up fourteen-year-old Cuban girls and tossing coins to make men scramble in the gutter." Says one of Fernández

Robaina's informants, "We were always glad to see the U.S. fleet come into the bay for one of their 'good will' visits, and we lived in such a world of our own that we thought it was funny when they went charging into decent houses by mistake. On the other hand we weren't fools. We knew what they were like, and we tried to take them for whatever we could."

High or low rollers in search of sex or drugs were not the only market for services that were illegal or unsafe to buy at home. Though abortion was nominally prohibited in Catholic Cuba, abortion clinics catering chiefly to American middle- and upper-class women were also a growth industry. This business too involved investment by organized crime and the promise of political officials to look the other way in return for a share of the revenue under the table.

At the same time, of course, Havana continued to attract U.S. businesses of a legal sort. In the 1950s, the Cuban capital developed its most sizeable colony of resident Americans (some of Cuban ancestry), many married to Cubans and living their lives on both sides of the Florida Straits. A look at the annual Anglo-American Directories of Havana for the years of the mid- and late 1950s reveals several thousand such residents, living alongside members of the Cuban elite in places like the new thirty-two story FOCSA condominium tower near the Capri and the Nacional, or the Riomar and Rosita de Hornedo apartment buildings developed by Alfredo Hornedo at the mouth of the Almendares on the Miramar side.

One Nelson Alfred Anderson, for instance, president of firm selling electrical, mechanical, and industrial goods, lived in the FOCSA, had his office nearby in the Radiocentro building on La Rampa, and belonged to the Havana-Biltmore Yacht Club and Havana Country Club. (Cuban-run with English-language titles, these private preserves had given birth to suburbs called "Biltmore" and "Country Club" too.) His neighbor Pastor Lagueruela, listed as a lawyer and industrialist, lived with his U.S.-born wife Rae Casas and their son Andy in one of the FOCSA's two twenty-ninth-floor penthouses; their club was the Miramar Yacht. Dr. Twyla Smell, who lived on the fourth floor, taught English at the University of Havana and at the private bilingual Ruston Academy in the neighborhood of Country Club Park, which enrolled both Cuban pupils and North American ones. The school's director, James Baker, is also listed as a member of the Havana-Biltmore and the American Club.

In general, the marriage (literal and otherwise) of the descendants of the old landowning aristocracy and the new rich who owed their wealth to speculation in real estate, hotels, and casinos characterized the elegant venues of Havana in the 1940s and 1950s. Old wealth and new socialized in the top-rung clubs known as the Big Five: Havana Yacht, Vedado Tennis, Havana Biltmore, Miramar Yacht, and Casino Español. Sunday afternoon gatherings in these private enclaves for croquet, tennis, golf, swimming, boating, smoking, drinking, and gambling were the focus of the capital's Cuban and North American elites. The clubs' patriarchs were men like Juan Gelats, owner of one of the largest banks relying on Cuban capital; Néstor González de Mendoza, real estate magnate, congressman, and banker; Laureano Falla Gutiérrez and Manuel Aspuru, sugar millionaires; and the brewery owner Julio Blanco Herrera, also owner of the Tropical baseball stadium named after his beer. Their membership included not only temporary Havana residents who maintained their U.S. citizenship, but Cubanized ones such as the textile magnates James and Burke Hedges, or the contractor Frederick Snare, president of the Cuban Country Club.

The case of Burke Hedges is illustrative of the social relations among industrialists from the two shores. His properties included an apartment in Manhattan, several factories including a rayon plant (and accompanying house) in Matanzas, and a two-century-old hacienda in the other direction from Havana, in Pinar del Río to the west. This Yemayá estate—named after the goddess of the sea and protector of family love in the Lucumí pantheon—was famed for its private landing strip and yacht anchorage, a pool and cabañas for guests, barracks for the many servants, and a monumental bar carved out of Cuba's ancient precious woods like the decorations of El Escorial palace in Spain. The Hedges' adoption of Cuban citizenship brought them several advantages. They were exempt from U.S. taxation, on the one hand, and rewarded by General Batista, on the other. Thanks to his friendship with the general, Burke Hedges was able to unload his rayon plant in a sale to the government when it did not flourish as he had hoped. He became director of the Cuban Association of Manufacturers, a member of the presidential advisory council and, in the last months of Batista's reign, Cuban ambassador to Brazil.

Outside the upper crust, U.S. influence was primarily cultural rather than person-to-person. In the 1950s, the impact of American culture grew stronger than ever before. Only the well-heeled could go see Eartha Kitt in the show at the Nacional, Nat King Cole in the Tropicana cabaret, George Raft greeting guests in the Capri's Salón Rojo, or Ginger Rodgers in the Copa Room of the Riviera on its inaugural night. Almost everyone, however, could put together the price of admission to see American films premiere in La Rampa cinema, halfway up the glamorous slope of 23rd, or the Warner cinema in the Radiocentro complex at the top of the hill. Radiocentro, an updated version of Radio City Music Hall, also housed CMQ's new studios for both radio and TV. In the mind of most Havana residents, the United States was still identified with efficiency in business organization, modern technology, gadgets for the home, and a faster pace of life. Juan Valdés and his brother Tony Irízar were both habitués of La Rampa, where their employer, Max Lichy, had coincidentally opened a new branch of his Indochina department store. In 1957, Juan was dazzled when the Cine La Rampa installed a stereophonic sound system to premiere *Around the World in Eighty Days* in the new technology of Todd-AO. The next year Radiocentro premiered another American invention, showing *This is Cinerama* on its specially equipped screen. Tony, like much of Havana, was a devotee of Hollywood musicals, knew the songs of Bing Crosby, Doris Day, and Frank Sinatra by heart, and could describe perfectly the steps of Cyd Charisse and Fred Astaire in each shot of *High Society*. He regularly read the magazine *Show*, which published the lyrics of songs on the U.S. hit parade.

Television, meanwhile, had gone on the air in Havana in 1950, the second city in Latin America to offer the new medium, thanks to the efforts of the Cuban radio entrepreneur Gaspar Pumarejo in collaboration with RCA. Pumarejo brought color TV from the United States in 1958, making Cuba the second country in the world to present color on the small screen. Tony Irízar, counting on a knowledge of major league baseball which rivaled his knowledge of American music and cinema, auditioned for *El Show de los 64,000 Pesos*, directed by Pumarejo himself on his Channel 2. In a city where three out of every five male inhabitants were experts in the abstruse science of baseball trivia, Tony got lucky and made it onto the popular quiz program, modeled after *The $64,000 Question* in the United States. For several weeks he showed off his mastery of the bases once stolen by Lou Gehrig, the hits currently racked up by Bob Skinner, and the way the last game of 1955 World Series between the Brooklyn Dodgers and the New York Yankees was decided by the fielding of the Cuban Edmundo Amorós who doubled Gil McDougald off first base. Then he prudently retired from the program with the sum of $4000 pesos. Having been a wage worker since the age of eleven, he quit the Indochina and invested the money in his own shop, a photographic studio which he hoped he could keep afloat.

Havana was an easy place for North Americans to live or visit precisely because of the implantation of customs and consumption styles characteristic of the northern middle class. *Habaneros* who could afford it drank Coca-cola, Pepsi, Orange Crush, and Ginger Ale, dressed to the nines in MacGregor and Arrow shirts, washed their clothes with Fab and Tide as well as Jabón Cándado, ate canned peaches from Del Monte and Libby, brushed with Colgate (pronounce col-ga-tay), washed themselves with Camay or what they called Pal-mo-lee-vay, wore U.S. Keds, rubbed Mum and Arrid in their armpits, rode Niagara bikes, and of course drove Oldsmobiles, DeSotos, Studebakers, and Fords. In Havana it was possible to get through the day reading one of the many English papers, breakfasting on Kellogg's Corn Flakes with hot cakes and maple syrup, and listening to American radio without needing to resort to short wave. Besides the easily available Miami stations, two Havana stations played North American music exclusively. One of them, Radio Kramer, got a new shipment every week of the latest records of American rock and roll.

This coexistence of the *yanqui* and the Cuban left a singular imprint on the identity of Havana. At Christmas time, Alberto Motola filled the sidewalk outside his Buenavista variety store with Christmas trees imported from Canada, and the shelves inside with glass balls, plastic icicles, and other ornaments from Jesus to Santa Claus. Alongside the trees on the sidewalk were stands full of cheap toys and more expensive ones, including great numbers of baseballs and baseball bats, destined for the neighborhood children on the Día de Reyes, when the ancestors of many residents used to parade through Old Havana to the Plaza de Armas in full African dress.

Similarly Tony Irízar, when he was not arguing over the artistic merits of Bob Fosse versus Ginger Rogers with the other employees of the Indochina, devoted himself to working out his own choreography, not of Hollywood musicals but of *casino*, the sophisticated Havana dance style that was the rage in the 1950s and is still dominant among the young dancers of the city today. When he got off work he would rush across the river to the Tropical Brewery's

Salón Rosado, an extension of its old beer garden into a new space beside its stadium on Avenida 41. The Salón Rosado was a world apart from the tourist cabarets and exclusive clubs, or even from the societies of the white and colored middle class. It was the mecca of casino for the masses of Havana, its clientele predominantly black and mulatto but far from exclusively so. It was the place where local bands underwent their trial by fire. There the Conjunto Casino, one of the major dance bands of the 1950s, wowed the dancers with the hits of moment, from the most heartrending bolero to the most frenetic guaracha, behind the extraordinary and versatile voice of its leader and lead vocalist Roberto Faz.

So for thousands and thousands of Havana residents, the city's aural universe ran the gamut of a syncretic identity where the Spanish, the African, and the North American flowed together as never before. This explains why the culture of the North was generally not rejected even by the groups with the most nationalist consciousness, including those most determinedly on the left. Antiimperialist sentiment could run parallel to the inclinations and tastes of Cuban popular culture, and Cuban popular culture had been linked to that of the United States for a long time. Further, personal contacts with Americans were not always of the sort Arthur Schlesinger recalled. "For the immense majority of the population," Juan Valdés remembers, "an American was a tourist. Tourism was an activity which existed in the country and was accepted, the way we accept the Italian tourists today. After all, the gringos of that time were no more uninteresting than the Italians who visit us en masse now. The majority of the Americans came to blow off steam and to drink rum. The one who was drinking rum was accompanied by Cubans who were happy to be around him, because the gringo paid for the bottle. Only, when those three marines climbed on the statue of Martí in the Parque Central and pissed on it, everything was different. Then everybody said they were sons of bitches, and hated them."

That last incident, famously caught by a Cuban photographer, illustrated the other side of the eternal love-hate relationship with Americans and the United States. Darker-skinned Cubans had to contend with the more strident racism of the neighboring culture as well. When Carlos Larrinaga and his white Cuban boss went to Chicago for a two-month training course at Victor Adding Machine headquarters, his boss unthinkingly reserved them both rooms at a middle-rung commercial hotel. When they arrived, Carlos was refused admittance, and told to go stay at a colored hotel instead. In Havana itself, the more a private club or luxury commercial establishment catered to the U.S. tourist trade, the more likely it was to discriminate against Cubans of color. Even Batista was refused entrance to the Havana Yacht Club because his ancestry was mixed.

Architecture followed U.S. trends too, particularly those associated with the "urban renewal" of American cities in the 1950s. Besides the skyscraper hotels, a slum clearance project made way for construction of the Plaza Cívica, a vast but automobilized and sterile new seat of government offices and monuments between Vedado and Cerro—far different from the green space envisioned there by plans drawn up by French consultants in the 1920s, and never realized. The historical and architectural value of the old city, meanwhile, counted for little with investors intent only on the new. The colonial heritage continued to deteriorate under the combined assault of sun, sea air, storms, and time. Visitors noticed, as they had in other times, that one of the most striking characteristics of Havana was its decay.

In 1953, twenty-seven-year-old Allen Ginsberg, unknown and drunk on cheap rum and Coca-Cola in the Havana Club bar that used to face the Plaza de la Catedral, saw that plaza as "weather-beaten tropical antiquity, as if rock decayed . . . blunt cornucopias and horns of conquest made of stone . . . a great, dumb, rotting church." Similarly Graham Greene depicted what he called "the ruins" of Havana: "The pink, grey, yellow pillars of what had once been the aristocratic quarter were eroded like rocks; an ancient coat of arms, smudged and featureless, was set over the doorway of a shabby hotel, and the shutters of a night club were varnished in bright crude colors to protect them from the wet and salt of the sea. In the west the steel skyscrapers of the new town rose higher than lighthouses into the clear February sky."

In one of those skyscrapers, a gala celebration was in progress on New Year's Eve of 1958, the night that brought the year of publication of *Our Man in Havana* to a close. In the Copa Room of the Riviera, the sons and daughters of sugar and real estate magnate families like the Suárez Rivas, the González de Mendoza, the Lobos, and the Gómez-Menas danced in the company of the sons and daughters of the Cuban political elite and the American organized crime families. They all looked forward to a modern Havana, a Havana of greater luxury and brighter lights. Among the plans in the works for the Cuban capital of the 1960s was an artificial island to be built in the curve of the Malecón, straightening the graceful seaside drive and hiding its baroque and sea-battered architecture behind a complex of still newer hotels, casinos, and high-rise apartment blocks, Miami-izing the 450-year-old city as never before.

Old Havana, for its part, was to be populated by a new wave of modern buildings. A sample was the ugly utilitarian steel-and-glass box of offices that filled the square block behind the Palace of the Captains General, where the Royal and Pontifical University of San Geronimo de La Habana had been founded two centuries before. For its roof, nothing less than a helicopter terminal was planned. Another urban renewal plan called for bulldozing a strip through the heart of Old Havana to make way for a new, broad avenue built for automotive traffic to link the Capitol and the port. This project would have demolished the pattern of narrow streets and short blocks designed by the planners of the earliest eras to provide cooling shade for high-ceilinged houses of the old city, converting it to an open field for modern commercial investment and development. But most of these plans never left the drawing board, because a different transformation, unimaginable to those present in the Copa Room of the Riviera, intervened.

13

Havana in Revolution

Just a week after that New Year's Eve of 1958, an army of bearded rebels led by Fidel Castro entered the other end of the Malecón from the Hotel Riviera, packed aboard trucks, armored cars, civilian autos, and vehicles of every other type. The image of Castro and fellow *comandante* Camilo Cienfuegos mounted on a tank, followed by smiling young long-haired guerrillas and passing through crowds of cheering Havanans, circled the world within a few hours. Though this was clearly the opening of a new chapter in the city's history, few could foresee how different it would be. To understand the change, we need to go back to the first months of 1952.

Three days after the Batista coup, the junior partner of a law firm called Aspiazu-Resende-Castro presented a formal accusation that Batista had violated the Constitution of 1940, and requested a prison sentence for the usurper, but Fidel Castro neither expected nor received a positive response from the courts. Soon after, some University of Havana students organized the first anti-Batista *tánganas*, a Cuban term meaning a heated argument, now more specifically referring to spontaneous political actions in which a series of speakers shouted speeches or slogans from improvised platforms on the stairs and benches in the central plaza of the school. One of these *tánganas* led to a demonstration descending the broad neoclassical stairway from that plaza, below the statue of Alma Mater, scene of many other demonstrations in the Machado era and since. The demonstration proceeded downhill toward Centro Habana, but at the corner of Infanta and San Lázaro the police opened fire. By coincidence, the first student victim of the dictatorship shared the surname of "El Hombre," as Batista had styled himself in his electoral campaigns. Rubén Batista's funeral became the first popular repudiation of the regime.

January of 1953, ten months after the coup, marked the hundredth anniversary of the birth of José Martí, "The Apostle," who by then was treated with the kind of secular religious devotion that name implies. The new government attempted to capitalize on the birthday with a lavish official celebration, but on the night of January 27, on the eve of that commemoration, a procession of students, youth, and other citizens preempted it. Carrying improvised torches, they avoided the fatal stairway, marching down the Avenida Universidad toward the Fragua Martiana, a memorial containing relics of the Apostle on the site where he had toiled in the quarries as a teenage prisoner of the Spanish crown.

Within the crowd spilling down the hillside, one group of 200, mostly young men, formed itself into military style ranks and squadrons. These were a section of the group within the Ortodoxo youth organized by Castro and Abel Santamaría, beginning to prepare for an armed action against the dictatorship at a time and place not yet known. Santamaría, a twenty-seven-year-old bookkeeper at the local Pontiac dealership who had previously been an office worker for one of the Hedges family's textile firms, was more typical of the membership of this group than was Fidel. Son of a sugar mill carpenter in the interior province of Las Villas, Santamaría had come to Havana in search of education, advancement, and a wider world. He was belatedly putting himself through high school while reading widely in politics, history, and other spheres. Castro by contrast was the son of an Oriente sugar planter, a self-made Spanish immigrant who had flourished by selling cane to the large U.S.-owned mills, to the point where he could send his son to Havana for a Jesuit high school education and then a university law degree.

After participating in the demonstration, this group henceforth assembled only in small subgroups in sites spread out through the city such as the apartment of Abel and his sister Haydée on the corner of 25th and O, a block from La Rampa and the roulette tables of the Montmartre. Six months later, 165 of them, including both Santamarías, reassembled far from Havana in a small farmhouse on the outskirts of Santiago de Cuba. There they boarded a caravan of innocent-looking Oldsmobiles and Chevies and proceeded to attack the Moncada garrison, the country's most important army base after Columbia. The failed attack, which cost the lives of many including Abel Santamaría, was seen as an act of madness by many sectors opposed to the dictatorship, the communists included. After a week of fierce repression, including torture and assassination of many of those captured during the attack itself, the dictatorship put Castro, his brother Raúl, and the remaining leaders on trial. They were sentenced to long prison terms on the Isle of Pines, off the south coast of Cuba, opposite the area which the first founders of Havana had abandoned to the mosquitoes four centuries before.

Two years later, in a gesture designed to demonstrate his moderation and generosity and establish democratic credentials for his regime, General Batista decreed an amnesty for all political prisoners. Castro and his colleagues returned to Havana where, taking advantage of a pause in press censorship, they declared that they would continue to fight. After a few months they left for Mexico, leaving behind a new underground political organization, the 26th of July Movement, named for the date of the Moncada attack. By December of 1956, when the group (including new recruits such as Ernesto "Che" Guevara) left Mexico on board a yacht purchased from a Texan who had named it *Granma* after his grandmother, the 26th of July Movement could count on some degree of resources and organization for clandestine struggle in the cities, particularly Santiago and Havana.

The 26th of July was not the only organization to attempt to dislodge the dictatorship by any means possible. Three months after the landing of the *Granma* ("more of a sinking," as Guevara later wrote), the University Students' Federation (known by its Spanish initials FEU) assaulted the Presidential Palace. José Antonio Echeverría, the architecture student and FEU president who led the action, was a well-known figure in his own right. Nicknamed Manzanita (Apple) for his round face and rosy cheeks, he had been arrested many times at the head of student demonstrations, and publicly beaten by the police. A short time before the attack on the Palace, a group under his leadership sneaked a banner into the stands of the Grand Stadium in Cerro during a nationally televised playoff game. Eternal rivals Havana and Almendares were competing for the championship, and the Lions, under a new agreement incorporating the Cuban leagues into the farm system of stateside organized baseball, pinned their hopes on St. Louis Cardinals veteran hurler Wilmer "Vinegar Bend" Mizell, who was positioning himself for a comeback by playing winter ball. At the right moment, the students unfurled their slogan "Down With the Dictatorship" in the outfield. The banner stayed in place for the few minutes it took police to charge onto the field from their choice seats and rush across the diamond with truncheons at the ready, to administer punishment in full public view.

The action at the Palace was much more ambitious, an attempt to behead the regime by executing the dictator, on the assumption that none of his military or civilian subordinates would have the skill or prestige needed to reorganize the ranks of the dictatorship, much less gain the respect of the citizenry who were fed up with the Batista government. They almost succeeded. The group of attackers drove a truck with the emblem of the *Fast Delivery* service up to the front door of the Palace and poured out. Armed with submachine guns, they overcame Batista's personal guards and reached his private office on the second floor. But Batista had managed to escape through a back door they did not know about, and to reach the top floor of the Palace where the bulk of his guards had the advantage of better cover and heavier arms. The survivors among the attacking group had to retreat under a rain of machine gun fire.

While this was going on, Echeverría and a smaller group assembled on La Rampa, where they took over the offices of Radio Reloj in the Radiocentro complex opposite the construction site of the Hilton Hotel. Echeverría's sharp, high-pitched voice, honed in the university *tánganas*, went out over the airwaves, declaring: "People of Cuba, the tyrant Batista has met justice in his own lair. The University Student Federation, in the name of the people, has come to settle accounts." A few seconds later, Radio Reloj went dead, interrupted in its central transmission tower while residents of Havana listened, electrified. Echeverría then tried to reach the university on foot, but police opened fire from a patrol car and left him mortally wounded on the sidewalk below its walls. The Apple was one of many to fall on the afternoon of the attack on the Presidential Palace, and in the night and the days of retribution that followed.

To avenge the attack, Batista unleashed a wave of terror that reached far beyond the FEU. That same night of March 13, Dr. Pelayo

Cuervo Navarro, former leader of the Ortodoxo party, was taken from his home by eight armed men. Cuervo's offense was that he had denounced the abuses of the Cuban Telephone Company, hikes in the rates of the electric company in violation of public utility laws, and the government's complicity in both. He was transported to the shores of the Laguito, an ornamental lake in the exclusive Country Club district, and riddled with bullets. The message to the "legal" opposition was clear: regardless of ideology or social position, no one opposed to the regime should feel safe. Many other political figures received warning visits that night from the SIM (Military Intelligence Service), the most feared of the regime's political police.

The FEU, however, suffered the most. Esteban Ventura Novo, chief of one of the Havana police divisions, discovered that several leaders of the attack were hidden in an apartment near the Fragua Martiana. Ventura's men stormed the apartment and killed the young revolutionaries Fructuoso Rodríguez, Joe Westbrook, José Machado, and Juan Pedro Carbó Serviat. Their bloody corpses were dragged down the stairs of the apartment building to the street, in full view of terrified neighbors.

That night, nocturnal Havana ceased—for many—to be the dazzling world it had been up till then. The underground networks of 26th of July, the FEU (now renamed March 13 Revolutionary Directorate) and to some extent the communists' Popular Socialist Party counterattacked the repressive organs of the dictatorship on their home ground. Col. Blanco Rico, head of the SIM, was killed by a Directorate commando squad in Meyer Lansky's Montmartre cabaret. The 26th of July proclaimed a new slogan, "0-3-C," which meant "No Buying, No Movies, No Cabaret" (*Zero Compra, Zero Cine, Zero Cabaret*). Revolutionary graffiti and leaflets exhorted citizens to boycott stores and entertainment venues as a way to highlight the society's political ills and to mobilize the discontent of merchants and entrepreneurs. Homemade bombs called *petardos* were placed in streets, parks, and other public spaces to dissuade the populace from going out at night and to make the security forces feel that the city did not belong to them. One memorable night, 100 *petardos* went off in different locations around Havana. *Habaneros* could not tell which explosions were the traditional nine o'clock firing of the cannon in the Cabaña fortress, and which were detonations of another sort.

For most of his nearly seven years of dictatorial rule, Batista governed through a suspension of Constitutional guarantees and with iron censorship of the press. U.S. journalists who managed to reach the Sierra Maestra and interview Fidel Castro's rebels were deprived of their notes and film by the army. News of the rebellion was available only from Radio Rebelde, the clandestine Voice of the Sierra, where the *Granma* expeditionaries had been reinforced by volunteers from cities and, especially, by landless peasants and smallholders recruited in the mountains themselves. Gluing their ears to radios turned down to minimum volume, so that they could not be overheard a few feet away, Havana listeners tuned in at night to the Radio Rebelde announcers, making out the course of the battles in the Sierra through the constant hiss of the shortwave.

Juan Valdés, while part of an aboveground group trying to bring the employees of the Indochina department store into the commercial workers' union under the protection of the country's labor laws, was also working in the anti-Batista underground. So was his brother Tony, who had been a member of the 26th of July Movement since 1954 (unbeknownst, of course, to those who watched him field baseball questions on TV). Alberto Motola and María Roffe were quietly selling 26th of July bonds to their Buenavista neighbors and customers, to raise funds for the rebellion. Buenavista was a barrio divided, since many low-level army officers lived in the end of the neighborhood closest to Camp Columbia, but as Raquel Cañizares remembers, "there were all types here—there always are—but there were many us opposed to Batista, the young people especially. Young people always want change, and Carlos had his ideas that came from his father, too."

The closer the end of the dictatorship, the more intense the actions in the cities grew. A general strike called for April 9, 1958 was supposed to provide a final urban push needed to topple the regime, by combining shutdowns of all workplaces with daylight armed actions. Though the rebels gained control of some provincial cities, especially Cienfuegos, for a few hours, in Havana the concentrated power of the army and police was too great. The strike failed, as did any possibility that the revolution might be carried out in Havana this time. Juan Valdés and Tony Irízar were identified as conspirators in the general strike, possibly fingered by the owners of the Indochina. Juan was fired under a new Batista law removing labor law protections from subversives, and both brothers were jailed. Daniel Motola remembers watching his parents burn the clandestine 26th of July bonds before they could be found by the police. From then on, rebel strategy turned chiefly to the Sierra, to a war of attrition against the army on ground friendlier to the guerrillas and unfamiliar to the regime. That summer, an exasperated Batista launched an offensive of 20,000 men attempting to occupy the Sierra and root the rebels out. Their defeat by a much smaller guerrilla force marked the beginning of the end.

Between blackouts produced by sabotage of electric installations, explosions of *petardos* and nighttime shooting, *habaneros* heard over

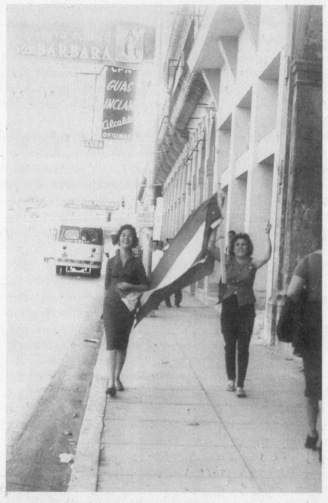

Celebrating the fall of Batista, January 1, 1959.

Photo: Instituto de Historia Archivo.

Radio Rebelde how the guerrilla war had spread beyond the Sierra Maestra in columns led by rebel commanders Che Guevara and Camilo Cienfuegos. The climax was the rebels' December siege of Santa Clara, the major city of the central region. Not many went out to enjoy Havana's legendary night life that tense New Year's Eve. Even the party at the well-guarded Copa Room of the Riviera received some two-hundred last-minute cancellations of reservations by phone. Just about midnight, Batista returned to Camp Columbia for the last time, to board a military aircraft that whisked him, his family, and closest associates to Santo Domingo. Havana awoke on New Year's Day to a state of delirium comparable only to August 12, 1933 when Machado fell.

In a city always filled with noise, the citizens outdid even themselves. Cars full of 26th of July and Revolutionary Directorate militia, now openly carrying weapons and wearing the armbands of their organizations, drove in all directions as they tried to capture remaining Batista henchmen. The crowds did not repeat the lynchings and sacking of mansions that had occurred in 1933, though they did direct their violence at parking meters and slot machines, both of which were believed to have directly fed Batista's pockets. The doors of the Castillo del Príncipe opened to let hundreds of political prisoners out. The rebel army column led by Camilo Cienfuegos soon arrived from Santa Clara, entering Camp Columbia by the same gate, number 4, through which Batista and his confederates had entered in the predawn hours of March 10, 1952. Cienfuegos, the son of a Spanish anarchist tailor, was the most prominent of the rebel commanders to hail originally from Havana. As a teenager he had participated and been wounded in early anti-Batista protests, then gone into exile in the United States where he worked as a waiter and dishwasher in New York. A few days after entering Camp Columbia, in a symbolic gesture to signify a break with the past, he personally took a sledgehammer to the wall that anchored gate number 4.

Che Guevara, in turn, arrived and set up his characteristically spartan headquarters in the fortress of La Cabaña, where the British gun emplacements had fired on the Morro 200 years before. On January 8, Fidel Castro and the main force of the Rebel Army arrived in a triumphal parade, passing through the city to cheers of jubilant crowds. Castro made his first postvictory speech in Havana at Camp Columbia to a gathering that numbered in the hundreds of thousands. "The tyranny has been overthrown," Castro said that night, "The happiness is tremendous, but nonetheless much remains to be done.

Perhaps all that lies ahead will be more difficult." He had already made clear—speaking from Santiago on his way to Havana—there would be no transitional governments or negotiations. The old armed forces had to surrender and be dissolved, and the old order would perish.

What would replace the old order was not yet clear. Whatever it was, Castro implied, would fulfill the hopes for social reform, national pride, and independence from foreign influence that had been frustrated in 1898 and in 1933. In the middle of his speech, two doves landed on the rostrum before him, and one on his right shoulder. The Catholics thought immediately of the Holy Ghost, and the *santeros* of the *orisha* associated with mental strength, Obatalá. Castro turned for a moment toward Camilo Cienfuegos and asked, "How'm I doing, Camilo?" Camilo smiled, and the crowd, charmed, burst into applause.

Outside the circles closest to Batista, enthusiasm for Castro and the bearded rebels was near universal in a jubilant Havana. Interviewed by the popular magazine *Carteles* as he strolled down Calle Maloja in Central Havana, the Caballero de París dropped his antique speaking style and declared, "I like the *barbudos*. Those boys are fine with me. My subjects are pleased to have them among us. But the issue of the beards should not be overlooked, because, just between us, they stole that idea. They're taking advantage of my popularity among the people of this town by imitating me."

Not all, however, was luminous in those initial glory days. Clouds appeared over the sky of Havana. The first, though not the only, blew in from the United States, which the rebels viewed suspiciously due to Washington's support of Batista, to whom the Eisenhower administration had supplied weapons until March of 1958. After cutting off the sale of arms, U.S. envoys had tried to convince the general to abdicate in favor of a successor who could take the steam out of the revolution and prevent it from coming to power.

"Never in any Latin American land has popular antagonism toward this country been more bitter than it is now in Cuba," reported U.S. journalist Carleton Beals, who had been covering the Caribbean and Central America since the 1930s. The Cuban press fiercely criticized U.S. ambassador Earl E. T. Smith for his past involvement in the granting of nickel mining concessions in Oriente to Bethlehem Steel, the shady agreements with the U.S.-owned Cuban Telephone Company which Pelayo Cuervo had denounced, and his support for elections that Batista had stage-managed in 1958. During the guerrilla war, Smith had denounced Castro in no uncertain terms, and had praised top Army figures even after the cut-off of arms sales.

In the event, the fundamental differences between the revolutionary government and the United States would hinge on agrarian reform and measures to undercut the traditional dominance of American companies—and, later, on Soviet ties and the fear of "other Cubas in the hemisphere." But the dominant theme in the first months of 1959 was the punishment of Batista officials judged guilty of violence against civilians. Starting on January 1, revolutionary tribunals organized by the Rebel Army had began to sentence army officers, policemen, and members of paramilitary groups in summary trials which led—if the accused were found guilty of killing unarmed civilians—to the firing squad. The Cuban press now reported the grisly details of murder, torture, and rape which they had been unable to report before. In profusely illustrated editions of upwards of 1 million copies, mass circulation magazines such as *Bohemia* and *Carteles* recounted the deaths of an estimated 20,000 victims at the hands of Batista's repression. They also listed the names of their killers, many now out of reach of the tribunals, having escaped to the United States or the Dominican Republic on the wee hours of New Year's Day.

While many Cubans found the trials and executions proof of the return of law and justice after long years of terror, they were counterproductive for the revolution's image abroad. "Spilling across Fidel Castro's Cuba," *Life* magazine reported, "an ugly tide of blood vengeance last week put a curious strain on relations between the liberated island's people and their friendly U.S. neighbors." The trials of Fulgencio Batista's "unlucky henchmen" lacked the necessary legal guarantees for the defendants, U.S. observers found, and were held before hostile crowds. Yet, as *Life* also reported, "Castro's support could not be doubted. Everywhere Cubans assembled to cheer him—and the executioners. 'There is hardly a family which has not felt the brutality of the Batista police,' cabled [*Life's*] correspondent. 'After seven years of rage, Cubans are now going to make the sadists pay.' "

One of the most controversial images to be reproduced around the world was a sequence of snapshot images of the firing-squad execution of Col. Cornelio Rojas, the same officer who had brought the Caballero de París to appear before President Prío ten years before. Under Batista, Rojas had become police chief of Santa Clara, where he had been responsible for numerous deaths and tortures which he carried out himself with instruments especially invented by an auto dealer friend. Nonetheless, the photographic sequence of his execution, as an old man in civilian dress, did not communicate any of the well-known sadism of the man. The volley of the bullets striking his head threw his hat several yards into the air, while his body shook from the impact of the blast.

The most famous of the public trials was that of army colonel Jesús Sosa Blanco, transmitted live on TV from the Sports Palace. Sosa was accused of causing the deaths of more than thirty peasants in the Sierra Maestra. The main witnesses were the survivors of the Argote family, the majority of whose thirteen members had been killed on his orders. Every Cuban with access to a television set saw Señora Argote point out Col. Sosa as the man guilty of the deaths of her parents and brothers, in a type of confrontation between the rural poor and the symbols of traditional authority that had never gone out over the airwaves before. Sosa Blanco lifted his hands and smiled, declaring, "I'm in the Roman circus, just like Jesus Christ." The colonel's statement and the photos of the angry crowd were circulated the next day by the AP and UPI wire services, as a proof that a spirit of vendetta dominated the revolutionary courts.

The prosecution of the killers of Dr. Pelayo Cuervo was typical in a different respect. The defendants were seven policemen (said to have also been involved in other, similar abuses and deaths), a sergeant from the Bureau of Investigation who was shown to have fired the six fatal shots, the ex-police chief of Havana, and the ex-chief of the SIM. The prosecutor demanded capital punishment for the killer and the seven participating policemen, and twenty years imprisonment for the two superior officers, Hernando Hernández and Carlos Cantillo. A private prosecutor, a well-known lawyer hired by Cuervo's widow, asked for the death penalty for Batista and two other superior officers as well. The tribunal's response was the death penalty for three of the police and long prison terms for the other four. Cantillo was sentenced to fifteen years in jail, and Hernández was absolved. The fact was, however, that neither Cantillo, nor Hernández, nor the sergeant who pulled the trigger stood at any risk. Like Batista, they were well out of reach, walking the streets of Miami or other cities abroad.

Beyond the trials, Castro converted the new medium of television into a nightly window into every home so equipped, a window that often remained open into the wee hours of the morning. On the small screen, he educated, chided, exhorted, explained, answered his enemies, and made decisions on the spot. On one occasion, while Castro was criticizing Francisco Franco's government's policy toward the Cuban revolution, the Spanish ambassador, the Marqués of Bellisca, burst into the studio to challenge him in the manner of a duel. Castro's idea of mobilizing voluntary teachers from the capital to begin reducing illiteracy in the mountains first appeared in the midst of a TV appearance, and before the program ended there were students signing up. At midnight, the *comandante* might turn up for a milkshake in the kitchen of the Havana Hilton—renamed Habana Libre—where the temporary headquarters of the rebel army had been set up, or he might drop into a crowded and inexpensive Chinese restaurant on the grittier Calle Infanta for a meal. In the Grand Stadium of Cerro, a team of Barbudos played exhibition games before the professional matchups, sometimes with Fidel on the mound and Camilo Cienfuegos behind the plate.

If much of that was theater, it was theater mixed with substantive measures too. Some of the government's early reform actions had direct and popular effects in Havana, like the institution of price controls that drastically lowered rents and electricity and telephone rates, or the abolition of private beaches and the end to racial discrimination in any venue open to the public as well as in private clubs. Casino gambling was banned quickly—though implementation was delayed for some months after croupiers, dealers, and other employers protested that they would be left without work. Renegotiation of labor contracts raised disposable income for many in the capital, in a variety of trades. But the agrarian reform, which broke up the large rural estates and guaranteed a minimum of land to any peasant, sharecropper, or squatter already working it, was a fundamental break with the past. It found echoes in the capital very soon.

To celebrate the 26th of July of 1959, poor peasants who had received land under the new law were invited to the city as honored guests, and Castro asked *habaneros* to express their respect by lodging these new landowners in their homes. The response to the slogan, "Open your home to a *campesino*" meant that half a million peasants, in their country clothes and straw hats, arrived in a dazzling city which received them with open arms. Those who couldn't find space in private homes were lodged on cots in the Hall of Mirrors, the Presidential Palace's gala main reception room. To be a *guajiro* (hick) in the capital suddenly lost its pejorative connotation, and became instead a kind of badge of citizenship, as normal as the bearded rebels—crosses, *santería* beads, and other amulets round their necks—scattering cigar ashes on the thick carpets of the Havana Libre before tumbling onto the nearest armchairs and sofas to sleep.

For the youth, especially, Havana in revolution meant new adventures and a redefinition of style. When they enrolled in the voluntary teachers' movements, and then in the "army" of the 1960–61 literacy campaign, they left behind electricity, air-conditioned movies, parental authority, and the pleasures of urban life to go to places reachable only on the back of a mule. Without pay, they taught reading and writing while relying on their own abilities and the support of people whose like they had never met before. For those remaining in or returning to the city, uniforms suddenly went from anathema to chic. Parading in militia outfit, carrying a gun, marching, and standing guard became the thing to do.

Juan Valdés, who had now finished three years of high school by attending at night, went to Oriente as a literacy teacher. He was followed two years later by Carlos & Raquel Larrinaga's first-born son Pablo, namesake of his great-grandfather the tamale vendor. Over the objections of fearful grandparents, but with the support of Carlos and Raquel who had both (as contemporary language had it) "incorporated themselves" into the revolution by taking up posts in new neighborhood organizations, Pablo went off with schoolmates at the age of twelve to help harvest coffee on lands redistributed by the agrarian reform. In inspiring youth to go to the countryside or join the militia, the revolution ruptured tradition in another way. It included girls in these mobilizations as well as boys. Particularly for girls of the white middle class, this was a radical break from the old attitudes of the capital. The writer Mirta Yáñez later described this rupture in her story "All us Blacks Drink Coffee" (the title taken from a song popularized by Rita Montaner), in which a middle-class white teenager goes to pick coffee in spite of her mother's dismay: "And who knows, your mother demands in a powerless rage, if out there you won't go so crazy as to fall in love with a Negro. And you know what it means to be a nice white girl, as white as the paper daisy that your mother crushes nervously between her hands in your birthday photograph, its yellow heart overflowing with innocence . . . How times change."

As the story indicates, the honeymoon between all of Havana and the triumphant revolution did not last very long. Antagonistic economic, social, and political interests emerged, and the first signs of a political opposition and a hostile emigration started to appear. Batista allies and business partners like the Hedges brothers departed first, as they lost their properties to the new Department for the Recovery of Stolen Goods. The owners of the Indochina also left, accused of having informed on the underground, and their department store was confiscated under a new law governing property left behind. Then the cross-class alliance that had temporarily accepted Castro's leadership against Batista began to break down over the radicalism of the reform program, and the increasing hostility between the new government and the United States. The interests affected by the agrarian reform included large cattle ranches and sugar mills with extensive landholdings, many of them owned by American concerns such as the King Ranch or United Fruit, and others by the upper crust of the Cuban bourgeoisie. Owners, executives, and stockholders of the casino hotels and the U.S.-based utility companies saw their power and income threatened, and many in the upper class were unnerved by the loss of the privileged physical spaces they had exclusively enjoyed until then. The moderate anti-Batista figures who had made up Castro's first cabinet saw that real power lay with the Rebel Army, and over one or another issue, they began to resign.

Within the first few months, by late spring of 1959, the State Department and CIA had decided that it was "impossible to carry on friendly relations with Castro government" and that it was necessary to "devise means to help bring about his overthrow and replacement by a government friendly to the United States." One by one the mansions of Biltmore and Country Club and many in Miramar and Vedado began to empty out, as their residents emigrated for what they thought would be a temporary stay in Florida or New York until things got back to normal again. In turn, the affected sectors of the professional class who had traditionally gone to American-affiliated private schools and worked for the Americans or the Cuban upper crust began to take sides one way or the other. The conflict between the revolution and an emerging counterrevolution began to fill more and more public space.

At night, the ghostly silhouettes of airplanes without running lights flew over the city and strafed certain buildings, or dropped fire bombs on outlying fields of sugar cane. These planes took off from airfields in Florida, flown by pilots from Batista's air force or by ex-rebels who opposed the direction taken by the revolution since its triumph. Nighttime explosions began to be heard in Havana, summoning echoes of the struggle just concluded against Batista. Those ensconced in Miami publicly announced their crusade against Fidel Castro, and boasted that they had the support of the United States. Of the various assassination plots later revealed by the Senate Select Committee on Intelligence hearings in 1975, one involved the CIA's top directorate, two mafia figures recommended by a former FBI agent, an ex-official of Grau San Martín's cabinet now organizing anti-Castro forces in Miami who was suggested by former Havana mafia boss Trafficante, and poison pills supplied by that chain of command to an agent working in the cafeteria of the Habana Libre. By some accounts, the cafeteria worker had the pills in his hand and was ready to introduce them into Castro's milkshake, but at the last minute lost his nerve or changed his mind.

In this history of Havana, we will not rehearse the four-year-long series of back and forth, tit-for-tat Cuban and American government actions—economic reforms, economic sanctions, nationalizations, subversion, repression, new sanctions and threats, new nationalizations, and new aggressions—that marked the breakdown and then final rupture of all trade, transportation, and diplomatic relations between Cuba and the United States. One end result was the Cuban adoption of a Soviet alliance, a Marxist-Leninist ideology, and a state socialist system in which all major industry, commercial establishments, media outlets, and entertainment venues came into the hands of a state that defined itself as representing the poor, the patriotic, and the revolutionary against the conservative, the American-dominated, and the rich. Another was the exodus, over the years 1959–62, of some 200,000 Cubans out of the 6 million population, primarily from Havana and including the bulk of the elite.

Those who stayed got to keep their homes, cars, furs, art works, and bank accounts, and they often lived off these for many years, islands in the sea of change around them. One of them was ex-president Ramón Grau San Martín, who continued to live in his Miramar home as we have mentioned above. Another was Dulce María Loynaz. In a philosophical prose poem written many years before, she had compared physical pain to a civil war in which the body, always taken for granted and obedient, suddenly rebels against the mind, seeking compensation for its losses and defending its rights. "It never demanded anything," the mind complains wonderingly about the body. "Now it comes . . . shouting its name in the silence of my nights . . . the simple, angry beggar who used to sleep every night outside my door."

After the actual revolution of those previously taken for granted, Loynaz withdrew more and more behind the pillars of the house in which she and Pablo Álvarez de Cañas had entertained at the Vedado corner of 19th and E. The rejection was mutual, as the cultural figures of the revolution had little use for her Catholicism or her intimate and personal style of verse. But she was too Cuban, too nationalist, and too *habanera* to leave. "Keep giving birth to me always," another equally prescient poem had asked of her island, "and pluck away my attempts to leave you, one by one." Her sister Flor, in similar fashion, remained ensconced in her estate in La Coronela, on the city's western outskirts, where the revolutionary 1930 Fiat was still hidden in her garage and she was accompanied by a collection of thirty pet dogs.

Dulce María's husband, on the other hand, left his adopted island behind. His employer Hornedo had gone, there was no more *El País* nor any more society pages, and out of whatever calculus of his own Pablo Álvarez de Cañas went to the United States for eye surgery and then resumed residence in Spain. He returned only much later, in the 1970s, old and sick.

Still others of the family, however, "incorporated themselves." Dulce María's younger half brother and his wife, both doctors, were among the half of Cuba's physicians who did not join the exodus to Miami but rather stayed to build the new state-run health system. "They didn't become Party members or Marxist-Leninists or anything like it," recalls their daughter Verónica, "but they were humanists and Cubans and they threw themselves into the public health work that the revolution undertook."

In the course of these transition years, from 1959 to 1962, Havana faced two moments of high drama, known in Cuba by the name of a beach and a date—Playa Girón and the October Crisis—and in the United States as the Bay of the Pigs and the Cuban Missile Crisis.

On April 13, 1961, a phosphorus bomb set the historic and nationalized El Encanto on fire, burning the department store to the ground and causing the death of one employee. Two days later, B-26 bombers bearing Cuban air force insignia attacked the military airports of San Antonio de los Baños, to the south of the capital, and Ciudad Libertad (formerly Camp Columbia) in the city itself. Raquel Cañizares and Carlos Larrinaga were on a train to Camagüey at the time, when word spread of the attack. "You can't imagine our panic, as close as it was to where we lived, and our children back there with my godmother and cousins. When we got to Camagüey we got hold of a phone, and called. They told us it was terrible, that they could hear the explosions, that they hid under the bed. But they were okay."

The next day, from a podium at the busy commercial intersection of 23rd and 12th, a block from the Cemetery of Colón, Fidel Castro spoke at a memorial for the seven who were not so lucky, who died in the raids. He announced that the planes had not been flown by defecting Cuban pilots but by members of an invasion force based in Nicaragua, trained and supplied by the CIA, for an invasion that might come any day. Paraphrasing the Gettysburg Address, he referred to a revolution "of the humble, by the humble, and for the humble." But pointedly departing from such antecedents, for the first time he used the word "socialist" to describe the revolution he asked his listeners to defend.

The invasion came that night, at two beaches along the Bay of Pigs on the southern shore of Matanzas, about three hours from the capital by road. "After you make the landing," one of the CIA trainers had said in a morale-boosting speech to the expeditionaries, "all you have to do is drive your trucks to the Central Highway, stick out your arms for a left turn, and head for the capital, because the *habaneros* will be waiting for you with open arms."

In fact, thousands of Havana militia members—some already trained and some newly signed up—piled into hastily conscripted trucks and city buses to go and fight. What had been chic had become real, and militia from Havana (as well as Cienfuegos, Santa Clara, and small towns closer to the main battlefront at the beach called Girón) fought, bled, and died in the fifty-six hours of combat which resulted in the defeat of the invasion force before it could secure a beachhead as planned. U.S. strategists relying on information from their traditional Cuban allies, mostly in exile, had vastly underestimated the support that the Cuban government could count on, especially against an operation evidently sponsored by a foreign power. Any potential for an internal rising was neutralized by a wave of preventive detentions and arrests, most of them temporary, whose effect was to strengthen the new regime. The nearly 1200 survivors of the invading force did arrive in Havana—but as prisoners. In another round of trials broadcast on TV and radio late into the night, they were sentenced to prison terms ranging from fifteen to thirty years—or, as an alternative, wholesale ransom by their sponsors for food and medicine to the tune of $5000 apiece.

After the Bay of Pigs, Havana once again became the sort of fortified garrison that it had been in its early centuries of pirate attacks and interimperial wars. On the horizon, instead of the sails of British and Dutch privateers, the watchful destroyer *U.S.S. Oxford* became a familiar and permanent sight. The gardens of the Hotel Nacional reverted to their original use when trenches, sandbags, and the antiaircraft guns popularly known as *cuatro bocas* (four mouths) appeared. It was the same elsewhere along the seafront as the population awaited a new invasion that could include a full-scale air attack on the capital. Military radar receivers swivelled day and night on top of the Habana Libre, Riviera, and FOCSA, while on the Puerto Rican islet of Vieques, U.S. Marines trained in landing exercises against an imaginary regime presided over a dictator called Ortsac, a name which could be read backwards with ease.

Among those most severely affected by the atmosphere of polarization leading up to and following the Bay of Pigs invasion were some of the youth just a bit younger than those in the militia and the Literacy Campaign. Worried parents put 14,000 unaccompanied children onto planes at the Havana airport, for delivery to the uncertain mercies of churches, foster families, orphanages, relatives, or special camps in the United States. What became known as "Operation Peter Pan" was concocted by the CIA, the Catholic Church, and Cuban and U.S. citizens active in the underground opposition to Castro. One of its founders was James Baker, headmaster of Ruston Academy, the private school that had served the Havana's American residents and their associates among its Cuban upper- and upper-middle class. Urging the proposal for a children's exodus on authorities in Washington, Baker argued that, "As the programs for turning more and more children into Communist robots are accelerated, we become more than ever eager to try to save more children." Washington empowered Msgr. Bryan Walsh, a Catholic welfare agency official in Miami, to use clandestine channels to issue special U.S. immigration visa waivers to any and all Cuban children between the ages of six and sixteen. Evidence of the new social fault lines running through Havana is the identity of one of the operatives in the Peter Pan network: María Teresa Cuervo, daughter-in-law of the murdered Pelayo

Cuervo, who used her position at an Old Havana travel agency to make reservations for children brought to her by lay-attired Catholic priests.

The generally white and well-to-do parents who sent their children out of the country were motivated by real fears (as in the Mirta Yáñez story) that they were losing the hearts and minds of their children to the new ideals of the radicalized revolution, and by the prospect that the government would soon close the private and parochial schools that they had always counted on. These parents were also stampeded into panic, however, by false rumors spread through underground leaflets and telephone campaigns and shortwave broadcasts on the CIA-operated Radio Swan. Chief among these rumors was that a new law was about to transfer *patria potestad* (legal authority over children) from parents to the state, which would send them off to Russia for years of indoctrination and return them as "materialist monsters" beyond their parents' control.

Most parents who entrusted their children to Peter Pan expected the separation to be temporary, until the government fell or they too were able to emigrate and join their children in the United States. But the government did not fall, and air traffic to and from Miami ceased permanently in October, 1962. Many of the children ended up separated from their parents for years, and some forever. The parents' worst fears had been realized, but in an unexpected way.

The catalyst to the end of air service was, of course, the Cuban government's acceptance of Soviet short and intermediate range missiles to be stationed at various points throughout the island, which from the Cuban point of view would serve as a deterrent to any further invasion attempt. In the ensuing showdown, Havana's horizon filled with far more numerous and threatening U.S. naval vessels than the World War II vintage *Oxford*. Between October 22 and November 20 of 1962, Havana lived in a state of high alert. Children continued going to school, theaters kept showing films, the cafeterias on La Rampa stayed open to the wee hours as usual, but teachers, service workers, and bus drivers alike went about their business in blue and green militia uniforms, the radio broadcast a steady stream of patriotic songs new and old, and trenches and antiaircraft emplacements multiplied from the sandy beaches east of the capital to the coral reefs on the west while the city braced for an invasion which half of John F. Kennedy's advisors were urging him to launch during those tense days.

When Kennedy and Nikita Khrushchev instead agreed on a Soviet withdrawal of the missiles in return for an unwritten U.S. promise not to invade Cuba in the future, Havana breathed a sigh of relief for the end of the crisis. But many felt let down by the way the Soviets had left Cuba out of the negotiations and failed to openly declare the results. Their mixed sentiments were reflected in a new rhyming tune that Havana high school students sang and danced in their conga lines: *Nikita, mariquita, lo que se da no se quita.* Nikita, you sissy, giving should be for keeps.

When the Bay of Pigs prisoners finally left their Havana prisons in late December of 1962, in return for 53 million dollars worth of baby food and medicine, they were feted in Miami's Orange Bowl by John and Jackie Kennedy, with the First Lady greeting them in Spanish and the president promising that their flag would "fly over a free Havana" before long. The main weapon of U.S. policy was implemented in February 1962, a complete economic embargo that banned not only trade with the United States but also trade with Western Europe and Latin America insofar as this could be enforced. Over the next year the number of Western ships docking in Havana and other ports dropped from 352 to 59, and the capital's remaining commercial air links dwindled to three, with Mexico City, Prague, and Madrid. The city once preferred by American corporations for testing their latest consumer goods had lost its borrowed glitz. The Sears & Roebucks, the new Studebakers and DeSotos, the Chesterfields and Salems preferred by many smokers over their traditional brands, the premieres of the films of Marilyn Monroe and Marlon Brando, vanished along with the rest. More important to the economy, the managers and technicians who had overseen everything from electricity generation to beer bottling were gone too, as were the inputs and spare parts that had always been just a day away.

Yet, despite shortages and dislocations, Havana would remain the capital of the triumphant revolutionaries through the terms of eight more U.S. presidents after Eisenhower and Kennedy, through five decades which would involve great breaks with the past and great continuities too. JFK's Orange Bowl speech was broadcast and reprinted in Cuban state media as the year 1962 ended, but this did not dampen New Year's Eve festivities in Havana. The residents of the capital imbibed great quantities of beer and rum and danced until dawn.

14

Revolution with *Pachanga*: Havana Transfigured

Last Saturday I couldn't get a seat at the Tropicana. After a long wait I got a chance to applaud the most extraordinary choreographic spectacle: The Agrarian Reform, a sumptuous, dynamic, and inspiring ballet that's an excellent example of revolutionary theater . . . Let visitors to Havana go to the beaches, let them enter the stores, stroll the streets, loiter in the cafés . . . They will feel they have landed in a transfigured city.

(Alejo Carpentier, "A jubilant Havana," July 1959)

In this journalistic portrait of the changes in his city, the fifty-four-year-old novelist Carpentier marveled at much that he saw: Toy stores awash in dolls of bearded guerrillas, exhibitions of tractors and other farm implements multiplying throughout the sophisticated capital, vendors of tamales and *fritas* displaying signs that said, "Eat what Cuba grows." This was not the city of American postcards and films, of Hemingway, Graham Greene, and Guillermo Cabrera Infante, of bright lights and carefree people, the bongo player Ricky Ricardo of *I Love Lucy* or the crafty, smiling mulatto gambler with a wisecrack always on his tongue. This city was undergoing a profound transformation, not just in its appearance but deep inside.

The wave stirred up by the revolution—including its wave of discontents—inundated everything. Throughout the country, the thick soup of Cuban nationalism boiled over. Into the old simmering ingredients of Spanish sausage, African root vegetables, and Chinese or Arabic spices profusely sprinkled with American cocktails, new liquids now dripped. The peculiar ideology of "creole communism" blended idealism and personal sacrifice, volunteerism and collectivity, exaltation of the figures of the worker and the guerrilla, a spartan style and a radical ethic of doing away with the old and inventing the new. It affected every class and race, and every barrio of the capital. Still in love with its new heroes and new slogans, Havana did not stop dancing and enjoying with every pore. "This is Revolution with *pachanga* (raucous partying)," many Latin American radicals visiting the city in the early 1960s said. Yet the city submitted to the nation's long-deferred dream, for which many of its residents had fought in 1895, in 1933, and in the struggle against Batista and against U.S. domination.

In a space of barely four years, Havana was abandoned by its elite and invaded by the poor people of the countryside. Its enclaves of middle-class comfort, its glamorous theaters and concert halls, and its towering hotels all opened their doors much wider than had ever been imagined before. Its connections with the North abruptly cut, more and more isolated from the South as well, the city had to lay new and unexpected supply lines from the remote East, whose strange languages had to be learned in a rush. The most cosmopolitan and culturally diverse city of the region, born as the crossroads of the New World and accustomed for centuries to international commerce and instant familiarity with strangers, now underwent a test of survival. Its transfiguration was part of the survival strategy, but was also a product of its culture, old and new.

First and foremost, the experience of the revolution made the citizens of Havana conscious as never before that they inhabited the privileged capital of an island whose countryside had long teemed with poverty, hunger, curable diseases, illiteracy, and neglect. When the Rebel Army marched into Havana in 1959, four out of every five of its soldiers—recruited largely in the mountains of the east—did not know how to read or write. The same was true of nearly one out of every three Cubans throughout the country. Yet the illiteracy rate in the capital was only one out of eleven.

The cities of the interior, not just the remote countryside, suffered from such imbalances too. The only three television stations on the island were based in the capital. Havana had 123 movie theaters, while no other city had more than five. Commitment to rectify this disparity, together with ideological radicalism and the politics of state socialist centralism, meant that the victorious revolution would pour more resources and energy into the interior than the capital. Thus, the hundreds of thousands who assembled in the Plaza de la Revolución—many of them with experience as militiamen and women, literacy teachers, voluntary cane cutters and coffee pickers, administrators of sugar mills, or simply considering themselves revolutionaries—applauded economic policies that prioritized the construction of roads, hospitals, utilities, and schools in the mountains instead of the capital.

Parallel to this movement, the resources of the capital were redirected internally from the rich to the working class and the poor. The exclusive private yacht and beach clubs of Miramar and Playa Marianao were thrown open to the public for admission fees of fifty cents, or turned over to labor unions for their members' use. The Country Club became the site of a new, free-of-charge National Arts College—an innovative design of red-brick beehives and sinuous paths and corridors, some of them later encroached by the jungle of vegetation along the narrow Río Quibú. Alfredo Hornedo's mansion on Carlos III became Centro Habana's Casa de Cultura, where would-be writers could join workshops and the modern equivalents of Chano Pozo played not for patrons but for those who would have previously gathered in the courtyards of El África or El Ataúd. The Grand Stadium became the Latinoamericano, where all ties to U.S. professional baseball were cut.

The Habana Libre, when it ceased to be a makeshift Rebel Army headquarters, became a crossroads for international revolutionaries and radical activists of many stripes. Its rooms and night clubs and swimming pool, like those of the Riviera and the Nacional and the Capri, also became a playground for Havana honeymooners of all classes and races, for Cubans from the countryside attending political events in the capital, and for young dating couples who could save up twenty pesos for decaying luxury, privacy, and a bed. The nearby FOCSA apartment building, twenty-eight stories of luxury condominiums, became a dormitory for students from the interior who came to study in the capital. The older estate across the street—a mansion house and carriage house, with steep, green-tiled roofs that seemed to belong in Switzerland—became an elementary school. Many abandoned or confiscated apartments went to Rebel Army soldiers and their families, who stayed in Havana to fill new or old government posts. So did great homes newly subdivided into apartments or single rooms. The old and crumbling Loynaz estate on Calle Línea, where the salons of the 1920s and 1930s had taken place, was partitioned by new residents, adapted, and partitioned again. The same fate befell the house of General Enrique Loynaz in suburban Lawton, after the aged general went to live in the seaside town of Santa Fé.

Other classic buildings became museums of what was gone: The Presidential Palace turned into a Museum of the Revolution, in fact a museum of all of Cuban history from the revolutionary point of view. The politician Orestes Ferrara's Tuscan mansion alongside the wall of the university became the Napoleonic Museum, housing the departed Ferrara's imperial French art collection and that of émigré sugar magnate Julio Lobo (equally obsessed with Bonaparte) who owned, among many other treasures, a lock of the emperor's hair. The Palacio de Aldama, rescued from its fate as a tobacco factory, was restored to become the home of the Historical Institute. The mansion and gardens of sugar heiress María Luisa Gomez-Mena, the Countess of Revilla-Camargo—famed for parties with 100-pound gold candelabras, 5000 dozen gladioli, and 500 pheasants flown in from the United States—became the Museum of Decorative Arts.

When the Literacy Campaign ended, Juan Valdés, at the age of twenty-three, was offered a job as manager of newly nationalized sugar mill in the central province of Las Villas. Still without a high school diploma, though self-taught in philosophy and mathematics, he knew nothing of sugar or agriculture. But like thousands of others whose political militance or trade union activism qualified them to take the place of former owners and administrators, he threw himself into this work. In his few free weekends, especially between harvests, he returned to Havana. There he walked in his muddy Russian boots and olive green military pants past the famous corner of Galiano and San Rafael, where El Encanto had burned to the ground. In the windows of the Indochina, Poljot and Raketa wrist watches from Moscow, ugly but cheap, had replaced the glamorous Swiss timepieces of a few years before. To the east, in the Barrio Chino where Valdés had spent part of his youth, the photo of Chiang Kai-shek had come down from the Casino Chung

Wah, the offices of the Kuomintang had been closed along with the pornographic cinemas, and a militia brigade had been named after the fallen Cuban revolutionary José Wong.

The other way, in the barrio of Colón through which Juan had once walked to work at the laundry, the brothels had gradually been shut, their employees enrolled in school or retrained for other jobs. "I wasn't one of those who rushed out with an armband on January 1 to pretend I'd been a Fidelista all the time," a former prostitute named Violeta recalled. "After the triumph, at first we were happy as clams, because everybody in the city felt safe and had money and came out to enjoy the new times, and we didn't have to pay any more bribes to cops or mafias of any kind. I was making more money than ever before. Then the rumors started to spread: that they were going to round us up, move us someplace us else, put us in jail. We thought it would be one more crackdown like with other politicians before. The first shock was the urban reform. It was radical, it made us the owners of our rooms. Then they rounded up the pimps, who had to shut up shop for good, and many of them left the island, and others went to jail or went to work. It was hard for us to adjust, some more than others, because we never thought that way of life would end—much less considered whether we could have had a role in contributing to the change. But many of us, when we saw it was really different from the past, then we joined up. And there was one of us, Cuca, whose boyfriend had been in it, always running from the police who accused him of distributing leaflets or setting bombs. He went to the Sierra, and six months later Cuca disappeared. Afterward she was one of those coming to us and telling us we ought to give up that work."

Despite all the changes, *la bulla* continued apace. Radios and televisions blared with broadcasts of all sorts of ceremonies, assemblies, and new soap operas featuring stories of patriotic struggle alongside the latest hits of Roberto Faz and Beny Moré. The resonant Cuban dance music now shared airtime with militia marches and songs. At certain hours, the auditory thread that linked one block to another in Centro Havana was Fidel Castro reporting on his recent trip to the USSR or Minister of Industry Che Guevara detailing ambitious plans. This background competed with truckloads of students chorusing carnival-style congas that insulted the president of the United States, or floats of the Carnival itself in whose three-story towers young dancers wiggled to the beat of rumbas dedicated to construction workers, or cars with loudspeakers announcing assemblies in the "Red Plaza of La Vibora" or dances in the Parque Central and Prado, where the city's most famous bands played deep into the night for free.

In the meantime, new lines of division opened, with the city's patchwork of religious beliefs as the terrain of one such split. Havana's Catholic clergy were mostly Spanish-born and conservative. Their initial coolness to the revolutionary ideology, and their outright opposition once it took Marxist-Leninist form, rapidly divided the political terrain into camps of believers and nonbelievers. Eduardo Boza Masvidal, the parish priest of the church of La Caridad across from the Valdés family's temporary Chinatown home, had become auxiliary bishop of Havana. He wrote passionate homilies against the government, excoriating its atheistic communism, its catering to foreign interests (the Russians), and its disrespect for private property (including the nationalization of private schools, particularly Catholic ones).

However, in Cuba the Church hierarchy did not have the following it could count on in many other parts of Latin America. There had been only 232 priests in Havana in 1953, for a population of over a million residents, and most of them had taught in the private schools attended by the children of white middle and upper class. Though a majority of Cubans declared themselves Catholic, mid-1950s surveys by the Church itself showed that only 11 to 18 percent of the country's population were orthodox Catholics who regularly attended mass. Another 6 percent of the population were members of Protestant churches, most of which sought an accommodation with the revolution. But the great majority of Cubans believed in God and/or gods "after their fashion," practicing grass-roots religion that mixed various proportions of Catholic, spiritist, and African rites. The atheism newly embraced by the leaders of the revolution drew on utopian sentiments embedded in each of these faiths, on the belief that a better world could be formed.

Bishop Boza Masvidal was among 130 priests expelled from the country as counterrevolutionaries five months after the Bay of Pigs. The catalyst for this move was a combination of religious procession and political demonstration that he convoked outside the church of La Caridad. The conflict between the Catholic Church and the new state played a major role in the departure of thousands of the capital's middle-class children in Operation Peter Pan, and practicing Catholic adults also left the country in much higher numbers than nonpracticing ones. A survey of Havana parishes taken in the late 1960s estimated that 50 to 70 percent of their members left the island in the decade after the revolution came to power. Churches of all faiths continued to operate, but among the hundreds of thousands of believers of one sort or another who stayed in the capital, the majority let go of their religion, kept it quiet, or something of each.

Those most accustomed to such an uneasy balance, of course, were the practitioners of Afro-Cuban religions, whose predecessors had spent centuries balancing conflicting traditions and public versus private display. Pragmatic and polytheistic, the African elements emphasized personal faith and daily conduct above catechism and had no official hierarchy or institutions to defend. The rebel troops had entered Havana wearing not just crosses but the beads of *santería*. For many believers in the "people's faith"—blacks and whites living in those barrios that once had been Havana outside the walls—the top leaders of the revolution were illuminated and protected by the *orishas* of the Yoruba pantheon. Otherwise, it would have been inconceivable that they should escape from death and designs of their powerful enemies. Among Fidel Castro's popular nicknames was El Caballo, the horse, a reference not only to his stamina but to the Chinese charada, in which the horse represented Number One. There were those who felt he had been bathed in the virtues of the Three Warriors of *santería*—the strength and battle spirit of Changó, the tenacity and will of the blacksmith Oggún, and the ability and vision of Elegguá, lord of the roads and opener of doors. It was well known that some of his closest collaborators, like René Vallejo, his personal doctor, and Celia Sánchez, his closest aide, were hidden believers who consulted with distinguished *babalawos*. The layer of official atheism brought the unwieldy word *oscurantistas* (obscurantists) into daily vocabulary to describe religious practitioners of all sorts, and it frowned heavily upon the *toques de tambor* celebrated in the courtyards and rooftops of the city or the annual San Lázaro's eve procession to the outlying chapel of El Rincón in honor of Babalú Ayé. Underneath, however, the old beliefs not only maintained themselves but functioned as a social glue.

Further, what the revolutionary ideology did not tolerate as religion, it celebrated as culture, giving Afro-Cuban traditions an official nod they had never received before. Audiences crowded into what had previously been the Tacón Theater and then the National, now renamed in honor of Federico García Lorca, to see the dancers of National Folklore Ensemble perform the traditional dances invoking Yoruba *orishas*. They packed the former Rodi movie theater in Vedado, renamed Julio Antonio Mella, to see the Modern Dance Ensemble interpret the Afro-Cuban poems of Nicolás Guillén dedicated to Sensemayá, the snake of the Mayombe rite, converted into subjects of much praised ballets and films.

More dramatically than religion, the private commerce that had sunk its roots deeply into the street life of Havana visibly withered away. Before leaving for the countryside as teacher and then mill administrator, Juan Valdés had won back his job at the Indochina, where he briefly became part of the management team of the nationalized store. Supermarket chains, which had time for only a brief appearance in Havana of the late 1950s and the early 1960s, were nationalized too. The change in the city's economic life also swept away local businesses the size of Alberto Motola's, which had lately added an appliance store, Motola Electric. Motola, already elected president of his local Committee for the Defense of the Revolution, cooperated with the new state employees sent to "intervene" his three linked stores, but when he continued to assist them in straightening out accounts and procedures, this was too much for the ideology to handle. " 'How can it be that this capitalist, this bourgeois, is working with you?' his son recalls the intervenors' superiors telling them. 'Kick him out!' He may have been president of the CDR, but Cuba is like that. Many contradictory things coexist." María Roffe, on the books as an employee, was immediately given employment at another store, as the new laws required. Alberto finally got a job as a warehouse supervisor in another newly nationalized Buenavista commercial establishment not far from home.

Unlike Alberto and María, the majority of Havana's Jewish population, including most of the Motolas and Roffes, left Old Havana, Vedado, and other neighborhoods to seek their fortunes in small business or professions in Miami or New York. The Arab stores on Montserrate, Bernaza, and Monte in the old city also closed their doors. But the smallest retail outfits were unaffected by the nationalizations of the early 1960s. The hand laundries and snack counters, many small bodegas and fruit stands, and the hundreds of varied carts and holes in the wall hung on, in the hands of Chinese-descended merchants above all. Then in 1968 a final wave of socialist radicalism known as the "Revolutionary Offensive" wiped out these last residues of the private urban economy, which would not reappear for another thirty-five years. The sole and honorable exceptions were the aged Fords and Plymouths whose proprietors made up the National Association of Revolutionary Taxi Drivers and continued to ply their trade. The Chinese entrepreneurs left little by little, especially for New York, where they opened Chinese-Cuban restaurants in whose menus egg rolls and Manchurian soup coexisted with demitasse cups of sweet dark coffee and specials like Cuban black beans with ground beef.

By then, the city's economic life had radically changed. The nationalizations of foreign businesses brought with them a patriotic sense of settling accounts, and a feeling among workers that they were in control of the factories at last. These new state enterprises tried to reproduce the rationalized efficiency of private monopolies. The big Crusellas and Sabatés soap and perfume factories, the paper and cardboard plants along the Avenida de Puentes Grandes, and the Antillana de Acero steel plant (formerly American Steel) in the southeastern suburb of El Cotorro had all been subsumed into large state corporations affiliated with the new Ministry of Industries. Former private service and commercial firms were now grouped along product and service lines and known as consolidated enterprises or, commonly speaking, *consolidados*. Victor Adding Machines became part of one of these, and Carlos Larrinaga was transferred to the new *consolidado* in Old Havana. From 1968 on, the tiny private workshops that made faucet washers or pressure cooker gaskets and storefronts that sold thread and fountain pen ink were dissolved in great conglomerates too—with acronyms that verged on the bizarre.

For example, the hundreds of retail sellers of cigars and cigarettes known as Romeo y Julieta, Partagás, Bauzá, or Hoyo de Monterrey, had been subsumed in a company called ECODICTAFOS, whose hermetic Spanish initials meant Consolidated Distribution Enterprise of Cigarettes, Cigars, and Matches. The monopoly wholesaler of the old beverage brands from Tropical or Hatuey beer to Coca-Cola was now in the hands of ECODICEMARAM (Consolidated Enterprise Distributing Beers, Maltas, Soft Drinks, and Mineral Waters). The entity in charge of distributing many products formerly available in stands and storefronts (buttons, brushes, barrettes, combs, and mops, cleansers, and hundreds of small useful objects) answered to the improbable title of ECODOQUINLIM. Although the majority of the streets and places in the city were still known by the same names as always, most of them as old as the Spanish colony, the commercial establishments were draped in these new, Orwellian names. So the shoe shop *La complaciente* ("at your service") became Unit 023-4577 of ECORERCARCU (Consolidated Repair Enterprise of Shoes and Leather Articles). Centralized decision-making and supply, combined with the mushrooming of administrative regulations and the growing effect of the U.S. economic embargo, kept the new business from running with the expected efficiency. When the customers of United 023-4577 of ECORERCARCU did not feel it was "at their service," they were often dismayed to be told, "those are our instructions," or "that service is not foreseen in the Ministry's regulations," or simply "we're all out of that."

On the edges of this state economy, small gray markets of semilegal private activity continued to exist. Alberto Motola, once he retired from his warehouse job and from another in the Sports Ministry as a judge of marlin fishing contests, found that he could not sit home idle, and that business was in his blood. He went to an undeveloped green area near the coast below Buenavista and beyond Miramar, known as Monte Barreto, and made an arrangement with a longtime squatter who had built himself a shack there. Together, Alberto, María and the squatter grew tomatoes, cucumbers, and other vegetables to eat and to sell. Later he got in the business of recycling wholesale-sized cans of lard and jam from bakeries. Though these activities were sometimes questioned by the police, his standing in the community and—he always claimed—his ties to old Popular Socialist Party leaders always prevailed.[1] Similarly on the edge of legality, many other families bartered rationed goods that exceeded their needs, or odd lots of hardware brought home from the workplace, all of which took the place of the street hawkers and small shops that had just about vanished from the city's mix. One other form of commerce that neither revolutionary morality nor state enforcement eliminated was grassroots gambling. The casinos, the mafia, and the National Lottery were gone, but *la bolita* (the numbers game) survived, as did *la valla* (the cockpit) in rural areas and on Havana's outskirts.

An issue weighing much more heavily on the minds of residents of the capital was putting a decent roof over their heads. Within the limits of its orientation toward the countryside, the revolutionary government attempted to do something about this. The original urban reform and later legislation eliminated the problem of prices, reducing rent to a maximum 10 percent of income and giving rights of perpetual occupancy and inheritance to many citizens. Throughout the formerly middle- and upper-class barrios of the city, housemaids and cooks and gardeners often went from being live-in servants to owners of the places they had worked. More difficult to tackle, however, was the problem of supply. In spite of the exodus of the elite, the growing migration to the capital, combined with a baby boom of 1960–65, increased the population of the city to a million and a half.

A slum clearance plan eradicated more than thirty squatter settlements and other unhealthy barrios of Havana, including Las Yaguas, The Cave of Smoke, and Llega y Pon, whose residents moved to new projects. These projects were originally financed through an imaginative system which made use of the profits of the century-old National Lottery. The later political decision to shut down all types of gambling, along with the increasing centralization of the state, and a desire to discourage immigration from the interior to Havana, all meant that these building projects began to decline after 1963–64.

The decision to reduce housing construction, together with the growth in employment, education, public health, and social services in the rest of the country, was highly effective in reducing the Cuban capital's rate of growth. Today's Havana has barely twice the number of inhabitants of 1959, an exceptional case in a region which produced megalopolises like Mexico City, Sao Paolo, Caracas, and Buenos Aires during the same period of time.

Nonetheless, the decline in the construction of new houses contributed to decay in the traditional centers of the city and later to the creation of new makeshift settlements like El Romerillo near the Playa de Marianao, El Fanguito alongside the Almendares below the heights of Vedado, or La Güinera in the southeastern district of San Miguel de Padrón. The nationalization of the small shops in 1968 converted many storefronts into improvised living spaces that housed those most in need while accelerating the deterioration of the buildings and the decay of the cityscape. Most of the old solars, if they were not leveled, gradually got individual plumbing and cooking and lighting facilities. But the mazes of gas, electric, and water lines were like spiders' webs, and the buildings' structural deterioration was often not addressed. By the end of the century, more than half of the buildings in Cuba characterized as being in substandard condition were concentrated in the capital.

During the 1960s, nonetheless, whatever the problems in housing, the overall living standards, work and educational opportunities,

public health services, and cultural life of Havana grew tremen-
dously. There were more schools, colleges, daycare centers, clinics,
theaters, museums, libraries and bookstores than ever before. Not
only rent but prices of basic food (a market basket of rationed
goods), public transit, concerts of all sorts, books, a ballet in the
García Lorca, and an occasional dinner in a luxury restaurant or
night at the Tropicana or in the Hotel Capri were within the reach of
all or almost all. Even the poorest Havanans could attend a decisive
game in the baseball finals at the Latinoamericano, send their children to study trumpet or violin, or get psychiatric or dental attention, or a heart operation, or funeral services—all completely free.

Juan Valdés climbed the ladder of the sugar industry to the point
of becoming director of agriculture for the whole province of Las
Villas, and finally returned to Havana as national vice minister in
charge of agricultural labor, but his true vocation still lay in ideas and
books. He was a friend of every used book dealer in the capital and
spent a good deal of his salary on works of history, philosophy,
and social science. Eventually he got the chance to study sociology
in the university, left his post in the Ministry of Agriculture, and
fulfilled his dream of becoming a professor of philosophy himself.
His children, named Elena and Alejandro out of his admiration for
classical Greek culture (after Helen of Troy and Alexander the
Great), took swimming lessons in the pool of a state sports academy in Miramar. Divorced some years before, he married a young
doctor, recently graduated from medical school. The white philosophy professor and mulatta doctor lived with the aunt who had
raised her, in the crowded, racially mixed, prerevolutionary
workers' housing development of Pogolotti in Marianao.

The Motolas, meanwhile, had paid for their middle son, León, to
attend junior and senior high school at the private Candler College
in the years before its nationalization, but their youngest son
Daniel went to the same school, now part of the state system, for
free. Both continued on to get university degrees. Isaac, the oldest
son, became a bus and truck mechanic, as he had determined to be
when he sneaked off from school to the bus yard at the age of
twelve. He studied mechanics in nearby Ciudad Libertad, the educational complex that had been Camp Columbia. That was where
he met his future wife, who had come from the provinces to study
biology in the teacher's college there.

Verónica Loynaz went every day from her parents house in
Lawton, near where the Loynaz family arms could still be seen on

the crumbling former home of the general, to the high school of La Vibora (a former convent school), where she mixed with all classes and races. General Loynaz's granddaughter regularly visited her aunts Flor and Dulce María in their secluded retreats, and also joined the Communist Youth. She went on to the university to study law. When she was criticized by fellow students there for her "bourgeois" speech and reluctance to curse, she declared in a Youth meeting that revolutionaries did not have to abandon the manners they had been brought up with, which were part of who they were.

In the cultural sphere, in the 1960s the reverberant Havana that had once been the Paris of the Caribbean filled again with illustrious visitors and cutting-edge international cultural events. The city received intellectuals and entertainers ranging from Jean Paul Sartre to Gabriel Garcia Márquez (who worked in the Cuban news agency Prensa Latina), Graham Greene (who came back to see what had changed), Julio Cortázar, the French film and stage star Gerard Philipe, Gina Lollobrigida, Mario Vargas Llosa, Carlos Fuentes, and Josephine Baker. Allen Ginsberg returned in 1968, no longer unknown, at the invitation of a Cuban-based publishing house to judge a poetry contest, though his advocacy of homosexuality and marijuana got him expelled after a few days.

The most famous French modern art exhibit, the Salon de Mai, was held on La Rampa that same year, and ordinary Havana was astonished to see for the first time, live, Warhol's soup cans and the smashed cars of César Baldaccini, as well as original paintings by Picasso and Braque, Jackson Pollock and Vasarely. Art found its way even into La Rampa's sidewalks, repaved to include colorful mosaics by the Cuban artists Wifredo Lam, Amelia Peláez, Mariano Rodríguez, and René Portocarrero. At the top of the hill, also in 1968, the Habana Libre hosted more than five-hundred artists, philosophers, writers from seventy countries in a legendary Cultural Congress of Havana. From Belgium, Maurice Béjart's Twentieth Century Ballet brought thousands of delighted spectators a whole new way of imagining dance. In the meantime classical romantic ballet provided the name for Coppelia, the new, modernistic ice-cream palace and park built catty-corner from the Habana Libre, with more flavors than Howard Johnsons, as *habaneros* who knew the northern chain proudly said.

The hundreds of thousands of readers who visited bookstores also discovered American literature, translated and distributed in the 1960s more than ever before or after. For a price that never exceeded three pesos, they could buy the novels of Dos Passos and Steinbeck, the stories of Hemingway and Faulkner, science fiction of Asimov and Bradbury. Theaters put on works of Leroi Jones, Edward Albee, Arthur Miller, and Eugene O'Neill. Certain radical U.S. political figures, such as Malcolm X, Angela Davis, Martin Luther King, Jr., and the leaders of the Black Panther Party received widespread exposure and were seen as heroes in the city and beyond.

Popular Cuban music continued as dynamic as ever, with a proliferation of groups and genres and new dance styles. In the mid-1960s emerged the Mozambique, developed by Pello el Afrokán and his band led by a phalanx of drums and trumpets at the head of the floats and conga lines of university students groups in the annual Havana carnival. The Mozambique caught on for its new dance steps, reminiscent of the traditions of rumba and danced en masse rather than in couples, as well its catchy lyrics and the volume of its great chorus of drums. Even Fidel Castro, known for being among the minority of Cubans who did not dance, was said to have invented a Mozambique lyric about voluntary cane cutting, which could be attacked with the same infectious "crazy pleasure" as dance.

Another famous dance band, Los Van Van, took its name from the mobilization around the 1970 sugar harvest, whose slogan was los diez millones van ("we'll make 10 million tons"). Los Van Van recovered the tradition of the charangas, the big dance bands of the 1940s and 1950s, which had incorporated the wind instruments of jazz groups into the previous sextets and septets of son. They added their own rhythms including those of rock and roll. The complex choreographies and steps invented by the dancers at the Salon Rosado of La Tropical served as inspiration for bandleader Juan Formell. His electric bass, almost unnoticed on the far left end of the big band, set the beat for the dancers whose improvisations he carefully observed. Van Van was an instant success among the youth, and their lyrics introduced new slang and mythical characters into popular speech.

Where Havana gave birth to something almost completely new, however, was in a genre where up till now the city had produced very little—film.

As consumers, the capital's residents in the 1960s had a shrinking number of cinemas but a broader access to world cinematography.

In 1960, more than 200 of the 380 films shown in the capital were still American, but later years brought not only numerous Soviet and Eastern European films, previously almost unknown, but those of Japan, Italy, France, England, Spain, and Latin America. Tony Irízar, still an incurable moviephile, now haunted the first-run cinemas to feast on the images of Roman Polanski's Warsaw, Pasolini and Antonioni and Fellini's Rome, Truffaut, Resnais, and Godard's Paris, Milos Jancsó's Budapest, and Milos Forman's Prague. Yet Hollywood films never disappeared, trade embargo or none. By 1980, there were as many U.S. films shown, by hook or by crook, as British and Italian ones.

For almost the first time since the early productions of Enrique Díaz Quesada, Cubans now got in the act as significant producers of cinema too. What had been made in Havana in the interim had been mostly melodramas and musicals produced by short-lived and poorly funded movie firms doing their best to imitate either Hollywood or Mexico. The first cultural institution created by the revolutionary government, in March of 1959, was the Cuban Institute of Cinematographic Art and Industry (ICAIC), established on one floor of the Atlantic office building at the busy Vedado intersection of 23rd and 12th. When the building was nationalized two years later, ICAIC got the whole thing. The film institute excelled first at politically innovative, fast-cutting and intellectually challenging newsreels and documentaries in the style pioneered by Santiago Álvarez. Álvarez, born in Old Havana in 1919, had worked in Pennsylvania and New York in the late 1930s and early 1940s as a coal miner and dishwasher, and returned to Havana where he studied philosophy and joined the Popular Socialist Party and then the anti-Batista underground.

Other ICAIC directors, influenced particularly by the Italian New Wave, made feature films on a wide variety of Cuban themes (rural, urban, contemporary, and historical) which soon began to win awards in European festivals both East and West. Some of the most notable features focused on the life of Havana and the complexities of its transformation. Tomás Gutierrez Alea's *Memories of Underdevelopment* (1968) sympathetically portrayed the alienation of a member of the old bourgeoisie on the eve of the Missile Crisis. Staying but not belonging, he observes the city as a spectator, through the telescope set up in the spacious living room of his high rise Vedado apartment. Alea returned to this theme again in *The Survivors* (1978), story of an aristocratic family that tries to maintain the *ancien régime* within a compound of their own. *The Survivors* was shot at Flor Loynaz's suburban estate, where she still lived. It starred Germán Pinelli, the radio newsman who had narrated the events of Orfila and gone on to be a prominent television host.

In the meantime, however, the *pachanga*—as well as the epic and drama of the early years of the revolution—was coming to an end.

15

Russian Meat, Miami Butterflies, and Other Unexpected Adventures

Havana's cultural effervescence went into decline toward the late 1960s as the Cuban attempt to invent an experimental socialism different from that of the Soviet Union entered a critical phase. Che Guevara's death among a group of Cuban guerrillas in Bolivia, the accumulated effects of the U.S. embargo and international isolation, and the Revolutionary Offensive of 1968 all contributed to chilling the old atmosphere of cultural diversity. The margins between what was considered to be within the revolution and what was seen as antagonistic grew more rigid, and the syndrome of Cuba as besieged fortress made prohibitions multiply. Homosexuality and religion were already seen as stains left over from the capitalist past, and their practitioners as people who had to be reeducated through work and study of "scientific atheism." Now the hunt for such deviation (especially in the previously more tolerant spheres of culture and education) became more intense. Unorthodox strains of Marxism, potentially critical of the Soviet model, also found themselves hemmed in.

The philosophy department at the University of Havana, of which Juan Valdés was a member, published a journal of Marxist theory called *Pensamiento Crítico* (Critical Thinking), which published articles from Europe, North America, and Latin America including Cuba. The young professors who had founded the journal, convinced they were carrying out a task of the revolution, were surprised to learn that they had been criticized by Raúl Castro, Fidel's brother and Minister of Defense, for circulating the ideas of writers critical of Soviet Marxism and exposing their students to this influence. *Pensamiento Crítico* was closed in 1972 and the philosophy department reorganized as the department for the teaching of Marxism-Leninism. Juan had to return to his post in the Ministry of Agriculture, and his other colleagues also moved to other jobs for the duration of the 1970s.

Prohibition of contacts with emigrants grew more rigid, as did strictures on rock music and even jazz, because these supposedly represented imperialist culture—as did miniskirts on women, long hair on men, and beards that did not sprout during the guerrilla struggle itself. A puritanism alien to Cuban culture took over radio stations and schools, periodicals, and political discourse.

At approximately the same time, the attempt to produce 10 million tons of sugar in 1970 led hundreds of thousands of Havanans to cane-cutting camps. The streets lost their old nocturnal vibration, while generalized shortages affecting the whole country left their mark on Havana as well. The accumulated costs of U.S. hostility and the unprecedented effort required by superambitious economic plans led to virtual paralysis of the economy. Unlike the later crisis of the 1990s, when dollar stores and a thriving black market would constitute an escape valve for some, the severe shortages at the end of the 1960s simply distributed nothing among all. When the 10 million ton goal was not reached in 1970, the government recognized the need for a change. It could not keep asking the people to sacrifice while the stores remained empty and a long wait in line was required to eat in a restaurant or buy food beyond the ration or an appliance as humble as an electric fan. The revolution could not maintain the extreme egalitarianism that meant the salary of pizza parlor employee and a cardiovascular surgeon bought almost the same in the market, if there was anything to buy. Castro made a speech accepting responsibility for the 10-million-ton debacle and offering to resign. The multitude assembled for the speech did not take up the offer, and government policy thereafter changed course.

To provide more consumer goods while maintaining the vital supply of petroleum and arms, the government made a new arrangement with the USSR and the socialist bloc. Among the main characteristics of the new period would be the implantation of a much more strictly Soviet model in the economic system, government organization, national constitution, Cuban Communist Party, armed forces, and communications media. A futuristic new Soviet embassy (half modernist skyscraper, half medieval watchtower, and popularly dubbed "the robot") would eventually come to tower over Miramar, dwarfing the nearby Jesús de Miramar cathedral that had formerly served the capital's well-to-do. Well before that, Marxism-Leninism came to be taught in state schools in the same rote form that catechism and Bible had been taught in the parochial schools before. This new bargain took its toll on consciousness and culture, but the flip side was that living standards grew steadily throughout the next twenty years.

An example of problems and solutions in the realm of housing is the case of Teresita Roca, who in 1970 got on the bus from Santiago de Cuba with her four children to escape from an alcoholic husband and start a new life. For a week the five of them stayed with her sister, who had come to the capital long before the revolution to work as a housemaid. Then they slipped into a former storefront on a main thoroughfare in Marianao, while Roca got a job in a daycare center nearby.

"We lived in a room right on the main sidewalk," Teresita recalls. "It was an illegal residence but the law also said we couldn't be thrown out. That was the story of those places—each time the housing agency talked someone out of there or found them a new place, somebody else slipped in before they could close it up or tear it down. We were just one in that series, and we lived there for almost two years. I felt happy just to have a roof over my head, even though the ceiling was falling down, and it leaked in the rain."

After two years, the state housing agency finally found the Roca family an apartment on the Calle Montserrate at the edge of Old Havana, in a former hotel with an intriguing history. The Hotel Montserrat was "one of the most modern and luxurious hotels of Havana, containing eighty splendid rooms with all the comforts including telephones and private baths," an advertisement a year after its opening had claimed. The site had once been occupied by a Carabalí cabildo, the Isuamo Isiegue de Oro, which later became a colored mutual aid society. It was bought by Spaniards toward the end of the colony, and in 1924 a Spanish-born investor opened the new hotel, a five story steel-and-concrete edifice with an open-cage wrought-iron elevator, balconies shaded by awnings that faced the bustling street, and a penthouse apartment on top.

By the time of its nationalization the Montserrat had become a residential hotel, and the only old residents still left when Teresita Roca arrived were a pair of French women, probably former prostitutes, who had remained in Havana. The rest of her neighbors were a mix of Cuban whites, blacks, and mulattos including a flower arranger, a steelworker, a sculptor, a ship captain, a bartender, a policeman, a dining hall worker, and a novelist. "When I was still in Santiago, I dreamed of a balcony," Teresita recalls. "So I figured this was that vision, come true." Blacks, practitioners of *santería*, and descendants of slaves, the Rocas had in a certain sense come home. Teresita set about subdividing the bathroom to make a tiny kitchen and bath, and expanding the living space by building what tens of thousands of Havana families in tight quarters had recourse to, a *barbacoa* or loft. Teresita Roca went to work in the personnel office of an electric plant, and later sewed and crafted wigs and candles in her home. Her children all went to boarding school for either junior high or high school, relieving the crowding somewhat.

The exact etymology of *barbacoa* is lost in conflicting claims and legends, but it is the same as barbecue, and the coinage referred either to its being built on a rack of crossbeams like a cooking grille, or to the heat produced by this arrangement, or both. Though the practice in Havana must date back to the late nineteenth century (because regulations prohibiting it were adopted at that time), the great flourishing of the barbacoa came after the revolution. Families who found themselves new owners of high-ceilinged houses or apartments did not feel the need to ask anyone's permission. They invented. A stroll down many streets of older neighborhoods revealed new ceilings and floors, visible through open shutters that had once sat high on single-story walls.

Despite the Soviet influence within Cuban ideology and political culture, some of these critical issues were addressed by filmmakers. Sara Gómez's *De cierta manera* (One Way or Another, 1974–77) looked at working-class Afro-Cuban culture, including its machismo, through the contrasting eyes of a white schoolteacher in an area slated for slum clearance and the black factory worker with whom she becomes involved. Throughout this story, the film intersperses documentary footage of the actual demolition of the El África solar in the barrio of Cayo Hueso (childhood home of Chano Pozo and a cradle of both crime and *rumba*) for replacement by a new housing project.

The relative abandonment of the housing stock during the 1960s was replaced by a new initiative in the early 1970s. This program attempted to decentralize the city by building bedroom communities on the east side of the bay (Alamar and Bahía) and the west side of town (San Agustín). The new concrete five-story apartment buildings—modeled after those of East European capitals like Moscow, East Berlin, and Sofia—were an escape valve for the pressure created by the lack of homes. They made use of a labor force of voluntary workers known as microbrigades, who built their own housing under the supervision of the universal state-sponsored unions. In a latter-day transfiguration of the Jabón Candado soap-bar lottery, microbrigade two- and three-bedroom apartments were distributed to union members by workplace assemblies on a mixed basis of participation, credentials, and need.

This novel incorporation of rank-and-file Havanans into housing construction succeeded in resolving some of the needs, but it brought new problems in its wake. Microbrigades turned out to be costly in terms of time and materials. Under the pressure to deliver the houses to those anxious to get out of their cramped spaces in the old neighborhoods, the brigades cut corners. The design— foreign to the architecture of Havana and to proposals developed by Cuban architects of the time—was repetitive and both functionally and esthetically not very good. Alamar, for instance, became a sprawl of hundreds of nearly identical rectangular five-story concrete walkups spread out between a highway and the sea. The *cinco plantas* (five stories), as the design became universally known, had low ceilings by Havana standards, weak electrical and plumbing connections, leaks in the walls, and doors and windows with little resistance to hot sun and tropical storms. When the designs were increased beyond five stories, the buildings needed elevators, which generally could not withstand the number of residents they had to carry. Finally, many residents of the *cinco plantas* added makeshift extra rooms, closed in common spaces or used them as garages or patios in which to grow bananas, or sat on the stairways as they were accustomed to using the sidewalks and courtyards of older neighborhoods, to play dominos and drink rum. Some began to call the microbrigade buildings "vertical solars."

In the area of food supply, imports of cattle feed and powdered milk gave birth to a sophisticated Cuban cheese industry, its products within the reach of all. Waiting lines for ice cream cones or three-scoop platters at Coppelia, which had become a fact of life in

Alamar housing project residents playing basketball.

Photo: Greg Cluster.

the early 1970s, dwindled to fifteen minutes or so. The shelves of the capital's stores filled with consumer products from Eastern Europe including canned meats and new televisions from Moscow, wines and fruit preserves and canned vegetables from Bulgaria, blenders from East Germany, and more. Many of these goods were sold in a so-called parallel market at elevated but not astronomical prices. The best-supplied of all the parallel market stores, where shoppers went to stock up for a special occasion, was located in a spacious building in Centro Habana across from the old site of the Plaza del Vapor. Its official name was Supermercado Centro, but most people still called it by its old name, Sears.

Though only a minority of the capital's residents had opportunity to buy a private car, still the numbers multiplied thanks to the purchases by state companies and some designated categories of managers, professionals, and outstanding workers. Alongside the pre-1959 products of Detroit circulated more and more Russian Volgas and Ladas, Czech Tatras, and Yugoslavian Yugos. By the 1980s rush hour traffic jams returned to Havana. They were called *tranque*, the word for what happens in Cuban dominoes when the game gets blocked. Day trips from Havana to Varadero beach by bus, complete with lunch and cabaña at a hotel, were cheap and easy to book.

At the Czech Culture Center on La Rampa, meanwhile, anyone could buy hand-blown glassware from Bohemia, pick recordings of the Prague Symphony playing Mozart, or enjoy imported Pilsen beer in glazed ceramic mugs. Across the street, where the Montmartre cabaret had been, the Restaurant Moscú offered the chance to try out a Russian soup, a *salianska* or *borscht* washed down with a cup of Ararat cognac or Stolichnaya vodka. Textiles were abundant, varied and cheap in Havana dry goods stores thanks to imports of natural and synthetic fibers from Eastern Europe. They combined with old Singer sewing machines and sewing skills to produce a variety in clothing styles and colors that surprised visitors expecting a population dressed in army fatigues or like Chairman Mao. When Carlos Larrinaga traveled to Germany for a training course in the late 1970s, he brought back the finished outfit his daughter Santa would premiere at the traditional party celebrating her turning fifteen.

The close encounter with East left other marks in the city's culture beyond the culinary ones. The teaching of Eastern European languages, along with Vietnamese and Chinese, had been initiated in the 1960s, but now it turned into a whole branch of education. Free language academies operated in every neighborhood, offering classes in many tongues by day or by night. Daniel Motola, after starting at the University of Havana in pure mathematics, decided he was not a mathematicians but a linguist, and switched to Russian which became his career. His mother—Fidelista because of Castro's support for education rather than his ideology—told him this was a mistake, because Cuba was ninety miles from the United States and one way or another English would become the language to know once again. Meanwhile her son León became one of tens of thousands of Cubans to study in the Eastern Bloc, spending six years in Warsaw becoming a specialist in physics and an electrical engineer before returning to work for a good salary in the ministry of armed forces. Those who went to northern Russia returned from long cold winters with memories of friendly and extroverted dormitory mates who insisted that they sit down to breakfasts of sardines, black bread, sausage, and vodka. Many brought back shoes and scarves they had bought in the immense department stores around Red Square in Moscow. More than a few also returned with a spouse from Warsaw or Leningrad or Prague.

A quarter century later, one of Havana's angry young men of the generation born in the 1980s, the writer José Manuel Sánchez, known by his pen name Yoss and for his punk/heavy-metal attire, would sum up the effect of the Russian cartoons, household goods, and rock groups that permeated his childhood: "Russian culture was a muted but constant influence in many areas of daily life, a contradictory symbol of both modernity and ugliness, poor quality yet great durability, an ambivalence that for decades shaped Cuban attitudes toward everything Russian, and that underlies our calling them 'bowling balls.' " *Bolos*, bowling balls, was indeed the slang term Cubans coined to describe the Russian advisors and technicians who lived among them, especially in the capital. They lived alongside Cuban residents from before and after 1959 in the FOCSA in Vedado as well as Alfredo Hornedo's last two developments, the former Rosita de Hornedo and Riomar apartment complexes on the Miramar seafront, both renamed Sierra Maestra after the scene of the guerrilla struggle.

Bolos remains in the Havana idiom of those who lived through that period, and so do a very few words of Russian, out of many that were popular when enthusiasm for things Russian was at its height. An old automatic rifle used by the local militia is called a *pepechá* to this day, the summary of an academic dissertation in the University of Havana is still a *referat*, and many who studied in Kiev or Baku still call sausage *kalvasá* or say *smetana* for cream.

Foreign influence in those 1970s and early 1980s cannot be reduced, either, to Soviet Russia and the countries of the East. Cuban participation in wars in Angola and Ethiopia, the Sandinista revolution in Nicaragua, and the official friendships with Algeria and South Yemen all opened paths to and from a variety of compass points. Beyond the thousands that fought in the battle of Cuito Cuanavale against the troops of the South African apartheid regime, many more doctors, teachers, and sports instructors traveled the greatest part of sub-Saharan Africa, Algeria, Yemen, Iraq, Iran, as well as Managua and Granada closer to home. From the early 1970s on, the medical schools of Cuba and especially Havana produced an ever greater supply of doctors, who came to constitute an exportable surplus, ambassadors of a significant part of the country's foreign relations effort.

At the same time, thousands of foreign students came to study at the University of Havana, which took in Palestinians, Ethiopians, and Afghans, as well as Ukrainians and Vietnamese. So *habaneros* of those years—and not only the middle class—came into contact with more new cultures than ever before. House-seeking immigrants from Oriente like Teresita Roca were dubbed *palestinos* by the longer-time residents of the capital, who saw them as uprooted and homeless like the Palestinians whom they met.

Nor was the study of English completely neglected. Tony Irízar, who had once practiced the words to "Somewhere Over the Rainbow" on his way to and from the movies, became an English professor after earlier stints as an agrarian reform official, security officer, and principal of a junior high. Teresita Roca's daughter Gloria and the Larrinagas' son Carlitos became professors of English as well. "We had no money for me even to buy an alarm clock," Gloria remembers, "but I figured out how to tell the time before dawn by the position of the stars against the nearby buildings. So I could get up, do everything I had to do, and catch the bus to my college class."

In 1978, another group of Spanish-speaking strangers appeared on the streets of Havana, the opposite of the *bolos* in a certain sense—culturally Cuban yet distinct from those who lived there now. These were Cuban-Americans from Miami, invited back in a sudden thaw.

Since the early 1960s, Cubans who left for the United States had been condemned in official discourse as traitors, excoriated as *gusanos* (maggots or worms). Popular language had picked up the term as a synonym for those disaffected from the revolution, *gusanos* even if they lived in Regla, Vedado, or Marianao. On the other hand, family loyalty ran deep, and many in Havana kept up with their Miami relatives in spite of prohibitions (just as many of their opposite numbers swallowed pressures from the most rightwing Miami groups to cut all ties with "Communists" left behind). This contradiction had torpedoed what would have been Carlos Larrinaga's first trip abroad since Chicago, for a training course in Italy in the late 1960s, because the local CDR president denounced him for lending his phone to a neighbor to receive phone calls from her ex-husband in Miami. The implication was that he, despite his and Raquel's own service as officers of the CDR, would seek political asylum while in the capitalist West.

In 1978, however, this picture abruptly changed. Among the causes were the stabilization of the economy, the recovery of commercial ties with most Western countries other than the United States, and a certain temporary detente with the Carter administration (which for two years allowed U.S. residents to travel legally to Cuba for the first time since 1962). In this context, the Cuban government began a dialogue with a portion of the Florida émigré community. Those who had left were henceforth not *gusanos* but "the Cuban community abroad." They could board special charter flights to Havana's José Martí International Airport to see family and revisit old homes and haunts. Or, as the street humor of Havana described this sudden turnaround, "the worms have metamorphosed into butterflies now." Almost 100,000 butterflies came in the first year, in a spirit of reconciliation and with suitcases packed full of American consumer goods.

These visits, however, were soon overshadowed by the pent-up desire of a minority on the Havana shore to make the hop the other way, and permanently. In the spring of 1980, ten thousand of them crammed into the grounds of Peruvian embassy on Fifth Avenue in Miramar, seeking asylum not in Peru but in the United States. This chapter in the drama of migration to the north led to an organized exodus of 125,000 Cubans, some 80 percent of them from Havana. By an accord reached between the two governments, for a period of five months those who wanted to make the trip could board small craft from Miami which were allowed to land in the minor port of

Mariel to the west of Havana, where the British had sheltered some of their ships while waiting to fight their way into Havana Bay in 1762. Those who left through Mariel spanned the spectrum of the society—white and black, employed and unemployed, with all levels of education and jobs, and including about 10 percent who were released from mental hospitals and jails.

In some cases their departure was no surprise, as was the case with the writer who lived across the hall from Teresita Roca. Gay, censored, and forced to publish the majority of his work by smuggling the manuscripts abroad, Reynaldo Arenas had been jailed, released, and in search of a way to leave the country for years. In the meantime, he lived in the Hotel Montserrat, thanks to a thousand peso bribe to the official resident of the room, where Arenas too built a barbacoa and a terrace out the back. In *Before Night Falls*, his phantasmagoric first-person novel written in the United States, Arenas went on to describe the Montserrat as "a real jungle on the far side of the law," a den of feuding families, witches, sex slaves, and thieves. Or, according to Teresita Roca's less sensational version, "We got along fine with him, we helped him, but later everybody got fed up with what he wrote about us that wasn't true."

In the cases of others who made their way to Mariel, however, the surprise of friends or families was complete. Isaac and Nirma Motola, mechanic and biology teacher, announced suddenly that they were going to join Nirma's relatives in Florida. The rest of the family had never heard them express this degree of disaffection, but two days later they were gone.

Though Alberto Motola later went to visit Isaac, and even put in some time selling shoes with him in a Miami flea market, in general Mariel set the clock of family reconciliation back many years. The official classification for those who left this time was neither *gusanos* nor *mariposas*, but *escoria*, the scum that floats to the top. On arrival in Miami, they were received as *marielitos*. Both terms were derogatory. In Havana they were labeled criminals, and repudiated in public marches and sometimes by mobs outside the homes they were leaving. In South Florida, white and upper-class Cubans considered them inferior, because among them were too many blacks and people who didn't speak English.

Family visits to Havana were severely reduced—until the 1990s—while visits the other way, such as Alberto Motola's, continued on a limited scale. In a curious footnote, the CDR president who had nixed Carlos Larrinaga's trip to Italy in the 1960s went on a family visit to Miami in the 1980s and decided to stay. "Behind every extremist there's an opportunist," goes another piece of Havana street wisdom, chosen by Raquel Cañizares to explain this event.

Those who fit in neither category went on with their lives in Havana, but the theme of family reunion did not disappear. In the 1985 film *Lejanía* (Distance) by Jesús Díaz, a mother who had left her teenage son behind returns for a visit ten years later. Her attempt to revive the relationship runs up against the toll taken by distance and the lack of a shared life. The young man does connect, however, with the female cousin who has also come to visit, as their shared memories form a bridge across the cultural and geographic divide.

Other Cuban films of the 1980s also touched on sensitive spots. No female directors took the place of Sara Gómez, who died young. However, Tomás Gutiérrez Alea's *Hasta cierto punto* (Up To a Point, 1983) reprised the themes of class and gender with the story of a single mother who breaks barriers by going to work on Havana's docks, and the male filmmaker, working on a documentary, who falls in love with her. Pastor Vega's *Portrait of Teresa* (1979), begins and ends with still shots of its title character, a Havana textile worker—one on the Malecón and the other at the corner of San Rafael and Galiano, where a band is performing in the park where El Encanto once stood. Vega wanted to make a "problem" film and so surveyed a number of psychologists about the most prevalent dilemmas facing their patients. *Teresa* examined the "double shift" and double standard faced by the women of the capital: plunged into paid work and cultural activity but at the same time confronted with all their old household duties; given economic freedom by employment and divorce laws but subject to the sexual double standard of old.

Cuban film, along with simultaneous work in Brazil, Argentina, Bolivia, and Mexico, kick-started the birth of a new film aesthetic throughout Latin America, whose products were (and continue to be) hosted in Havana's annual Festival of New Latin American Cinema. Begun in 1979, the Festival projected its entries on screens throughout the barrios of Havana, and after the cinemas closed its participants and public partied all night in the Hotel Nacional.

The socialism of some abundance, which counted on the Cuban-Soviet alliance as its central pillar, began to falter in about 1985.

Bureaucracy and overcentralization wore heavily. The prolonged
economic growth began to stagnate, and despite equal educational
opportunity it grew more difficult to rise on the social scale. It was
evident, for instance, that few youth, blacks, or women were getting into positions of power, and that religious believers were dis-
criminated against for such posts. People complained that less and
less could be settled in the meetings of local assemblies, while the
number of bureaucrats multiplied in all parts and the mass media
reflections of daily reality were boring and unreal. In the second
half of the 1980s, trade union meetings, student meetings, and
meetings of professionals and intellectuals discussed these problems. These were called "the process of rectification of errors and
negative tendencies," or Rectification in brief.

Among the problems discussed in the Rectification assemblies
were absenteeism and lateness at work, shrinking productivity in
factories, the inefficiency of the city's buses, the critical housing situation and lack of stable water supply in many barrios, and a lack
of entertainment venues for young people. Another theme was all
the red tape that had to be negotiated by the citizens as they
bounced from one office to another, which popular language called
exactly that, *peloteo*, being tossed around like a ball. In this context,
a certain air of renewal suffused the press, especially the radio,
which reported some of these heated assemblies. What began as a
discussion of the causes of economic slowdown ended up being a
debate about the role of the bureaucracy and party officials in all
the organs of government, about rigidities of ideology and political
mistakes.

Where this would have led if the economic base had remained
intact is impossible to say. Once again, as many times before, the
economies of the capital and the nation were about to be affected by
events taking place somewhere far away. In the late 1980s, through
the ten thousand kilometers of intense traffic and communication
that linked and separated Moscow and Havana, the echoes of glas-
nost and perestroika could be felt. In Soviet publications such as
Sputnik and *Moscow News* and *Literary Gazette* on sale in Spanish
versions at the newsstands of Havana, a discourse which questioned the socialist system from top to bottom left Cuban readers
astounded.

In August of 1989, *Sputnik* and *Moscow News* were removed from
sale, but that summer the populace was busy dealing with yet
another shock. General Arnaldo Ochoa, hero of the wars in Africa

and one-time commander of the Western Army in charge of the defense of Havana, was put on trial along with other high officials of the armed forces and the Ministry of the Interior, accused of corruption. The public trial electrified the TV viewers of the capital and the island. At the end of the trial, Ochoa and others convicted of drug dealing and personal enrichment were sentenced to death. A few months later, the announcement of the demolition of the Berlin Wall closed this year full of surprises. Consequences now lay ahead that, like those following the bearded rebels' triumph of 1959, almost no one accustomed to the Havana of the past three decades could guess.

16

The Blackout: Havana in the "Special Period" and Beyond

In part of a former mansion just off the Plaza de Armas, the gallery of the artist Pedro Pablo Oliva displays his paintings, among the most sought-after in Cuban art today. Oliva comes from the generation that studied in the 1960s in the National Art School, the fantastic complex of brick beehives and sinuous paths designed by Ricardo Porro on the former golf course of the Havana Country Club. Unlike the majority of students from the provinces who came to study in the capital, Oliva returned after graduation to his native Pinar del Río, a hundred miles to the west, where he went on creating his distinctive works. The human and animal figures in his canvases float in the air or recline in large armchairs, sofas, or beds, apparently sleeping and with peaceful expressions on their face. Unlike that of his contemporaries, his work does not usually feature explicit ideological challenges, irony, or commentary on other works of art. Knowledgeable viewers are surprised, therefore, to discover "The Great Blackout" (*El gran apagón*), an enormous canvas that fills an entire wall of his gallery. In this painting, numerous creatures—children, grandparents, cats, youths, birds—are curled

254

Pedro Pablo Oliva, "The Big Blackout" (1994). Oil on canvas. 290 x 520 cm.

Photo: Oscar Llanes.

up in a sort of tunnel lit only by a single candle. The painting is swathed in darkness and shadow except for the feeble glow that illuminates the inhabitants of the space. Among them, not particularly standing out, appear the serene faces of José Martí and Fidel Castro. Everyone seems to be asleep.

The fall of the Berlin Wall in the autumn of 1989 and the breakup of the Soviet Union in summer of 1991 were, for Cubans, the entrance into a tunnel, a prolonged *apagón*. Unlike residents of Warsaw or Prague or Budapest, the *habaneros* never had Red Army tanks patrolling their avenues or squares. So for them, the breakup of the Soviet bloc was not a moment of independence, a thrill of freedom or renewal. Rather, its effect was devastating. It brought an economic depression—not only a lack of light and electricity, but a simultaneous shortage of nearly everything else.

The demise of its special trade and aid agreements with Eastern Europe cost Cuba 80 percent of its export-import trade, brought an end to cheap oil and stable sugar prices, and cost the economy its main source of loans as well. As had happened with the loss of U.S. trade thirty years earlier, spare parts for machinery and inputs for agriculture and industry disappeared. Sixty percent of Cuban factories shut down or produced at bare minimum capacity. Electricity generation plummeted, as did supplies of food. "The revolution has only three problems," a typically ironic joke in the capital had it: "breakfast, lunch, and dinner." Most households in Havana had cooked on gas stoves or kerosene ones, supplemented by electric hot plates. Even when there was food to cook, now all three of these sources of energy might fail. Planned blackouts, by neighborhood, were instituted to share the electricity shortage equally. Unplanned ones added to the burden. Residents of the capital began to speak of *alumbrones*—brief periods when the lights went on. Those responsible for cooking, usually the women, often had to wait at home for the moment during the day that gas or electricity would come on. Those responsible for finding some food to cook, frequently the men, might be out scouring markets, legal or underground.

By Latin American standards, no one was malnourished or starving in the Cuban capital, though the daily intake of vitamins and protein fell drastically. Havanans' anxiety about what they would eat and when grew even faster. For those still working, lunchrooms at their jobs continued to serve a free basic meal, often just rice and beans—except when there was no fuel, and both lunchroom and workplace shut down at midday. Schools, hospital and clinics, and other essential services all kept functioning, if on a shoestring. Many other facilities did not. Coppelia stayed open, but going for ice cream became an activity for an entire afternoon or evening, with lines often four hours long. The government called the wartime-like austerity a "Special Period in Time of Peace." The euphemism stuck, and "Special Period" became the name of this crisis time.

Verónica Loynaz was living in Miramar in a large house surrounded by fruit trees and vines of blue bellflowers entwined in the fence. Unlike her aunt Flor, she did not live with thirty dogs, but rather with her husband, two small sons, two aging parents, three aunts, two dogs, and reasonable number of cats. She worked at a research center that studied European affairs, where she enjoyed a professional's salary that through the 1980s had guaranteed a comfortable life in socialist Havana's terms.

When the crisis broke out, what she could buy with her ration book suddenly shrank. The vegetable oil, soap, and detergent she was accustomed to getting at the state-run corner *bodega* nearly disappeared, as did the chicken and eggs. In the capital's always evolving slang, eggs were known for a time as *americanos* "because no one knows when they are coming or how many they will be." The monthly ration of beef became a mixture of ground-beef and soy powder of dubious flavor. The liter-a-day ration of milk still supplied to her younger son (as to all children seven or below) would not stretch to allow everyone in the household the morning *café con leche* to which all Cubans were accustomed. Off-ration sales of milk and other dairy products in Cuban pesos came to an end. There was no wheat flour, and the bread ration shrank to one small roll per person per day. The parallel market located around the corner from the bodega shut down. There were no more Bulgarian canned vegetables, Russian canned meat, German sausages, or Hungarian wines and sweets.

Although she was among the lucky ones who still had work, Verónica had to get there every morning by bike or on foot, because the city's bus service was decimated by lack of gas and spare parts. Hundreds of thousands of Chinese bicycles, distributed through workplaces, practically replaced cars on the streets. The Flying Pigeon, Forever, and Phoenix brands took the place of Ladas and old Chevies and Fords. Though these bikes were sturdy—the Flying Pigeon was said to have been used by Chinese peasants to bring harvests to market and by the Vietnamese to transport ammunition on the Ho Chi Minh Trail—they were heavy and limited to one gear. La Gran Habana had reached a total of 2 million inhabitants, spread out over an area of 280 square miles, a low-slung city with few tall buildings outside of El Vedado. For many thousands, the Special Period brought a bicycle trip of five to fifteen miles every morning and afternoon.

José Ramón Rojas, a cousin of the younger Larrinagas, worked as personnel specialist at the Pedagogical University in Ciudad Libertad. The job had formerly involved a bus commute from home to office, followed by many trips in a Ministry of Education car from his office to the Ministry in Old Havana, other offices, schools, teachers' residences, and student dorms. All of that now had to be done by bike. Throughout the city, three and four people, parents and children, could be seen perched on handle bars, cargo racks, and makeshift extra seats of a single bicycle. At night, in blacked out zones devoid of the usual sound of radios, TVs, or record players, the ghostly sound of whizzing tires was punctuated by hisses of breath to warn other cyclists, or the tinkling of old-fashioned spring-action bells. Between the biking and the reduced diet, Havana became a city of citizens who ranged from slender to skinny. Very few looked like their photos of a few years before.

In spite of being a committed member of the Communist Party, Verónica Loynaz found herself with no alternative but to buy food on the mushrooming black market. There one could find beans or eggs or vegetables brought privately from the countryside, as well as powdered milk and cheese and other commodities stolen from the hard-currency stores in tourist hotels or those maintained for diplomats. In relation to salaries, prices were high in the black market and astronomical in the dollar stores. The black market value of the Cuban peso dropped to 150 per dollar. Verónica's and her husband's salaries plus her parents' pensions equaled less than seven dollars a month.[1] Taking advantage of the yard surrounding the house in Miramar, she decided to create her own subsistence economy on the side.

This generation of Loynaz harvested the fruit from the trees of their garden to supplement their diets. Luckily, their plantain trees yielded *platanos burros*, a banana variety that could be eaten either raw or cooked. Above all, however, they devoted their yard to raising chickens, rabbits, and piglets. They acquired the animals from friends who went to the countryside to buy from farmers, or sometimes from government stores in the city that offered them for this purpose. Thousands of families did likewise, using porches and makeshift window-boxes if they didn't have yards, so that the conflict between treating these animals as pets or as food became a staple of Havana humor and literature in the 1990s. One joke—or true story—told of the parents who named their chickens Breakfast, Lunch, and Dinner so the children would not lose sight of the problems they were intended to solve. *La Manteca* ("Lard"), a popular theater piece, revolved around a family raising a clandestine pig inside their apartment, an animal none could bring themselves to kill.

Over every extra duty that the economic crisis brought to the households of Havana hung the threat of the *apagón*, whether scheduled or unforeseen. After finishing her daily work as a researcher, Verónica Loynaz hurried home to face her domestic tasks before night fell. She had to see whether anything new had come in at the bodega, take care of the animals, invent a supper menu out of whatever was at hand, and urge the children to do their homework while daylight lasted—all before a blackout hit. On weekends, she went to the countryside in search of feed or fodder for the animals, and melted cakes of soap to serve in place of detergent in her washing machine, ready for the hours when there was electricity to make it run. She picked bellflowers from the vine to marinate for the week's vegetable salads. And finally, when they could, she and her husband went out to visit a pair of lucky friends who lived beside a maternity hospital so their current never shut off.

In March of 1993, Havana was hit with yet another calamity, a vast and unruly winter hurricane later dubbed the "Storm of the Century" which drove the sea over the seawall and inland for as many as five blocks. This catastrophe flooded the home of the lucky friends who lived next to the maternity hospital. While helping them rescue their furniture and television set, Verónica decided it was time to change her life. The next day she went to see a friend of her father's who worked in the import-export firm CIMEX, one of the state corporations newly created to earn foreign exchange for the public treasury. She decided to leave the research work which she had always enjoyed so much, and submerge herself in learning business, so she could earn a part of her salary in the hard currency which was becoming essential to daily life. She went to work for CIMEX in the commercialization of such Cuban products as commemorative and antique coins. To deal with the crisis, the government legalized possession of dollars by Cuban citizens, and made them the legal tender in an ever-broadening network of stores no longer limited to tourists and diplomats. On the import side of CIMEX, Loynaz worked on the acquisition of clothing and shoes to sell in these dollar-only outlets, *el shopping* as they soon became known.[2] CIMEX flourished as Cuba slowly went about reinserting itself into the capitalist world market. Today its offices occupy the former Rosita de Hornedo (later Sierra Maestra) apartment-hotel on the Miramar seafront, recovered from the inroads of the Storm of the Century. In the meantime, as Cuban economic policy made room for more foreign companies and joint ventures, Verónica went to work for the Havana branch of an Indian home appliance firm.

The foreign business sector, however, was unknown territory to most of the city's residents. Among *habaneros* of color, the feeling was common that in this sector old patterns of racial discrimination had reared their head. The foreigners that most of Havana saw were the growing influx of Italian, Spanish, German, and Canadian tourists, as the government promoted tourism for a quick source of foreign exchange. These tourists increasingly monopolized the few nightlife venues that were able to stay open. The Turquino Bar of the Habana Libre, the new Salsa Palace recently opened in the Riviera, the disco in the Comodoro and the emblematic Tropicana cabaret became exclusive sites for visitors with dollars. So what Havanans began to call "apartheid tourism" made these years of lean cows especially bitter.

Unlike the depression of the 1930s, this one took place in a city all of whose people had grown used to having access to these particular playgrounds—to not having to stop "at the door of a *dancing* or a bar/or at the desk of a hotel" as the triumphal verses of Nicolás Guillén's poem "Tengo" proclaimed from the pages of schoolbooks, a poem that practically everyone had learned by heart. The Malecón, eternal nighttime porch of the Havana coast, now literally filled with people who brought portable radios, guitars, and bottles of homemade rum in search of recreation in a city battered by crisis and disillusion. The nicknames of the Cuban-style moonshine testified to its kick—*Chispa de Tren* (Train Spark) or *Saltapatrás* (Jump Back).

More than half of Havana had not experienced any earlier time to which the Special Period could be compared. The majority hadn't been born or couldn't remember the scarcities of the first years of the American embargo or the 1970 harvest, nor the inspiring hurricane of revolutionary ideas that had raged alongside. Many fewer could remember the ills of the decades before 1959. Those who did remember often believed that this last decade of the twentieth century was the worst they had ever known, and they felt the wind blowing in a completely new direction. The restoration of capitalism in Eastern Europe not only shook the daily economy of Cubans, but also shocked their way of thinking. On August 5, 1994, hundreds of them poured into the streets near the Malecón in Centro Habana, from the Prado to the Parque Maceo, in the first tumultuous demonstration of popular discontent in Havana in twenty-five years.

Although the initial motivation of this gathering was a rumor that a ship would arrive to take on passengers for a new version of the Mariel boatlift, the anxiety of the groups in the street overflowed into disorder, violence, and vandalism. They broke the windows of a dollar store and chanted slogans including "Down with Fidel." Castro himself, about to turn sixty-eight years old, promptly appeared on the same streets, walking down Calle San Lázaro toward the heart of the disturbances. Those who had silently watched the angry demonstrators a few moments before now welcomed Castro with applause and *vivas*, testimony to the volatile mixed emotions with which many in the city confronted these years of crisis, paralysis, and change.

Although this demonstration ended without significant effects on political stability, it was clear that the city was teetering on an edge. A few days later, the government announced the opening of new farmers' markets, long requested at workplace assemblies and neighborhood meetings, where small farmers, cooperatives, and state farms could bring fruits, vegetables, and pork from the countryside to sell at prices regulated by supply and demand.[3] While very expensive by Cuban standards, these *agromercados* were significantly cheaper, more accessible, and less morally compromising than the black market. Together with other measures they quickly boosted the purchasing power of the Cuban peso, which soon traded for the dollar (in new legal state exchange booths) in the range of twenty or twenty-five to one. More unexpectedly, the doors to northward migration were thrown open, without any kind of control.

Along the thirty miles of coral shores, inlets, river mouths and sandy beaches of greater Havana, would-be emigrants launched every imaginable sort of boat and raft. This time, unlike the Mariel exodus of 1980, those who wanted to try their luck in the United

States did not need a boat to come from Florida to fetch them nor a predetermined place to meet. An even greater difference between this and all other emigrations since 1959 was in the attitude toward those who left displayed by those who stayed behind.

In Pogolotti, a few doors down from the home of Juan Valdés and his wife Daisy—where the CDR headquarters of the block were located—an entire family set to work building a raft in their own house. Laboring night and day, fastening pine boards to tractor inner tubes, they fashioned a craft which took up all of their modest living room. They made oars out of baseball bats and mops, and a sail out of an old sheet, and found a way around a moment of crisis when it seemed they wouldn't be able to fit the raft through the door. Then they carried it to the coastline accompanied by young and old neighbors of the barrio, all offering advice about the voyage or helping to convey the saints from the altar that the mother of the family had maintained in the back room of the house. Particular care was paid to Yemayá, goddess of the sea, and Elleguá, opener of doors and roads. The raft was launched, loaded down by the number of passengers and the weight of provisions they'd put together for the perilous trip. It promptly sank. After rescuing the saints, the family and its supporters returned to Pogolotti and got busy building a new boat.

This scene was repeated up and down the coast, from Mariel to Cojímar where the British had landed and Hemingway fished, to the beaches of Guanabo where tourists watched Cuban families send off their relatives among a mixture of cheers, tears, and entreaties not to risk their lives. "It was a kind of hysteria you had to see to believe," reported a resident of Calle 60 at the edge of Buenavista who watched the parade of rafts on trucks, carts, and shoulders proceed down hill past her house toward the coast. "It was shocking to me, but it showed how people wanted to do something, anything, anything at all."

Things did not go exactly as planned. Facing an unprecedented numbers of rafters, the U.S. Coast Guard did not do what it had done with the scattering of rafters or boaters who had taken this plunge and eluded Cuban patrols over the past thirty-five years. Instead of bringing these migrants to Miami and granting them resident status, U.S. authorities sent them to the naval base in Guantánamo and interned them in a tent city under the searing sun of Cuba's southern and easternmost part.[4] There they waited almost a year, 35,000 of them, the great majority from Havana, until the two governments could agree on what to do. When they finally got to Florida, this wave of Cubans would not be called exiles, or freedom fighters, or *marielitos*, but just *balseros* (rafters), a plain unvarnished fact.

After that summer of 1994, the doorway from Havana to Miami closed again from both sides. Thereafter, by official agreement, the only migrants to be accepted would be those who traveled on the 20,000 annual visas that the United States agreed to give, for which the residents of Havana could enter a lottery or apply in long lines that formed outside the United States Interests Section on the Malecón. Those who launched themselves into the sea knew that if they were intercepted by either U.S. or Cuban coast guard patrols, they would be brought back. But paradoxically, the *balseros* of 1994 (along with those who had left through Mariel fourteen years earlier) continued be a presence in the life of Havana, much more so than those who left in the 1960s and 1970s and cut their ties. Fifty or a hundred dollars sent or brought each month by relatives and friends living abroad began to signify, for many families without other income in dollars, a way to keep their heads above water. Soon the total of such remittances sent by Western Union or silently carried by visitors reached a total of 800 million dollars throughout the island. The majority of these came to rest in Havana, in its widening network of dollar stores and currency changing stands. A CADECA (currency stand) went up outside every new farmers' market, so the remittances could be changed in Cuban pesos to buy vegetables and meat. Though corner bodegas continued to distribute minimum rations of certain staple foods, the dollar stores became the main source of other basics like cooking oil, pasta, canned goods, dairy products, and soap.

In the second half of the 1990s and first years of the new century, the injection of hard currency from tourism, remittances, and new exports, and the continued growth of farmers' markets of various types, provided an escape valve from the reigning tension. By and large, *habaneros* gained back some of their lost weight. Blackouts, the symbols of the worst years of the crisis, decreased but did not go away. The twenty-centavo "camels," officially called Metrobuses and denominated with routes running from M1 through M6, took the edge off the transportation crisis. Along the same routes, for those who could afford a quicker and less exhausting alternative, state-regulated private taxis began to ply, mostly Detroit products of the 1950s. Because they cost ten pesos, they went by the popular name "M-10." Private cars, tourist rental cars, and state or company cars gradually began reclaiming the streets from bicycles, though the bikes in no way disappeared. Meanwhile, other novelties began changing the physical the face of the city, always in contradictory form.

To the west of the Almendares, where urban planners of past periods had called for preservation of a coastal strip that would truly let residents *mirar al mar*, new hotels grew up to house new waves of tourists, clashing with the ambience and blocking the view. The grassy, wooded Monte Barreto, where Alberto Motola had gardened in the 1970s, disappeared under an anonymous office-park-style hotel built in a joint venture with the French chain Novotel. Walking along still-elegant Fifth Avenue, with its green median and leafy trees, one came to not only the ex-Soviet (now Russian) embassy and the nearby towers of the 1980s-built Hotels Tritón and Neptuno with a whiff of the microbrigade about them, but also to the new Hotel Panorama which appeared to have been flown in from Cancún, and a square, undistinguished office block hopefully called the Miramar Trade Center, built to house foreign firms.

In spite of these eruptions of contemporary bad taste, the drive to convert Miramar into an international commercial district also brought benefits to the old buildings of the neighborhood. Hotels such as the Copacabana and the Comodoro were renovated, and many of the mansions along First, Third, and Fifth avenues were restored and rented to foreign firms such as Castrol, whose sign figured prominently in front of one of them, or new Cuban state corporations like CIMEX. A much larger wave of restoration swept through the older parts of city—along the Prado and especially in Old Havana, the former walled city between the Prado and the bay.

Around the Parque Central, the revival of tourism brought the resurrection of tattered monuments like the hotels Inglaterra, Plaza, and Sevilla. The nineteenth-century Telégrafo rose literally from its ashes on the corner of Prado and Neptuno. The restoration of the Centro Gallego, Centro Asturiano, Capitolio, and other nearby buildings brought some of the old splendor back to this former showpiece area, which had been abandoned by both the capitalist development of the 1950s and socialist priorities of the decades after that. Tourists followed, drawn away from Vedado by the architecture, atmosphere, proximity of the colonial quarter, and the animation of city life. In the "hot corner" of the park, to the south side of the statue of Martí, Cuban men of all descriptions

gathered as they always had to argue about baseball: the make-up
of the Cuban national team which they patriotically supported, or
the merits of famous players of the past, or developments in the
U.S. major leagues which they continued to follow from afar—
including the key games won by El Duque Hernández and other
Cuban stars.

In Old Havana, the pace of restoration and improvement in the
late 1990s and early 2000s seemed to quicken month by month. The
priority granted to tourism brought unprecedented resources and
authority to the office of the Historian of the City, in charge of pre-
serving the nearly five centuries of national heritage and putting it
on display. Through drive, creativity, and ability to gain the trust of
the predominantly working-class residents of this historic district,
the office and its director, Eusebio Leal, managed to win direct

Plaza Vieja, Old Havana, after restoration. At back left is the Fondo de
Bienes Culturales art center and gallery, formerly the Palace of the Counts
of Jaruco (see chapter 3). The restored buildings also house an elementary
school (note uniformed Cuban school children), a hard-currency microbrewery and café (back right), and a rooftop *camara oscura* for viewing Old
Havana as a whole.

Photo: Greg Cluster.

control over the redevelopment of the old city. Above all, they won the authority to tax tourist and commercial development and directly reinvest a share of the profits into both historical reconstruction and improvement of the water and gas supply and other imperatives or enhancements of daily life.

In the Plaza Vieja, where the old mansions had long deteriorated into overcrowded apartment buildings and solars, the Historian's office gradually restored them and put part of the space to new uses to serve both tourism and the city's artistic and cultural life. The Palace of the Counts of Jaruco, which we have mentioned before as the colonial home of the family of the Countess of Merlín and ex-owners of the fictional food vendor Genoveva de Santa Cruz, was restored and given to an arts organization for its exhibit rooms and office. The ground floors of other buildings on the one-time market square became galleries and even a microbrewery. On the rooftop of a renovated apartment building, a *camara oscura* periscope was installed, allowing guided "tours" of the old city and the bay as seen from above. Unlike in New York's Soho or the historic districts of Paris, however, these improvements did not price the old residents out. The renovated apartments on the upper floors of most of the buildings on the Plaza Vieja and nearby streets were returned to former residents, who had meanwhile been housed in temporary units nearby—though, to be sure, to reduce density others of the former residents were given apartments in outlying districts such as Alamar. The *camara oscura*, like almost all historic monuments, museums, concerts, and other attractions in the old city, charges tourists and residents differentially. It admits Cubans for one peso and foreigners for one dollar apiece.

In the Plaza de Armas, the former palace of the Counts of Santovenia became the Hotel Santa Isabel once again, a luxury tourist spot as it had been in the nineteenth century under the management of Colonel Lay of New Orleans. But the office building that had once housed the U.S. Embassy, now restored from its deterioration, became home to a new neighborhood library on the ground floor and Cuba's Museum of Natural History on the floors above. The former home of the freedwoman Juana Carvajal, which had deteriorated from solar to uninhabitable ruin by the 1980s, was meticulously restored to its eighteenth-century appearance, its murals carefully uncovered from beneath successive layers of a plaster in paint. It now serves as the city's archeological museum, displaying the artifacts dug up in the course of the efforts to rescue

Old Havana from neglect. Elementary school classrooms in the barrio have also been distributed among its many old and new museums, so the heritage can be built into their curricula.

Other resurrections brought by the renewal of tourism and a dollar economy were not so positive as these. The ghost of Havana as the city of sin, temptation, and pleasure-for-hire rose from the coffin where it had been resting for a third of a century. Alongside retired Canadian or German couples and groups of adventurous backpacking youth, the planes touching down in José Martí International Airport began to unload single men and women, above all from Spain, Italy, and Mexico, who came not only for sun and sea but also for the smiling and seductive mulattas and mulattos who appeared in advertisements and postcards in the foreground of beaches and cabarets.

In search of the necessary dollars to get through the month, and also of bridges to emigration, hundreds of young Cuban women and men began to circulate in the tourist areas as part- or full-time sexual companions. The majority were well educated, many of them with professions and jobs. The city's hotels, discos, and beaches became centers of this new prostitution, which the language of the street baptized as *jineterismo*. To *jinetear* (derived from the word for horseman or jockey) previously meant to bust ass in pursuit of something, and had therefore been identified with hustlers who changed money or acted as informal concierges for the relatively scarce foreign visitors. Now it came to mean selling one's ass to tourists. The image of Havana as a destination for sexual tourism, reproduced in the tales of travelers, gave the *jineteras* and *jineteros* a mythic status reflected in films, novels, and even salsa songs that circulated on the world market. Havana resident and leading crime novelist Daniel Chavarría, a Uruguayan exile whose pre–Special Period books had featured Cuban spies and grassroots characters outwitting agents of the CIA, tells how in the late 1990s he invented *jineteras* as his new heroines to meet the expectations of foreign publishers (though his new characters, like his old ones, usually turned the tables on the foreigners at the end).

In its sex industry, as in its dependence on remittances, Havana came to inhabit not so much a "Special Period" as the real world of late twentieth-century Latin American capitals, from Santo Domingo to Buenos Aires to Bogotá. It did not, however, return full-blown to the era of Graham Greene or *Godfather II*, either in the size of this industry or in its place in the city's social life. Many of the young *jineteros* of both sexes were not looked down upon in the barrios where they and their families lived. Their contribution to the domestic economy, especially in families that had no aunt or uncle or son or daughter abroad, could be decisive in the attempt to make ends meet every month. In more than a few cases, the *jineteros/as* ended up maintaining lasting and long-distance relationships that their families could look upon as a sort of engagement—and sometimes it was. The embassies of Spain, Italy, Mexico, and other countries processed more and more marriages between foreigners (generally middle aged) and their younger Cuban partners, who eventually emigrated and came to form parts of families regarded as respectable in their new homes.

Emigration in the 1990s and 2000s was not limited to balseros, U.S. visa lottery winners, and *jineteras* or *jineteros*. Many professionals sought or found work in Europe or South America, teaching courses or designing computer systems or training athletes or using whatever skills the Cuban education system had given them. Some went temporarily, on short-term contracts. Others went for good.

Daniel Motola went to Bolivia on a temporary contract, negotiated by the Ministry of Education, to teach educational methods at a provincial university. In the meantime, his mother's prediction was proven right, as he and hundreds of other professors of Russian retrained to teach English—newly revalued as the language of international commerce, tourism, and academic exchange. Teresita Roca's daughter Gloria married an American colleague who had been invited as a visiting professor in the university English department where she taught, and she went to the United States to teach Spanish and study for a Ph.D. Others who had studied languages found jobs on both sides of the Atlantic. Of two brothers who had been undergraduates in Gloria's department, one went to Spain to work in tourism and then as an English teacher, while the other set to work at home learning Italian, which allowed him to specialize in freelance translation of bureaucratic documents for the binational marriage boom.

One profession that figured heavily in emigration and work abroad was music. Sergio Larrinaga, Carlos and Raquel's third son, left for Europe in 1995 to follow the market for Cuban music, pursuing his career as a percussionist in Italy and Holland. He was far from the only Cuban musician in search of hard-currency employment. The renewal and dollarization of the Havana music market had begun in 1994 with the inauguration of the Palacio de la Salsa in the Hotel Riviera and other dance venues like La Cecilia near the Playa de Marianao and Papa's in the modernized yacht basin formerly called Barlovento, now rebaptized as Marina Hemingway. The best bands in the country rotated through these stages, especially Los Van Van (still adapting and going strong a quarter century after the 1970 harvest), NG La Banda, the always provocative Charanga Habanera, and the groups headed by Adalberto Álvarez, Isaac Delgado, and Paulito F.G. At the tables and on the dance floors of the clubs, a new breed of clients joined the tourists and the few fortunate Cubans there. These were minor league talent scouts seeking acts for bars in Amsterdam or Hamburg, and major league recording executives intent on investing in the juicy and undercapitalized capitalized Cuban music business and building its international appeal. Suddenly, the musicians in top bands began to earn dollars and drive Audis around Havana, inaugurating a new style of life which was equally vilified and admired.

The most famous case of the resurrection of Cuban music in the world market was the Buena Vista Social Club. The Social Club phenomenon was the result of a careful merchandising operation which made use of the formidable talents of old smiling musicians who smoked big cigars, drank rum, and played acoustic instruments. The Cuban music of the 1920s and 1930s, already familiar to North American and European ears, thus made a new appearance as a natural product uncontaminated by technology and splendid in its simplicity. In the concert film that followed the initial success of the album, these engaging musicians appeared against the background of a dirty but imposing city, unpainted and enchanting, whose beautiful buildings and residents shined in the midst of physical decadence just as the aged musicians did. Above all, the film and the music evoked the magical images of Graham Greene and Ernest Hemingway buried in the memory of the West. The popularity of Buena Vista Social Club spread like wildfire and opened a new path in Cuban music.

For their own part, Havanans without dollars, who were the majority, kept going to the Salon Rosado of the Tropical, where the famous bands often played in between their more lucrative engagements and international tours. At La Tropical, a new music was taking shape. This was *la timba*, an updated evolution of *son*. Extending the experience of salsa, la timba added new elements of musical fusion, sprinkled extremely rapid rhythms into the mix, and led the dancers to show off their abilities with abrupt, fluid, sensual moves not easily accessible to European tourists. Timba, Los Van Van's Juan Formell explained in one interview, "is any Cuban rhythm, then mixed with Afro-Urban American styles— funk, jazz, soul, blues, rap, anything that jives the hips."

Timba brought different subjects and languages into the mix as well as new rhythms and steps. Invocations of the gods of Afro-Cuban religions, which had practically vanished from Cuban popular music, reappeared in the new lyrics. Changó, Orula, and Yemayá were acclaimed from the leading stages and their names chanted by thousands of excited dancers. In a song called ¿Y qué tu quieres que te den? ("What do you want them to give to you?") the lead vocalist of Adalberto's band declaimed a rap-style lyric that spread from mouth to mouth, asking the "packed house" of the dance hall not to hold back, but to make their requests of Elegguá (who "opens the roads, and that's the truth") and other orishas. The packed house always repeated along with the singer: And what do you want him to give to you?

Outside the dance hall, of course, asking and waiting were not enough. Cuban orishas also helped those who helped themselves. Economic reforms that accompanied dollarization and farmers' markets also legalized small-scale self-employment in a variety of trades. Following this reversal of the "revolutionary offensive" of 1968, many in Havana set up shop as auto mechanics, carpenters, manicurists, or plumbers. Pablo Larrinaga, an office machine mechanic like his father, began to repair essential home appliances in his free time, from electric fans to rice cookers. Fast food stands like that of his great-grandfather repopulated the streets of the city, offering homemade sweets and drinks and fritters and sandwiches. More new services flourished with government licenses or without them: baking birthday cakes to order, teaching private classes of English or Italian, selling crafts, gardening, cleaning houses, catering weddings (with photos, dresses, video, food, and drink) and renting rooms and houses to tourists along with food or city tours or classes in Cuban dance. Approximately a quarter of the workers who had previously worked for the state now lived on income from this type of work.

Clandestine restaurants in private homes had emerged in the early 1990s and were legalized soon after. Their popular name, paladares, came from that of a fast food chain established by the villainess of a popular Brazilian soap opera to which most of

Cuba's TV viewers were addicted for entertainment and escape. Paladares sprang up in the living rooms of elegant houses and in garages and bedrooms of more modest ones. One, the famous Juana la Cubana in Vedado, served its fried pork, fried fish, fried plantains, rice, and beans in the single room of an apartment-with-barbacoa in which the beds were folded up against the wall during business hours. Paladares, however, remained subject to strict inspection as to the sources of their ingredients, some of which were available or affordable only on the black market. So they inhabited a gray area much like the *casabe* vendors of the sixteenth century who had to establish where they got their yucca from.

Luchando (struggling) is the universal term for this process of finding some way to make a necessary buck. Not everyone could set up a paladar or had a saleable skill. Thus some dedicated themselves to *bísnes*, to buying and selling things obtained legitimately like cigarettes or sugar from their ration or things stolen from the warehouses of the state. All told, the ingenious residents of the city came up with hundreds of such activities—illegal, semilegal, or quite legal but not quite by-the-book. Exaggerated descriptions popped up in the fiction published in Cuba in the late 1990s and 2000s just as the clandestine pigs had nosed their way into the plays and films of the years shortly before.

In Leonardo Padura's *The Novel of My Life* (2002), one character describes his friend's business this way: "He makes rum in his own house, and has a machine to seal the caps the same as in the factory. Then, with two or three contacts he has, they sell this rotgut rum in the dollar stores and he takes the same number of bottles of good rum and sells it himself at a lower price. So his confederates in the store never get caught stealing, because there aren't any bottles missing, and he's always got steady customers. He told me that soon, he's going to start making Coca-Cola too." In Mylene Fernández's *Other Answered Prayers* (2003), the heroine's neighbor invents the expedient of renting spots on her balcony to foreign tourists, who can enjoy Havana's glorious sunsets for a dollar a pop. Besides stretching the hostess's budget, the practice helps out the visitors who "prefer enjoying the Havana of their dreams without having to actually rub elbows there." Low-level corruption has of course accompanied all these activities, as inspectors and functionaries of various sorts are bribed with money or services to look the other way.

Equally important, however, is the fact that most of these forms of extra-legal activity also support the safety net (or high-wire act) of free or very inexpensive state services that continue to function despite the crisis. In any family, someone's racket may allow someone else to dedicate herself or himself to a job in a hospital or clinic or theater, and the same individual often works in both spheres. The teacher who coaches would-be emigrants in English for dollars also teaches in a high school or college with equal care. The electrician who moonlights installing cables for pirate internet access also keeps the low-rent apartment building's collective water pump working. The bus driver who sells gas on the black market also drives the *camello* bus, under very difficult conditions, every day.

One way or another, and thanks also to other economic policies and events that lie outside the scope of this history of the city, the crisis in its original form began to fade. Most *habaneros* gained back the weight they had lost, and the sea of bikes in the streets ebbed, so that Havana in peak commuting hours no longer seemed so much like Hanoi. A light grew visible at the end of the long, dark tunnel, but everyone emerged into a very different place than the one from which they had entered a decade before. What protection the tunnel had offered them had been distributed unequally, which became markedly visible when they came out. Some now had children abroad, while others had retired from old jobs and taken new ones. A good many had better salaries, sometimes double, and some (such as doctors, teachers, sports instructors, and artists) now counted on regular stints working in other countries of either the First or Third World, with modest hard-currency salaries to subsidize their Havana lives. Another obvious fact was that Havana had more old people and fewer young ones than ever before, thanks to the combination of continued broad health services, insecurity about the future, and reduced births.

Racially as in every other way, the effects of the ten-year tunnel were mixed. Some neighborhoods with the highest concentration of black population, like Old Havana, breathed a certain optimism exhaled by the restored buildings and the prosperity that tourism brought. In others, like Cerro or La Lisa (beyond Marianao), the shortage of employment and housing, exacerbated by a surge of immigrants from the eastern provinces seeking the opportunities of the capital, could be felt in the streets. With relatively fewer relatives abroad and less presence in the well-paid posts in tourist hotels administered by foreign firms, black Havanans—whose ancestors had lived in the capital since the days of the free Africans of the sixteenth century—did not so much try to escape the city as to find new niches which would permit them to advance.

All told, Havana emerged from the tunnel into a twilight zone, something that was no longer the Special Period but as yet had no name. On the one hand, it was a city in the grip of disillusion and abandonment. On the other, it was animated by a drive for reconstruction which sought to offer jobs and social protection to young and old, black and white. In the midst of such contradictions, as had been true ever since the appearance of Francis Drake's fleet outside the mouth of the bay, the population continued to unite and cooperate in the face of any external threat.

In the late summer of 2005, an enormous hurricane called Wilma moved steadily toward Havana, its size and strength presenting a threat almost like an impending nuclear attack. As the hurricane approached from the east, the *habaneros* boarded up windows, took shelter in the more solid houses of their neighbors, bought great quantities of bread and crackers, warehoused potable water, and teamed up to push Chevies or Ladas awaiting repair or gas to safety. They lit candles to Yemayá Olokkún, the patroness of storm-tossed waters, and to St. Christopher after whom San Cristóbal de La Habana had been named. They sat religiously in front of the television to watch the weather report which showed satellite images of the monstrous hurricane blowing toward the bay where the treasure fleets had sheltered.

Miraculously, Wilma skirted the southern shore of Cuba. Havana got drenched but avoided taking a direct hit. The hurricane then hovered over the Yucatán peninsula 120 miles to the west, and finally followed the Gulf Stream toward Florida, leaving Havana behind. That night Juan Valdés, the Larrinaga-Cañizares, Daniel Motola, Verónica Loynaz, and all those who lived away from the sea went to bed relieved to escape hundred-plus mile an hour gusts, and glad that the rain had subsided. But in the predawn hours the sea rose and began to pour over its wall and into the city, from the rocky coast of Miramar to the Bay of Carenas itself. Salt water penetrated block after block of streets and houses in Vedado and Centro Habana, especially between the Hotel Riviera and the Parque Maceo, land stolen from the sea a century before. The flood destroyed walls within the massive and newly restored Castillo de la Punta, the fort that had defended the mouth of the bay during the taking of Havana by the English in 1762.

When day dawned, a Monday, the coastline had moved. The only vehicles cruising up and down the Calle Calzada, where the gardens of the Loynaz de Castillo had looked toward the coast in the 1920s and 1930s, were lifeboats rescuing the residents of flooded homes. A few days later, the sea decided to retreat as suddenly as it had advanced. The neighborhoods all along the Malecón seemed to have emerged from a shipwreck. The flood had dragged huge boulders five hundred yards inland to the Calle Línea, beyond Calzada—along with boards, planks, tree branches, lampposts, and even six-packs of beer which the sea had plucked from the expensive stores and cafés bordering the Malecón. The ornamental plants, the bushes, and the grass along sidewalks and in the yards of the houses had changed color. There was no electricity, and government crews were supplying free canned goods, pasta, and powdered milk to all the families of the inundated zone.

Even in the midst of the flood, however, the families who lived in the water-soaked houses had come out at first light to witness the spectacle of the sea breaking noisily over its wall. They stood watching with their eternal curiosity, joking with those who came from other parts of the city to observe the taking of the Malecón by the sea. Then it was time to come back to life, to clean up the ruins, to set up the domino table on some dry sidewalk or corner while the sea went back where it belonged. Time, as a smiling mulatto said as he watched the sea retreat, "to go on *luchando*," the way residents of the port city had always done.

Notes

1   KEY TO THE INDIES

1. Governor and captain-general were originally separate positions, the one civil and the other military, but from the late sixteenth century on they were combined. In our discussion of colonial officials from this time on, we have used the terms interchangeably.

2   THE HOUR OF THE MAMEYS

1. Cuban historian Gustavo Placer Cervera, author of several recent works on colonial military history, suggests that legend may have overtaken fact in the many earlier biographies of Pepe Antonio and accounts of the siege. He points out that the guerrilla leader is likely to have died of the same epidemic of tropical fevers that decimated the British attackers and that archival evidence does not confirm the long-held tradition that he was deprived of his command.
2. In the original Spanish, the women are hiding in *bocoyes de arroz* (casks or barrels for rice), which rhymes with *Dios* (God). In all our translations of songs or verse we've taken liberties to preserve rhyme where appropriate.

3 PARIS OF THE ANTILLES

1. What we are calling the Paseo del Prado, running from La Punta fortress by the seafront south to the Campo de Marte parade ground (since the 1920s the Parque de la Fraternidad) has gone through a succession of official names. It was originally called the "Nuevo Prado," presumably in comparison to the old one in Madrid, which was originally a field or "pasture" as the name implies. After improvement in the nineteenth century, Havana's Prado was officially renamed Paseo de Isabel II in honor of the Spanish queen. Postindependence, it was again renamed, this time in honor of José Martí. But the old name has stuck, as is the case with many other streets.

   At the Campo de Marte began another broad avenue, the Paseo de Tacón, which ran westward to the Príncipe fortress, along the present-day streets Reina and Carlos III, the route of the M2 bus.

5 STIRRINGS OF NATIONHOOD

1. Until we come to our discussion of Domingo Del Monte and his circle, later in this chapter, we are omitting other anticolonial conspiracies and reform efforts mounted by liberal white Cubans. We do not mean to underestimate the importance of such crucial figures in the formation of Cuban national identity and in the fields of poetry, religion, political economy, and education as José María Heredia, Félix Varela, José Antonio Saco and José de la Luz Caballero.

6 REVOLUTIONS AND RETRIBUTIONS: FROM THE TEATRO VILLANUEVA TO THE *MAINE*

1. The legendary William Randolph Hearst quote comes from a memoir by James Creelman, who had been a Hearst correspondent in Madrid. When the quote was later picked up by a London paper, Hearst denied having sent such a telegram. The artist, Frederick Remington, and the reporter who accompanied him, Richard Harding Davis, neither confirmed nor denied Creelman's report.

7 MANY HAPPY RETURNS?: U.S. OCCUPATION AND ITS AFTERMATH

1. The suffrage rules included only males over the age of twenty-one who were either Cuban-born or Spaniards willing to take on Cuban citizenship, and who in addition could read and write, owned property worth at least $250, or had served in the Liberation Army. The last was a

compromise the occupation government could not avoid. Still, given illiteracy rates, poverty, and the numbers of ex-slaves born in Africa, only about a third of adult Cuban males had the right to vote in these elections.

8 SYMBOL OF AN ERA: ALBERTO YARINI Y PONCE DE LEÓN

1. In some versions of the story the general is not Jesús Rabí but Florencio Salcedo—likewise from Oriente, black, and risen through the ranks of the insurgent army. Either way, the moral is the same.

9 CATCH A FORD ON THE MALECÓN: REPUBLICAN HAVANA'S GROWTH AND DECAY

1. To the confusion of North American audiences, the music of the "rumba" craze that swept the United States in the 1930s was not rumba at all, but a mixture of other Cuban genres, especially *son*. U.S. record labels recorded a wide variety of Cuban music, in sessions held both in Havana and in New York, and called all of it rumba. Authentic rumba never in itself became pop music, even in the Cuban cities where it grew up.

14 REVOLUTION WITH *PACHANGA*: HAVANA TRANSFIGURED

1. Cuba's prerevolutionary communist party had gone by various names, of which Popular Socialist Party was the last. In the 1960s, the 26th of July Movement, the Revolutionary Directorate, and the PSP merged into a single organization which eventually became the Cuban Communist Party, the ruling party of a Leninist-style single-party state.

16 THE BLACKOUT: HAVANA IN THE "SPECIAL PERIOD" AND BEYOND

1. Translations of Cuban salaries into dollar terms can be misleading, because housing, health care, higher education, and other services that consume a large part of a U.S. salary remain free or cheap in Cuba despite the economic crisis. Still, the comparisons are worthwhile in relation to the products Cubans do have to buy in hard currency or its equivalent.
2. Throughout the period under discussion, the U.S. trade embargo has remained fully in force, except for a loophole voted by the U.S.

Congress starting in 2001 for cash-only sales of U.S. agricultural goods. Most goods in the dollar stores were imported from Western Europe, Latin America, or Asia. Nonetheless Cuba's new hard-currency sector used the dollar as the standard international medium of exchange, as did all of the country's international trade.

In 2005, for use in the hard-currency sector in place of the dollar, Cuba adopted a new "convertible peso" (distinct from the regular Cuban peso or *moneda nacional*) that could be bought with U.S. dollars, Euros, Canadian dollars, and other hard currencies at international exchange rates (minus a 10 percent tax in the case of U.S. dollars).

3. There had been a previous and generally popular experiment with farmers' markets in the 1980s, on a more limited scale. They had been closed in the Rectification campaign, on the argument that they were promoting the growth of a class of rich middlemen and diverting personnel and equipment from regular tasks.

4. Since 1959, the Cuban government has taken the position that the perpetually renewable Guantánamo lease is invalid, having been coerced under the terms of the Platt Amendment. The U.S. government, however, has continued to insist on its right to occupy the base.

Bibliographic Sources and Suggestions

One of the pleasures of working on this book has been the opportunity to digest a great variety of primary sources, popular works, and scholarly research about Havana—books and articles, nonfiction and fiction, music, pictures, web sites mounted by individuals and institutions in and out of Cuba, maps and tourist guides both intact and disintegrating, memoirs, reminiscences, biographical dictionaries, census documents, and more. In addition we interviewed members of representative families and picked the brains of friends and acquaintances of all sorts. In this bibliographic essay we can't begin to provide a complete list of our sources. What we can do is guide interested readers to some of the historical works and to the sources of most of our direct quotations, and in the process acknowledge our own biggest debts to historians in Cuba, the United States, and elsewhere. A great many of our sources are, of course, in Spanish. Most, even if published in Cuba, are available via inter-library loan from at least a few university or public libraries in the United States.

I. GENERAL WORKS

Comprehensive general works on Cuban history in English include Louis A. Pérez, Jr., *Cuba: Between Reform and Revolution* (New York: Oxford, 1995) and *Cuba and the United States: Ties of Singular Intimacy* (Athens: University of Georgia, 1997), and Hugh Thomas, *Cuba, or The Pursuit of Freedom* (London: Eyre & Spottiswoode, 1971). For buildings, streets, and other constructions throughout the history of Havana and other Cuban cities, an invaluable resource is Juan de las Cuevas Toraya, *500 años de construcciones en Cuba* (Madrid: Chavín, 2001).

II. COLONIAL ERA (1500–1898)

One key source for our quotations from official records and correspondence, periodicals, and travelers' chronicles throughout the Spanish colonial period is Gustavo Eguren's fascinating collection of primary source excerpts, *La fidelísima Habana* (Havana: Letras Cubanas, 1986). Also very useful throughout this period have been Manuel Moreno Fraginals, *Cuba/España, España/Cuba: Historia Común* (Barcelona: Crítica, 1995) and Eusebio Leal Spengler, *La Habana, ciudad antigua* (Havana: Letras Cubanas, 1988).

For the sixteenth and seventeenth centuries (chapter 1), a great many quotations and details also come from Irene A. Wright's classic works based on documents in the Archives of the Indies in Seville: *Historia documentada de San Cristóbal de La Habana en el siglo XVI* (Havana: El Siglo XX, 1927) and *Historia documentada de San Cristóbal de La Habana en la primer mitad del siglo XVII* (Havana: El Siglo XX, 1930). In English, readers may also consult her *The Early History of Cuba, 1492–1586* (New York: Macmillan, 1916).

The account of Giovanni Francesco Gemelli Careri that closes chapter 1 is drawn from Eguren. (The original *Giro del mondo* was published in Italian in 1699, and was published in English translation in the eighteenth century but not since; the section dealing with New Spain has been translated into Spanish, most recently by the Universidad Nacional Autónomo de México in 1976.)

For information on the house of Juana Carvajal we are indebted to the Office of the City Historian of Havana.

The taking of Havana by the English (chapter 2) has been the subject of many military histories, at that time and ever since. Recent examples include Gustavo Placer Cevera's *Los defensores del Morro* (Havana: Unión, 2003), César García del Pino's *Toma de La Habana por los ingleses y sus antecedentes* (Havana: Ciencias Sociales, 2002), and Sonia Keppel's *Three Brothers at Havana* (Salisbury: M. Russell, 1981). The occupation and its effects have received less attention. Emilio Roig de Leuchsenring, ed., *La dominación inglesa de La Habana: Libro de Cabildos 1762–3* (Havana: Imprenta Molina y Cia, 1929) includes the letter of the Jesuit priest and other primary sources from which we quote, and a useful interpretive essay. Roig has also edited *Cómo vio Jacobo de la Pezuela la toma de La Habana por los ingleses* (Havana: Oficina del Historiador, 1962), containing four chapters from Pezuela's nineteenth century account. *Documentos inéditos sobre la Toma de La Habana por los Ingleses en 1762* (Havana: Biblioteca Nacional José Martí, 1963) includes further documents (including the statement by Benjamin Franklin) and an equally useful essay by Juan Pérez de la Riva. A different interpretation by a Spanish historian is Celia María Parcero Torre, *La pérdida de La Habana y las reformas borbónicas en Cuba, 1760–1773* (Madrid: Junta de Castilla y León, 1998).

For the Marquesa Beatriz de Jústiz and her writings, we are indebted to the work of Luisa Campuzano. See her "Las muchachas de la Habana no tienen temor de dios . . . ," in *Revista Canadiense de Estudios Hispánicos* 16, no. 2 (1992): 307–318, available online at http://www.lajiribilla.cu/2001/n17_agosto/516_17.html (accessed June 30, 2006). The texts themselves are also in "Memorial y décimas dirigidos a Carlos III en ocasión de la toma de La Habana por los ingleses," in L. Campuzano, ed., *Yo con mi viveza*, pp. 183–194 (Havana: Casa de las Américas, 2003). See, in addition, the chapter "La hora de los mameyes" in Reynaldo González, ed., *El bello Habano*, pp. 4–5 (Vitoria-Gasteiz: Ikusager, 1998).

Levi Redfield's 1799 memoir that includes his participation in the Havana expedition, *A True Account of Some Memorable Events and Remarkable Occurrences in the Life of Levi Redfield*, is available on microfiche. Roswell Park's memoir appears in "A Journal of the Expedition Against Cuba," forward by Julian Park, *University of Buffalo Studies* I, no. 4 (1920). For more on the role of North American provincial troops in general, see David Syrett, "American Provincials and the Havana Campaign of 1762," *New York History* 49, no. 4 (1968): 375–390. Maj. Joseph Gorham's diary (in its English original) is in *Cinco diarios del sitio de la Habana* (Havana: Biblioteca Nacional José Martí, 1963).

For the nineteenth century (chapters 3–6), we have drawn on a very wide variety of sources, including those noted above for the colonial period as a whole. Some of these are:

TRAVEL ACCOUNTS (CHAPTERS 3–6): Frederika Bremer's impressions come from her *The Homes of the New World: Impressions of America*, trans. Mary Howitt (New York: Harper & Brothers, 1853). We have translated comments by Nicolás Tanco, Edward Otto, and others from Eguren. Accounts by U.S. and British visitors (including Samuel Hazard and Richard Henry Dana) can be found in Louis A. Pérez, Jr., *Slaves, Sugar, and Colonial Society: Travel Accounts of Cuba, 1801–1899* (Wilmington: Scholarly Resources, 1992) and *Impressions of Cuba in the Nineteenth Century: The Travel Diary of Joseph J. Dimock* (Wilmington: Scholarly Resources, 1992), as well as in the original books by Hazard (*Cuba with Pen and Pencil* [Hartford, CT: Hartford Publishing Company, 1871]), Dana (*To Cuba and Back, a Vacation Voyage* [reprint, Carbondale: Southern University Illionois Press, 1966]), Matilda Houstoun (*Texas and the Gulf of Mexico, or, Yachting in the New World* [reprint, Austin, TX: W.T. Taylor, 1991]), and others. The Countess of Merlín (María de las Mercedes Santa Cruz y Montalvo) published her full three-volume account in French as *La Havane* (Paris: Librairie d'Amyot, 1844), and a shorter one-volume edition in Spanish, *Viaje a La Habana*, both 1844; our quotes are translated from the Spanish edition (reprint, Havana: Librería Cervantes, 1922).

CECILIA VALDÉS (CHAPTERS 3 AND 4): We have translated all the quotations from Cirilo Villaverde, *Cecila Valdés o La Loma del Ángel* (Havana: Arte y Literature, 1977). We have also benefitted from Reynaldo González's critical work on *Cecilia* and race in nineteenth century Cuba, *Contradanzas y latigazos* (Havana: Letras Cubanas, 1992). After a long absence from print in English, the novel is now available to English-speaking readers in a new translation: *Cecila Valdés, or, El Angel Hill*, trans. Helen Lane (New York: Oxford, 2005).

AFRO-CUBAN SOCIETIES AND RELIGION (CHAPTER 4): On the cabildos and their functions in private and in public, see Philip A. Howard, *Changing History: Afro-Cuban Cabildos and Societies of Color in the Nineteenth Century* (Baton Rouge: Louisiana State University, 1998), Daniel E. Walker, *No More, No More: Slavery and Cultural Resistance in Havana and New Orleans* (Minneapolis: University of Minnesota, 2004), and Judith Bettelheim, *Cuban Festivals: An Illustrated Anthology* (New York: Garland, 1993); the last contains a translation of Fernando Ortiz's classic work on the cabildos and the Day of Kings, as well as Ramón Meza's 1891 article in *La Habana Elegante* recalling the celebrations. On the Abakuá, see Tato Quiñones, *Ecorie Abakuá: Cuatro ensayos sobre los ñañigos cubanos* (Havana: Ediciones Unión, 1994). On religious practices deriving from Africa (subject of a recent research boom on the island) we have consulted Joel James Figarola, *Sistemas mágico-religiosos cubanos. Principios rectores* (Havana: Ediciones Unión, 2001) and Lydia Cabrera's classic text *El monte* (various editions) for symbolism including the myths of the ceiba.

SOCIAL AND ECONOMIC STRUCTURE IN DAILY LIFE: On the role and place of white women (chapter 3), see Luis Martínez-Fernández, "The 'Male City' of Havana," in Tamara Hunt and Micheline Lessard, eds., *Women and the Colonial Gaze* (New York: NYU, 2002). Most of our examples of black and mulatto families and workers in chapter 4 are drawn from María del Carmen Barcia Zequeira, *La otra familia: parientes, redes, y descendencia de los esclavos en Cuba* (Havana: Casa de las Américas, 2003) and Pedro Deschamps Chapeaux, *El negro en la economía habanera del siglo XIX* (Havana: UNEAC, 1971). See also Digna Castañeda, "The Female Slave in the Cuba during the first half of the Nineteenth Century," in Verene Shepherd, ed., *Engendering History: Caribbean Women in Historical Perspective* (New York: St. Martin's, 1995). Robert L. Paquette, *Sugar is Made With Blood: The Conspiracy of La Escalera and the Conflict between Empires over Slavery in Cuba* (Middletown: Wesleyan, 1988) also has useful statistics and examples on occupational distribution by color.

Maria del Carmen Barcia's research in social history has also been our main source for the information in chapters 4 and 6 on prostitutes and their magazine *La Cebolla*, and the descriptions in chapter 6 of life in the capital during the second Independence War. For the former, see her article "Entre el poder y la crisis: las prostitutas se defienden," in Luisa Campuzano, coordinadora, *Mujeres Latinoamericanas: Historia y Cultura, Siglos XVI al XIX*, vol. 1 (Havana: Casa de las Américas and Universidad de Iztapalapa, 1997); for the latter, *Una sociedad en crisis: La Habana a finales del siglo XIX* (Havana: Ciencias Sociales, 2001).

REBELLION AND REPRESSION (CHAPTERS 5 AND 6): On Aponte, see José Luciano Franco, "La conspiracion de Aponte, 1812," in his *Ensayos históricos*, pp. 143–90 (Havana: Ciencias Sociales, 1974). For La Escalera, as well as Domingo del Monte and upper class *criollo* attitudes toward slavery and independence, see Robert L. Paquette, *Sugar is Made With Blood*, cited above. For Manuel Moreno Fraginals and Jorge Lozano on the attempted Abakuá rescue of the medical students, see, respectively, *Cuba/España* (cited above) and Pedro A. García, "27 de noviembre de 1871: Culpables de cubanía," in *Granma*, November 27, 2001 available at http://www.latinamericanstudies.org/1868/culpables.htm (accessed June 30, 2006). For a judicious account of Evangelina Cossio, see the prologue to Jane McManus, *Cuba's Island of Dreams* (Gainesville: University Press of Florida, 2000).

CULTURAL TIES BETWEEN HAVANA AND U.S. CITIES: On the influence of education in the U.S. (chapter 3), baseball (chapter 6), and similar matters, see Louis A. Pérez, Jr., *On Becoming Cuban: Identity, Nationality, and Culture* (Chapel Hill, University of North Carolina, 1999). Many further sources on the early history of Cuban baseball may be found there.

ANTONIO MACEO AND JULIÁN DEL CASAL: Two articles on this tantalizing encounter (sources of our description and quotations in chapter 6) are: Victor Fowler, "Casal disputado y una nota al pie," in the Summer 2002 edition of the internet magazine *La Habana Elegante, segunda época* (www.habanaelegente.com), and Oscar Montero, "Casal y Maceo en *La Habana Elegante*," in *Casa de las Américas*, no. 225 (October–December 2001) and *Encuentro de la Cultura Cubana*, no. 10 (Autumn 1998) (http://arch1.cubaencuentro.com/pdfs/10/10om117.pdf [accessed June 30, 2006]).

III. OCCUPATION AND INDEPENDENCE (1898–TODAY)

For the complex tapestry of Havana's day-to-day response to the U.S. *occupation and its aftermath (chapter 7)*, we have drawn extensively on Marial Iglesias Utset, *Las metáforas del cambio en la vida cotidiana: Cuba 1898–1902* (Havana: Ediciones Unión, 2002). A complementary work that also contributed greatly to this chapter is Pérez, *On Becoming Cuban* (cited above).

For the political history of U.S.–Cuba relations and the Platt Amendment, see Pérez, *Cuba and the United States* (cited above), Philip Foner, *A History of Cuba and Its Relations with the United States* (New York: International, 1962), and Emilio Roig de Leuchsenring, *Historia de la Enmienda Platt: una interpretación de la realidad cubana* (Havana, Ciencias Sociales, 1973). The 1823 Thomas Jefferson quote is from a letter to

President James Monroe, and that of John Quincy Adams is from a letter to
the U.S. ambassador in Spain; for complete citations, see *Cuba and the
United States*, p. 276. The letter from Gen. Leonard Wood to President
Roosevelt about Juan Gualberto Gómez and the "degenerates" of the
Convention may be found in the Theodore Roosevelt Papers (Library of
Congress microfilm, Series 1, Reel 12, letter dated April 12, 1901).
R.F. Bullard's article on "How Cubans Differ from Us" is in *Century*,
November 1907.

Our account of *the life and death of Alberto Yarini (chapter 9) and the barrio
of San Isidro* comes primarily from Dulcila Cañizares, *San Isidro, 1910:
Alberto Yarini y su época* (Havana: Letras Cubanas, 2000), Tomás Fernández
Robaina, *Historias de mujeres públicas* (Havana: Letras Cubanas, 1998), and
Leonardo Padura Fuentes, "Yarini, El Rey," in his *El viaje más largo*,
pp. 231–48 (San Juan: Plaza Mayor, 2002). Quotations from prostitutes are
from Fernández Robaina (Consuelo) and Cañizares (Lulú); most quotations from other San Isidro figures are from Cañizares. For a study in
English, see Mayra Beers, "Murder in San Isidro: Crime and Culture
during the Second Cuban Republic," in *Cuban Studies* 34 (2003): 97–129.

On media-driven anti-black hysteria and the colored community's
response, see Alejandra Bronfman, " 'En Plena Libertad y Democracia':
Negros Brujos and the Social Question, 1904–1919," in *Hispanic American
Historical Review* 82, no. 3 (2002): 549–587. On Cuban musicians playing in
silent movie theaters, see Ned Sublette, *Cuba and Its Music* (Chicago:
Chicago Review, 2004). For Enrique Díaz Quesada and the early history
of Cuban cinema, see special issue of *Cuba Update* XIX, no. 1
(October–December 1999), and Arturo Agramonte and Luciano Castillo,
"Enrique Díaz Quesada: El padre de la cinematografía cubana" in the
Cuban Ministry of Culture's web site La Jiribilla (http://www.lajiribilla.
cu/2002/n70_septiembre/memoria.html [accessed June 30, 2006]). See
also Alejandro de la Fuente, *A Nation for All: Race, Inequality, and Politics in
Twentieth Century Cuba* (Chapel Hill: University of North Carolina, 2001).

The most detailed and best-documented history of Cuban filmmaking
from its origins to 1990 is María Eulalia Douglas, *La tienda negra. El cine en
Cuba, 1897–1990* (Havana: Cinemateca de Cuba, 1997).

Chapter 9, on Havana's *growth, decay, and culture in the 1910s–1940s*,
draws on an eclectic range of sources, including family history interviews
which extend through this and the following chapters of the book. Raquel
Cañizares and Carlos Larrinaga were interviewed by Dick Cluster and
Rafael Hernández in Havana in August 2005. Daniel Motola Roffe was
interviewed by Dick Cluster in Havana in December 2004.

A general work on the city's growth, planning, and architectural history
is Joseph Scarpaci, Roberto Segre, and Mario Coyula, *Havana: Two Faces of
the Antillean Metropolis* (Chapel Hill: University of North Carolina, 2002).
More specifically, for *solares*: Carlos Venegas, "Havana between Two
Centuries," *Journal of Decorative and Propaganda Arts* 22 (1996): 13–34; sugar

industry's role in the city's growth: Oscar Zanetti Lecuona, "La capital del azúcar," in Bernardo García and Sergio Guerra, eds., *La Habana/Veracruz, Veracruz/La Habana* (Veracruz: Universidad Veracruzana, 2002); El Vedado: Mario Coyula, "Más acá del río y bajo los árboles: a la sombra de un Vedado que ya es no más" (manuscript, forthcoming) and Jorge Pavez Ojeda, *El Vedado, 1850–1940*. *De monte a reparto* (Havana: Centro Juan Marinello, 2003), and "Veinticuatro horas en la vida del Dr Carlos Miguel de Céspedes," *Bohemia*, January 13, 1946. The quotation from Federico García Lorca at the beginning of the chapter is from *A Poet in New York*, ed. Christopher Maurer, trans. Greg Simon and Steven F. White (NY: Noonday Press, 1998), which includes one poem and three letters written in Havana.

On Dulce María Loynaz: Aldo Martínez Malo, *Confesiones de Dulce María Loynaz* (Havana: José Martí, 1999); Ana Cabrera Vivanco, *La voz del silencio* (Havana: Ciencias Sociales, 2000); Dulce María Loynaz, *Fe de vida* (Havana: Letras Cubanas, 1995). A bilingual selection of her poetry is Judith Kerman, trans. and ed., *A Woman in Her Garden: Selected poems of Dulce María Loynaz* (Buffalo: White Pine Press, 2002).

On Chano Pozo: Leonardo Padura Fuentes, "La noche triste de Chano Pozo," in *El viaje más largo* (cited above), pp. 277–94; Jordi Pujol, *Chano Pozo: El tambor de Cuba* (Barcelona: Almendra Music, 2001, issued as bilingual book and 3-CD set by Tumbao Cuban Classics, 2001). On the social development of the various genres of Cuban popular music, see Ned Sublette, *Cuba and Its Music*, cited above, Alejo Carpentier, *Music in Cuba*, trans. Alan West-Durán (Minneapolis: University of Minnesota, 2001), and Robin Moore, *Nationalizing Blackness: Afrocubanismo and Artistic Revolution in Havana, 1920–1940* (Pittsburgh: University of Pittsburgh, 1997). A panorama of genres of Cuban dance music from *contradanza* to *timba* may be found in the special issue no. 39–40 of *Temas* (Havana: October–December 2004) devoted to Cuban music. On Los Jardines de la Tropical and the colored social clubs, see Eugene Godfried, "Dialogue with Juan Cruz, Past President, Marianao Social Club," on AfroCubaWeb (http://www.afrocubaweb.com/eugenegodfried/juancruz.htm [accessed June 30, 2006]).

Chapter 10, on the revolution of 1933 and its context: Carlos Loveira's *Juan Criollo* can be found in many Spanish editions but has not been published in English. Cira Romero's prologue to the Letras Cubanas edition (Havana: Letras Cubanas, 1987) includes biographical details. For documentary sources on the Cuban labor movement in the nineteenth and twentieth century we drew from *El movimiento obrero cubano. Documentos y artículos* (Havana: Ciencias Sociales, 1977), and on strikes and other events leading up to 1933 from Julio Domínguez García, *Noticias de la República: Apuntes cronológicos 1900–1929* (Havana: Ciencias Sociales, 2003). On twentieth century Cuban feminism, see K. Lynn Stoner, *From the House to the Streets: The Cuban Women's Movement for Legal Change, 1898–1940* (New York: Garland, 1989).

An account of the events of '33 and their context published in the U.S. is Luis Aguilar, *CUBA 1933* (Ithaca: Cornell, 1972). Accounts published in Cuba include José A. Tabares del Real, *La revolución del 30: sus dos últimos años* (Havana: Arte y Literatura: 1971) and Lionel Soto's three volume *La revolución del 33* (Havana: Ciencias Sociales, 1977). The plan for the assassination attempt in the Colón Cemetery is described in the biography of its protagonist Pío Álvarez, Newton Briones Montoto's *Accion directa* (Havana: Ciencias Sociales, 1999). Luis Buch's memoir *Un insurreccional en dos épocas* (Havana: Ciencias Sociales, 2001) describes the underground activity in Havana through 1935, while Olga Cabrera's *Guiteras, la época, el hombre* (Havana: Ciencias Sociales, 1978) analyzes the government of the Hundred Days.

Chapter 11, Radio Days, draws particularly on Oscar Luis López's *La radio en Cuba* (Havana: Letras Cubanas: 1981, 2002), as well as Reynaldo González, *Llorar es un placer* (Havana: Letras Cubanas, 2002) on soap operas and the two principal magazines of the era, *Bohemia* and *Carteles* (1940–1948), for descriptions of the Constitutional assembly, violent crimes, and other events.

Juan Valdés Paz was interviewed in Havana by Rafael Hernández in June 2005. Various anecdotes about the Caballero de París (chapter 11 and elsewhere) come from the periodicals *Bohemia* (1945, 1949), *Diario de la Marina* (1944), *Gente* (1949), *Alerta* (1939, 1949) and from María Argelia Vizcaíno's collection "El Caballero de París" (http://freeweb.supereva.com/carlo260/caballero.html?p [accessed June 30, 2006])on Carlo Nobili's very useful website *Cuba. Una indentità en movimento* (http://freeweb.supereva.com/carlo260/ [accessed June 30, 2006]); there is also a collection called *Yo soy el Caballero de París*, edited by his doctor during the final years of his life, Luis Calzadilla Fierro (Badajoz: Diputación de Badajoz, 2000). The "events of Orfila" are narrated in Oscar Luis López, *La radio en Cuba* (1981) as well as periodicals of the time. Pedro Prada, *La secretaria de la república* (Havana: Ciencias Sociales, 2001) narrates the events surrounding the suicide of Eddy Chibás in the voice of his personal secretary Conchita Fernández.

In *chapter 12*, the opening story about Amletto Battisti and the painting stolen from Carlos Miguel de Céspedes is from the same *Bohemia* article of 1946 cited for chapter 9. Graham Greene's comments on writing *Our Man in Havana* are from his introduction to the edition published by Heinemann and Bodley Head, London, 1970.

J.P. McEvoy's article on Batista's coup appeared in the Spanish edition of *Reader's Digest* in July 1952 and in slightly different form in the English edition of that same month (vol. 62). Batista's statement about the "Monte Carlo of the Caribbean" comes from *Life*, March, 1958. Among many sources on the Mafia in Havana are Robert Lacey's *Little Man: Meyer Lansky and the Gangster Life* (Boston: Little Brown, 1991) and Enrique Cirules, *El imperio de La Habana* (Havana: Casa de las Américas, 1993), available in

English as *The Mafia in Havana* (Melbourne: Ocean Press, 2004); contemporary articles in the U.S. press include "Crime: Happy Days in Havana" (*Newsweek*, January 20, 1958) and "Not So Far from the Crowding Mob" (*Saturday Review*, April 19, 1958).

The sex worker's account is from Tomás Fernández Robaina's *Historias de mujeres públicas*, cited above (chapter 9). Arthur Schlesinger's comment comes from his memoir *One Thousand Days* as cited in Pérez, *Cuba and the United States*. On Burke Hedges, see "Cuba. Ambassador of Fun," *Time*, September, 1958. Alan Ginsberg's phrases on the Plaza de la Catedral are from his poem "Havana," in *Reality Sandwiches* (San Francisco: City Lights, 1963).

For *chapter 13* and beyond, Verónica Loynaz was interviewed in Havana by Rafael Hernández in October 2005.

Almost all of Fidel Castro's speeches, including the one from Camp Columbia in January, 1959, can be found online in English, translated by the U.S. government's Foreign Broadcast Information Service, at http://lanic.utexas.edu/la/cb/cuba/castro.html (accessed June 30, 2006). The Caballero de París quote on the rebels and their beards is from *Carteles*, May 3, 1959. Carleton Beals on the anti-American mood in Havana in early 1959 is from *Christian Century*, February 4, 1959. On the trials and executions of Batista's officers see *Bohemia* of March 8, March 15, March 22, and April 26, 1959 and *Carteles*, March 22, March 31, April 5, and May 31; *Life*'s report appeared in the January 26, 1959 issue.

Mirta Yánez's 1976 story "Todos los negros tomamos café" ("We Blacks All Drink Coffee") appears in English, trans. Claudette Williams, in Pamela Mordecai and Betty Wilson, ed., *Her True-True Name* (Oxford: Heinemann, 1989).

Among the many sources on the unfolding of Cuba–U.S. relations in this period, Jane Franklin's *Cuba and the United States. A Chronological History* (Melbourne: Ocean Press, 1997) offers a condensed summary of the events. On the assassination plots directed at Castro, see the 1975 U.S. Senate report, "Alleged Assassination Plots Involving Foreign Leaders" (republished with introduction by Sen. Frank Church, New York: Norton, 1976). The quotation from the CIA trainer of Bay of Pigs expeditionaries is from Peter Wyden, *Bay of Pigs: The Untold Story* (New York: Simon & Schuster, 1979).

The two Dulce María Loynaz poems referred to are from her *Poemas sin nombre*, XXXV and CXXIV; the latter appears in an English translation in the Judith Kerman collection, *A Woman in Her Garden*, cited above. Much of the information on Operation Peter Pan comes from María de los Angeles Torres, *The Lost Apple: Operation Peter Pan, Cuban Children in the U.S., and the Promise of a Better Future* (Boston: Beacon, 2003).

In *chapter 14*, Alejo Carpentier's opening quote comes from the article he published in the Venezuelan newspaper *El Nacional*, June 17, 1959, reprinted in the magazine *Universidad de La Habana*, September 1984.

The quote from "Violeta" about the closing of brothels is from Tomás Fernández Robaina's *Historias de mujeres públicas* cited above. On the emigration and expulsion of priests, see John Kirk, *Between God and the Party: Religion and Politics in Revolutionary Cuba* (Tampa: University of South Florida, 1989) and Margaret Crahan, "Salvation through Christ or Marx," in Daniel H. Levine, ed., *Churches and Politics in Latin America* (Chapel Hill: University of North Carolina, 1986). On the conflict over religion see also Aurelio Alonso, *Church and Politics in Revolutionary Cuba* (Havana: Editorial José Marti,1999).

On housing construction, see Scarpaci, Segre, and Coyula, *Havana*, cited above; on filmmaking and popular music in the 1960s and 1970s, *La tienda negra* and *Temas* no. 39–40, also cited above.

For *chapter 15*, Teresita Roca was interviewed in Havana by Dick Cluster in December 2004. For the prior history of the Hotel Montserrat and its site we are indebted to the Office of the City Historian.

The writer Yoss's statement about Russian influence is from his article "Lo que dejaron los rusos," *Temas*, no. 37–38 (April–September 2004). Reinaldo Arenas, *Before Night Falls*, is available in an English translation by Dolores M. Koch (New York: Viking, 1993).

On the social class of Mariel emigrants, see Rafael Hernández and Redi Gomis, "Retrato del Mariel: el ángulo socioeconómico," in *Cuadernos de Nuestra América* III, no. 5 (1986). On emigration as a theme in Cuban cinema, Desirée Díaz, "La mirada de Ovidio. El tema de la emigración en el cine cubano de los 90," in *Temas*, no. 27 (October–December 2001).

Our discussion of the crisis of the 1990s and the economic reforms of 1993–96 in *chapter 16* draws on *Temas*, no. 11 (July–September 1997) and no. 30 (April–June 2002), and on Rafael Hernández, "Toward a New Socialist Society? Changes, Crisis, and Social Configurations in Cuba," in his *Looking at Cuba: Essays on Culture and Civil Society* (Gainesville: University Press of Florida, 2003).

Among Daniel Chavarría's recent novels of Havana, *Adios Muchachos* has been published in English, trans. Carlos López (New York: Akashic, 2001). Leonardo Padura's *La novela de mi vida* was published in 2002 by Tusquets (Barcelona) and Ediciones Unión (Havana). Mylene Férnandez Pintado's *Otras plegarías atendidas* (Other Answered Prayers) was published in 2003 by Ediciones Unión (Havana).

Juan Formell's comments on timba music and dance come from Robin Davies, "Comenzó La Fiesta: Los Van Van Is in Town," http://www. salsasf.com/features/articles/vanvan01.html (accessed June 30, 2006). The song "¿Y qué tu quieres que te den?" by Adalberto Álvarez y Su Son, appears on their CD *Mi linda habanera* (Bismusic, 2005). For the Havana music market and *timba* in the 1990s, we drew on Emir García Meralla "Hágase la timba" (*Temas*, no. 39–40, cited above). For lyrics to songs by Los Van Van and other Cuban salsa groups, see also http://www. rosariosalsa.com.ar/letras/letras.htm (accessed June 30, 2006).

Index

Note: Boldface numbers indicate illustrations